Last of the Few

Last of the Few

The Battle of Britain in the Words of the
Pilots Who Won It

Max Arthur

2 4 6 8 10 9 7 5 3 1

Published in 2010 by Virgin Books, an imprint of Ebury Publishing
A Random House Group Company

Copyright © Max Arthur 2010

Max Arthur has asserted his right under the Copyright, Designs and Patents
Act 1988 to be identified as the author of this work

For legal purposes the Acknowledgements constitute a continuation
of this copyright page

Endpapers image reproduced by permission of the IWM (HU54418)

Every reasonable effort has been made to contact copyright holders of material
reproduced in this book. If any have inadvertently been overlooked, the
publishers would be glad to hear from them and make good in future editions
any errors or omissions brought to their attention

The Random House Group Limited Reg. No. 954009

Addresses for companies within the Random House Group can be found at
www.randomhouse.co.uk

A CIP catalogue record for this book is
available from the British Library

The Random House Group Limited supports The Forest Stewardship Council
[FSC], the leading international forest certification organisation. All our titles
that are printed on Greenpeace-approved FSC-certified paper carry the FSC
logo. Our paper procurement policy can be found at
www.rbooks.co.uk/environment

Mixed Sources
Product group from well-managed
forests and other controlled sources
www.fsc.org Cert no. TT-COC-2139
© 1996 Forest Stewardship Council
FSC

Printed in the UK by CPI Mackays, Chatham ME5 8TD

Hardback ISBN 9780753522271
Trade Paperback ISBN 9780753522288

To buy books by your favourite authors and register for offers visit
www.rbooks.co.uk

This book is dedicated to 'The Few' and those on the ground who supported them. We owe them an incalculable debt.

AUTHOR'S NOTE

For *Last of the Few* I have listened to hours of recorded interviews and read a number of personal testimonies, and interviewed many of the pilots who fought in the Battle of Britain. Throughout the book I have given some historical background, but the heart of the book lies in the personal accounts of those who fought and witnessed the battle. The accounts are not necessarily in chronological order and the ranks given are the ranks at the time. Through their words I have sought to capture the experiences and atmosphere of the battle: the waiting, the action and the consequences of those actions.

These are their words – I have been but a catalyst.

Max Arthur
London, 2010

CONTENTS

LIST OF ABBREVIATIONS

AAF	Auxiliary Air Force
AOC	Air Officer Commanding
CID	Criminal Investigations Department
CO	Commanding Officer
DF	Direction Finding
Do	Dornier
FT	Flying Training
FTS	Flying Training School
He	Heinkel
Ju	Junkers
LDV	Local Defence Volunteer (Home Guard)
LMP	lack of moral fibre
Me	Messerchmitt
MTB	Motor Torpedo Boat
MU	Maintenance Unit
NAAFI	Navy, Army and Air Force Institutes
OTU	Officers Training Unit
POW	prisoner of war
prop	propeller
RAF	Royal Air Force
RAFVR	Royal Air Force Volunteer Reserve
RCAF	Royal Canadian Air Force
RFC	Royal Flying Corps
RT	radio transmitter
VR	Volunteer Reserve
WAAF	Women's Auxiliary Air Force

An Air Administration map showing the air defences of South East England and the Midlands

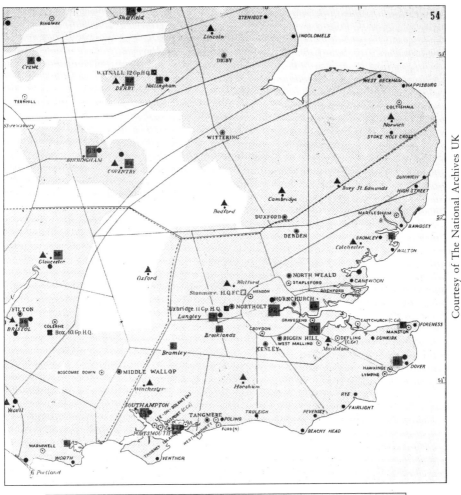

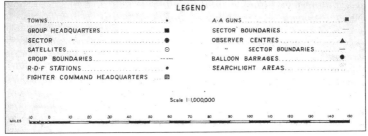

LEGEND

TOWNS.. •	A·A GUNS.. ■
GROUP HEADQUARTERS............ ■	SECTOR BOUNDARIES................ —
SECTOR " .... ●	OBSERVER CENTRES................ ▲
SATELLITES.................................. ⊙	" SECTOR BOUNDARIES........ —
GROUP BOUNDARIES.................... ----	BALLOON BARRAGES................ ●
R·D·F STATIONS.......................... •	SEARCHLIGHT AREAS................
FIGHTER COMMAND HEADQUARTERS .... ▨	

Scale 1:1,000,000

MILES 10 0 10 20 30 40 50 60 70 80 90 100 110 120 130 140 150

Courtesy of The National Archives UK

INTRODUCTION

During the First World War the Royal Flying Corps (RFC) had proved the value of air reconnaissance and bombing raids over the battlefields of France and Belgium – and in return, cities in Britain had come under air attack from German Zeppelin airships. The future of warfare had been changed for ever.

The aircraft of the Royal Air Force (RAF) – officially named as such on 1 April 1918 – were unsophisticated biplanes. Clearly, the aircraft deployed in any future conflict would be very different machines, but in the years after the Great War, aircraft development was slow. The Treaty of Versailles which dictated the terms of peace had effectively prevented Germany from developing any armed strength and the Allies retired to recover from their devastating losses. Sir Hugh Trenchard, a former pilot, became marshal of the new RAF, and it was his vision that shaped the role of the aeroplane in future conflict. He saw aircraft as an offensive tool, taking the war to the heart of enemy territory with bombing raids against communications, production and transport centres – so he ordered increased production of bombers. Fighters, he felt, were a sideshow

– a presence to boost the morale of the populace as they came under air attack. As politician Stanley Baldwin declared in 1932, 'The bomber will always get through.'

It was therefore fortuitous that Air Marshal Sir Hugh Dowding, Air Member for Research and Development, saw the need for new, faster and more manoeuvrable fighter aircraft and plenty of them. Certainly bomber production should continue, but fighters would be vital to take on incoming bombers and allow their own bomber force to fight on. He insisted that resources be dedicated to developing new fighter aircraft.

While Germany was still obeying the embargo on building military might the need for increased aircraft production in Britain was not deemed to be of paramount importance, but in 1933 Hitler's Nazi Party came to power in Germany. The build-up of German military power began – at first covertly, and then with no attempt at concealment – and the German threat was a reality. The new German air force – the Luftwaffe – was to be equipped with the best aircraft, and in 1935 Hitler commissioned the Messerschmitt 109 fighter. In the meantime, in Britain, in November of the same year, the Hawker Hurricane with its Rolls-Royce Merlin engine made its first flight – but at full speed it was still 30 mph slower than the Me 109.

The other British fighter innovation first took to the air in March 1936 – Reginald Mitchell's Supermarine Spitfire. At last there was a fighter to challenge the Me 109, and in 1938 first Hurricanes, and then eight months later Spitfires, started to be delivered to the squadrons.

All this would still be no defence against a determined invasion attempt – Dowding knew that he would need to put in place an advance warning system which would allow his fighters time to take off, gain the height they needed for effective attacks and confront the enemy before the bombers could drop their loads. This new detection system, radar, was developed and twenty-two

'Chain Home' stations were built along the south coast, with thirty lesser 'Chain Home Low' stations in support – and this, with the new Hurricane and Spitfire fighters, would be the technology on which Dowding would base his defence of Britain against invasion.

A Sergeant Pilot sits for a moment, reflecting.

1

Learning to Fly and Joining Up

Flying was new, exciting, inspiring – and following the First World War a generation of boys was growing up with pilots as their role models and heroes. For many, born among the more affluent classes, flying was the ultimate goal – and one which could be achieved by joining flying clubs or the new Auxiliary Air Force. The AAF squadrons were created to reinforce local squadrons and the sons of the well-to-do could learn to fly for pleasure. On the other hand, there was the RAF Volunteer Reserve, created in 1936 to support the regular air force. The volunteers, aged eighteen to twenty-five, were paid a retainer of £25 a year and trained at weekends – and once trained could be drafted to any squadron where they were needed.

As Hitler flexed his military muscles by invading Czechoslovakia in 1938, it became apparent that war was inevitable, sooner or later, and under Air Marshal Dowding's orders, aircraft production was stepped up and recruitment became paramount. And with the invasion of Czechoslovakia, then Poland, a new source of pilots emerged. Trained flyers from both countries abandoned their homelands and made their way, some by long and tortuous means, to Britain, where they would form the backbone of new squadrons – and having seen what suffering and loss Hitler's forces had inflicted on their homelands, they arrived burning with the desire to strike back and to wreak revenge on their invaders.

Dowding was adamant that the air force needed a new breed of fighter aircraft, but the powers that be, seemed to expect him to wage any future war using cumbersome, outdated Defiants. Although based on the same Rolls-Royce Merlin engine which powered the Hurricane and Spitfire, the Defiant was a two-man plane – the second man being an air gunner. There were no forward-firing armaments and the extra weight made the Defiant painfully slow and no match for the Luftwaffe's new Messerchmitt 109s. Dowding would not let the matter rest, and insisted stubbornly on proper investment in the RAF's fighter force – so making himself very unpopular with the Air Staff and at the Air Ministry.

One man supported Dowding – Air Commodore Keith Park, who was promoted to Senior Air Staff Officer in July 1938. Under their supervision regular RAF, Auxiliary Air Force and Volunteer Reservists were recruited and trained, as the pair of them took on the RAF establishment and stuck doggedly to their plan for the defence of Britain.

Pilot Officer Tim Vigors

222 SQUADRON

In 1929 I was sent to join my older brother at Beaudesert Park Preparatory School near Stroud. Throughout the first week I had not made any close contacts with my fellow pupils. Wallowing in my personal misery, I had refrained from trying to make friends, and now found myself too shy to intrude on any of the groups. Sadly I wandered across the field and sat down by myself under a tree. It was then that I spotted a lean dark-haired boy of about my own age, playing with a model aeroplane.

I watched with only a vague interest as the boy launched his flimsy wooden and canvas contraption into the air. Its propeller was driven by a large elastic band and once aloft it could achieve about twenty yards of powered flight before the band had fully unwound and it glided, powerless, to the grass. On the first couple of attempts its wing tip hit the ground first and it cartwheeled to a stop. But the third time the boy made some minor adjustment to the tail and when the propeller stopped, it glided to a perfect landing.

'Did you ever see a smoother landing than that?' the boy said, turning to me. The next time he flew the aircraft he allowed me to pick it up. As I held it, I felt an unaccountable shiver run through me. I could suddenly imagine myself sitting behind those wings and soaring into the sky.

I told him I was Tim Vigors and he told me he was Henry Maudsley, and new to the school. I said I was new too – and said how I hated it.

'Oh, it's not so bad, particularly if you have a friend.'

So started one of the closest friendships of my life. We shared an interest in aeroplanes which was to absorb us both for the next nine years and one that on a dark night over Germany in 1943, after the Dams raid, was to kill Henry – and one that so often nearly killed me too.

During my teenage years my thoughts were constantly on aeroplanes. My godmother, Pamela Wills, asked me to come and stay with her for a few days. Pamela had just learned to fly and was the proud owner of a de Havilland Hornet Moth. She knew of my interest in aeroplanes and suggested that I go flying with her each day during my visit.

Pamela met me at the Bristol airfield. Here she kept her own aircraft, so we loaded my suitcase into her Rolls Bentley and drove straight to the hangar where the Hornet Moth was housed. With the assistance of a mechanic we pushed the little aircraft out on to the tarmac and climbed in. The little cabin biplane was fitted with dual controls, and as I took my seat beside her, Pamela told me to be careful to keep my hands and feet away from the joystick and the rudder pedals. She then gave a signal and the mechanic swung the propeller and, at the second attempt, the engine roared into life. We taxied on to the grass field. Pamela looked over her shoulder to see that no other aircraft were in sight or landing, asked me if I was all right and strapped in, then opened the throttle. Off we sped across the airfield, running and bumping, and after some 300 yards Pamela pulled back on the stick and we were airborne.

We climbed out to the west of the field and when we had reached about 2,000 feet, levelled off and turned out over the Severn Estuary. We flew around for about five minutes and then Pamela turned to me and shouted to me to take the controls.

From reading books on aeroplanes I knew all about aircraft controls, but this was the very first time I had actually touched them. Gingerly I took the stick in my right hand and reached out with my left for the centrally situated throttle. Carefully I placed my feet on the rudder bars. I felt the nose going down and eased back on the stick. Of course, I overcorrected and the next thing I knew was that the nose was going up in the air and the right wing was dropping. I lifted it up quickly by pushing the stick to the left, but immediately found myself in a shallow left-hand dive. I glanced anxiously at Pamela, but she was smiling at my efforts and looking remarkably relaxed. Gradually I got the little aircraft back on to a level course and determinedly kept it there for at least two minutes.

I was beginning to get the hang of it when Pamela shouted at me that we must head back for the airfield or we'd be late for our dinner. Reluctantly I relinquished the controls. Pamela turned the aircraft back towards the airfield and, joining the circuit on the downwind leg, smoothly eased the Hornet into a left-hand turn and, losing height all the time, was soon on her final approach.

The next thing I knew we were bumping over the grass as she touched down in a reasonable three-point landing. I was ecstatic. At last I had actually flown an aircraft by myself.

For the next two days we flew for at least an hour each morning. I started to get a feel for what I was doing and by the end of the second day was completely confident of being able to control the aircraft climbing, diving and turning in the air. At the end of each flight my kind godmother allowed me to keep my hands on the controls while she landed and so, while I could not say that I had actually got the aircraft back on the ground by myself, I felt confident that should the necessity arise, I would be able to do so without undue damage to the undercarriage.

Something had happened to me which had made me different from my friends. I, Tim, had actually piloted an aircraft. I tried to while away the time which lay between the present and the moment I could join the RAF. My future was sealed.

Flight Lieutenant Johnny Kent
(CANADIAN) 303 AND 92 SQUADRONS

I was one whom the flying bug had bitten badly, long before Lindbergh's flight, and I was determined to learn to fly. I read everything I could find about my heroes of aviation – such men as Barker, Bishop, MacLeod, Mannock and McCudden. I suppose, like many others, I was most thrilled by the tales of the great fighter aces, but I never supposed that there would ever be a war which would allow me to take part in similar battles.

As a treat on my fifteenth birthday my father took me out to the Flying Club and I had my first flight. The pilot kindly showed me over the Gipsy Moth which the club had only recently obtained and then, thrill of thrills, I was put into the front cockpit, told what not to touch, and away we went for a most glorious half-hour over the city. I can still recall the terrific exhilaration that I felt and my surprise when I had no sensation of height. When we returned and landed my father saw from the expression on my face as I waved to him that there was no doubt about it – I had to fly.

Flight Lieutenant Johnny Kent, a Canadian pilot of 303 Squadron.

I was terribly keen to fly with the RCAF but when I found that this entailed undergoing a six-year university course, I decided, reluctantly, that such a career was not for me. There was, it turned out, only one possible way and that was for my long-suffering father to dig into his not-too-well-lined pocket and pay up. This he finally agreed to, on condition that I waited until I was seventeen and passed my Senior Matriculation examinations. Naturally I agreed most readily to these terms, but as time went on, I found it increasingly difficult to concentrate upon my studies.

Finally arrangements were made for me to start my flying lessons at the Winnipeg Flying Club under the tuition of Konrad or 'Konnie', as he was always called, Johannesson, a Canadian of Icelandic parentage who had served in the Royal Flying Corps and Royal Air Force in the First World War.

I worked steadily towards obtaining my Commercial Licence although I was still below the minimum age. It was an expensive business, building up the required number of flying hours and, like others, I was always on the lookout for some means of getting cheap flying. The sad fact was that the great economic 'boom' was over and we were now floundering in the awful 'Depression' of the Thirties.

In my constant lookout for a flying job I had, towards the end of 1933, come across an advertisement in the British publication *The Aeroplane* offering short service commissions of six years' duration in the Royal Air Force. I had made, along with several others, an application to be considered for such a commission, and in January 1934 I received a letter telling me to report to Fort Osborne just outside Winnipeg for a medical examination and an interview with the Brigadier Commanding. I duly attended and was both medically examined and interviewed – but nothing happened for a month or so, when I was again instructed to report for another medical examination. This happened four times and I got so fed up I wrote and asked for my papers to be returned and advised the authorities that I wished to withdraw my application. Back came a letter advising me that I had been selected as a candidate for a short service commission and that I was to make my own way to London and report to the Air Ministry not later than the beginning of March 1935. In February I said my sad farewells and set off for England and, I hoped, a career in the Royal Air Force.

After two weeks of square bashing, lectures and indoctrination, I was sent to No. 5 Flying Training School at Sealand near Chester. Initially the instructors and staff pilots flew us around the county in the Atlas and dual-controlled Bulldogs so that we could get used to the various landmarks, but after two weeks we started our proper training programme, which pleased me very much, as I found the Tutor such a delightful and easy aircraft to fly. After the official minimum of three hours' dual, I was sent solo.

Towards the end of the term various competitions were held and I was fortunate to win the forced landing silver cup – the only cup I have ever won. At the end of the term I was gratified to find that I was the only pupil assessed as 'Exceptional' as a pilot.

About this time the upsurge of militarism in Germany following the seizure of power by the Nazi Party brought to the Prime Minister, Mr Baldwin, the truth of his own words that our frontier was indeed on the Rhine. This and the knowledge that Germany was rapidly building up a modern air force convinced him of the need for a great increase in Britain's air power; the machinery was set in motion to implement the planned expansion of the Royal Air Force.

Flight Lieutenant Tom Morgan
43 SQUADRON

In less than nine months after I had turned eighteen, the air force told me I'd been accepted; I was interviewed and cleared the medical, then they wrote to me and said that I wouldn't be called forward for about seven months. We were living just outside Penarth in

South Wales so I borrowed my brother's bike, and I went to Cardiff Aeroplane Club and saw the chief ground engineer. I asked him if I could come into the hangar and familiarise myself with the aircraft – but I wasn't expecting to be paid. He had one licensed aircraft maintenance engineer – a very good chap – and that's where I started flying. I learned to hand-start the Gipsy Moths and the Tiger Moths, and Flying Officer Pope, the flying instructor, took me up. He showed me the effects of controls and over a few flights he showed me how to approach the landing and take off – so anyhow I could fly before I joined the air force.

Sergeant Pilot Iain Hutchinson

222 SQUADRON

I had a friend, Alec Green, who started flying at the Scottish Flying Club at the airport, and he took me up once or twice – and the bug bit, and I felt I really wanted to fly. I took a course and I started flying in May 1938. Then I realised that His Majesty provided a much better flying club, with more powerful aircraft, and so I applied to join the RAFVR. We flew at Prestwick about every second or third weekend, initially in Tiger Moths, and then we graduated to Hawker Hawks and Hinds, which was the first operational biplane that I flew – and I got my wings there.

The Volunteer Reserve was formed to complement the Royal Auxiliary Air Force. The Air Ministry wanted a more flexible reserve of pilots and navigators, and whereas the RAF was organised in squadrons, we were organised into town units. We were part of the City of Glasgow unit, but we were free to be posted to anywhere – as indeed we were when war broke out.

I expected to be called up when I was needed, but actually I wanted to fly the whole time, and I made a tactical error in going into the Volunteer Reserve. If I'd applied for a short service commission, I would probably have been able to do that.

Flight Lieutenant Peter Brothers, 32 and 257 Squadrons.

Flight Lieutenant Peter Brothers

32 AND 257 SQUADRONS

I learned to fly as a schoolboy, but my father hoped I would settle down and join his business. As soon as I was seventeen and a half, however, I pissed off and got a short service commission in the air force. That was in January 1936, and I was sent to Uxbridge first, for ground training, getting kitted out and so on.

At Uxbridge there was this splendid First World War pilot, Ira Taffy Jones, who stuttered terribly. One day he stood up and said, 'There is going to be a b-b-bloody wa-wa-war and you ch-chaps are going to be in it. I'll give you one piece of advice – wh-wh-when you fir-first get into a co-combat, you will be fu-fu-fucking fr-frightened. Ne-never forget the ch-chap in the other cock-cockpit is tw-twice as fu-fucking fr-frightened as you are.'

I reckon he saved my life with that piece of advice. In my first combat over France, I suddenly thought, My God, the chap in that other cockpit must be having hysterics, and shot him down. But I give all credit to Taffy.

I was posted to Biggin Hill in the autumn, and I operated there, flying Gloster Gauntlets and doing practice interceptions on civil aircraft. We were the first station to have an ops room. It was all chalk blackboards in those days, and one aircraft had a clock on the transmitter which transmitted for fifteen seconds every minute, so that the radio stations could get a DF (Direction Finding) bearing on you. Meanwhile, the radar was also checking on that, so we had a dual-fixing situation. The idea was to see how close the interception worked out on the incoming aircraft. The radar would plot incoming aircraft to Croydon, for example, and we'd go off to intercept them somewhere over the Channel or East Kent. We'd just fly past and report how close we'd been and when we first sighted them. That was very interesting and amusing, because the Station Commander would give you a course

Pilot Officer Ludwik Martel,
3 Regiment Polish Air Force.

to steer, vector so-and-so, and off you went. Then you'd hear him over the radio, saying, 'Vector . . . How the hell can I see the blackboard with your fat bottom in the way?'

The Gloster Gauntlets were biplanes, single-engine, single-seater aircraft. Very cold, with an open cockpit. In 1938 we converted to Hurricanes, and carried on doing the same sort of thing, plus gunnery practice. I never really bothered to think that we'd actually face an enemy. It was like being in a glorious, but expert flying club.

During 1938 Winston Churchill occasionally used to come into the mess at Biggin Hill, on his way home to Chartwell. The door would open just before six o'clock, and he'd come in. We'd say, 'Good evening, sir,' and he'd say, 'Would you mind turning on the radio, so that I can hear the six o'clock news?' Sometimes he'd have a glass of sherry, and then he'd ask us about our Supermarine Spitfires, whether we were content with them, and that sort of thing. He'd spend a few minutes with us, then he'd get on his way home. But we never told him that we were actually flying Hawker Hurricanes.

Pilot Officer Ludwik Martel
3 REGIMENT POLISH AIR FORCE

I went to technical college to go into the textile industry, and finished my education when I was nineteen. We had a professor in charge of physics and he was very interested in flying, and encouraged us to be interested too.

In 1936 I did a course in gliding – and that's where I fell in love with flying. Gliding was a very pleasant exercise. I did my course and was determined to continue flying afterwards. This was my vocation in 1936, and the next year I volunteered and went on a course to learn to fly. In Poland there was a system that all the young people who were willing and fit to fly were given a chance. We lived in a camp at the airfield. I volunteered to go and do my military service the next year.

The first plane I flew was a Polish construction called a Bartel. It was very exciting and very demanding – after gliding you find out that you have to concentrate when flying. It's quite a serious occupation – very pleasant – but you have to concentrate. I was very happy with it and in '38 I did my one year's National Service.

National Service was very demanding – before you were transferred to the air force, they sent you for one month to the army – which was very unpleasant. The people who were meant to train you as a soldier were not very nice, so people were rather jealous of those who were not staying in the army but going to the air force and there were some rude remarks.

I was with 3 Regiment in Posnan, then I went back home and back into civilian life. At Posnan we saw the German aircraft overflying us and people said this was very unusual, so we knew something was going on. I tried to get a job and wasn't very successful at first, then the time came at the end of 1938 that I got my call-up to join the Regiment again.

I flew the P7 and from then on I became a fighter pilot. It was my dream, but from then it was my tragedy – the start of the war and leaving Poland. On 1 September 1939 the Germans launched their first raid. It was serious and there was going to be a war, and I volunteered and joined the group outside Posnan when the war started. The idea was that there were some aircraft being sent from France and England to Romania. We knew the Polish forces were to be rebuilt in France and England, and I was in a group waiting and travelling all the time, until 7 September when I arrived in Paris and got all the necessary papers. There was no hope of our group doing any flying in Romania or collecting aircraft, so from then on our aim was to get to England. I waited in France for a few months – we tried to find out what aircraft we were going to fly – but that wasn't easy. It was depressing waiting, and what was more, I didn't speak any English at that time – nor did anyone else.

Pilot Officer Henryk Szczesny

(POLISH) 74 SQUADRON

As a boy at school, flying was my dream; flying was all I wanted to do because it lifts you up – you become like a bird. That is why, as soon as I could, I joined the Polish Air Force as a cadet and became a pilot officer in 1933.

I then taught pilots as an instructor. I emphasised the fighting skills of British pilots, most of all Mannock, from the 1914–18 war. I told them he was the best English fighter pilot. I got a photograph of him through the Embassy and put it on the wall – and he looked at me like 'Sailor' Malan did later. I told the student pilots about how he would fly and shoot, how he was always on the spot, and not afraid of anything. But I also talked to them about the tactics of Richthofen and of Polish pilots who had served with the Russian and German air forces.

In 1939 I was transferred to the east Polish border, teaching advanced flying in PZL7s. We knew the war was coming, so we were preparing – and indeed Poland was the first country to be invaded, on 1 September 1939. I was posted to a bomber station with six Polish cadets to fly defence for our bombers. I was lucky and shot down two Dorniers and damaged a couple more of them, but I was wounded. Then, as we were being beaten back, I flew to Romania, to Bucharest. There I had an operation on my leg because gangrene had set in. When I recovered, I made my way to Malta and then to France. I finally arrived in London on a foggy day, and I couldn't see a thing outside, but for the first time I had a lovely English breakfast of bacon and eggs.

All the Polish aircrew were sent up to Blackpool, where we just gathered together. The RAF sorted us out and I was sent to Aston Down for Spitfire training. It was very difficult for me because the Spitfire has the undercarriage down, flaps down, everything different! In Poland you pull back the throttle; with the Spitfire it was the reverse. I think the Spitfire was flying me!

Pilot Officer Henryk Szczesny, 74 Squadron.

Flight Lieutenant Tom Morgan

43 SQUADRON

About 1936 or '37 it began to look as though the Germans would come, so being a young man I thought I'd like to have a go at those chaps. The papers were telling us how nasty they were so, yes, I think I was ready for them.

When war broke out I was a junior officer with the Air Ministry. The air force was busy handing over the Fleet Air Arm to the navy, and we were not only transferring equipment, but training the naval pilots at Peterborough and Netheravon. Then one day, pretty near to the end of the job, my senior officer, Commander Atkinson, said he wanted to get back to sea. I decided to approach my director in the Air Ministry. I said, 'Look, sir, it's time I went flying. I haven't done much since I joined the air force.' And he said, 'Good for you, son' or words to that effect and said he would arrange it – which he did within a week. I was sent up to do a refresher course on Hurricanes and from there I was posted as 'B' Flight commander to 43 Squadron at Tangmere in 11 Group.

Sergeant Pilot Paul Farnes

501 SQUADRON

I was brought up by the lady who brought me into the world – she was a midwife at the little nursing home. My mother died there the day after I was born, and my father said the midwife was to get rid of me to Dr Barnado's. But this lady took a fancy to me – she was about forty at the time – and she adopted me. I had a wonderful upbringing, just she and I together. I couldn't have had a better life. But when I first found out about my father I was so angry.

I was working in London when I was about eighteen, and every morning I had to walk along the Embankment. I passed HMS *President*, which was a naval recruiting centre. I went in there one day and thought I wouldn't mind being in the naval reserve, so I got all the information and then not long after that I met a chap who was in the Volunteer Reserve, and he was flying, and he said, 'You don't want to join the navy – come and join the air force. Join the Volunteer Reserve.'

So I went with him down to the airfield where he was doing his training and by then he was flying Harts and Hinds. I thought this was much better than the navy, so I joined up. In view of my background – because I was illegitimate – I was a bit worried about whether they'd take me. But my adoptive mother supported me and wrote to the Air Ministry and asked if it would have any effect – and they said, 'No, if he can pass all the necessary tests, we'll be glad to have him.' So I joined the RAFVR.

Before the war began, in the VR you could volunteer to do six months with the air force proper – and so I applied. Your company you worked for had to take you back after this. I applied and they accepted me and on my birthday in July 1939 I was sent to St Athan in South Wales, and I converted to Hurricanes there. War broke out in September, and I was promptly posted to Filton, Bristol, as a sergeant pilot with 501 Squadron.

Pilot Officer Jocelyne Millard

I AND 242 SQUADRONS

My father was in the navy in submarines based at Troon Harbour, near Ardrossen, and all my schooling was in England. I went to a secondary school in Hitchin and a public school in Ware.

In 1932 I left school and went to work for a machine company. After four or five years I didn't seem to be getting anywhere, so I changed my job and went into engineering in a bigger way. I went to the 600 Group – a big steel manufacturer – and they had the national contract for locomotive wheels. I worked there for a while, then grew tired of that, then went on to a firm making industrial dust carts. I got tired of that as well, so I applied for a job with the de Havilland aircraft company in Hatfield, and I went there in 1935, and was there until war broke out.

At Hatfield I was doing development and production work. While I was there in 1937 I joined the RAFVR – one of the first people to join. Hatfield ran a flying school for the RAF, and it was very convenient for me as I worked and flew there as well. The medical exam took two days and I had to go to London, but I was accepted and tested in October and started my flying the same day, and I was there until 1 September 1939, when I was mobilised into the RAF.

I'd always wanted to fly, but I joined the air force against my mother's wishes – we lost my father in the submarine service in the First World War, and my brother moved away and married, so there was just me at home, so she was dead against my joining.

I got a letter saying that, because I was in a reserved occupation, they could have me withdrawn from the Volunteer Reserve. But I didn't want that – I'd joined the air force to fly. When I went for my interview at the Air Ministry, they asked me why I wanted to join and there were two reasons. I wanted to fly and I wanted to fly for my country – like my father, I was patriotic, so when they offered to withdraw me from the VR, I said no. I hadn't joined just for peacetime.

In October I had a letter saying 'Report to Euston Station at 10 pm', and I got on the train and found myself in Scotland at Prestwick, where I was set to do a flying instructor's course.

I didn't get into trouble, but my instructor did. He did a foolish thing – and so did I. We went off to do some instrument flying. When you're instrument flying in a Tiger Moth you go under a hood – and he went low flying over Ayr. Somebody reported him and I was called up before the CO and asked if I knew that my instructor had been low flying while instrument flying. I said I didn't realise it – and he said, 'You don't know when you're low flying? Then you're no good as a flying instructor.'

So I came off the course. I was sent down to Hastings and because of the chaotic state of the administration, I and one other were forgotten. We were down there from November 1939 to April 1940. Nobody knew where we were – or realised we hadn't been posted. I was then posted to a place called Anstey in Coventry where I did an advanced elementary course. Towards the end of the course, everybody was talking about their final test – and I thought that was funny because nobody had asked me about a final test – so I went to my instructor and he said I'd get a test all right, but it would be all on my logbook. When I got my logbook back I had been assessed an above average pilot and navigator.

I was posted to Grantham where they had Fairey Battles and Avro Ansons, which I flew. It took 159 turns of the handle to get the undercarriage up! You lumbered around the sky, and having been used to flying all these lovely light aircraft – Hawker Harts and so on – I found the Anson burdensome. I didn't like that very much. I went to the squadron commander and asked if I could have a transfer to Battles.

'I'm not going to cope with this Anson,' I said. 'I can't put my heart and soul into flying these things, not when there are Battles around.'

'I'll give you a transfer,' he said, 'but you'd better justify what you've asked for.'

Halfway through the course we had a flight commander's test and it lasted twenty minutes. I was assessed an above average pilot and above average pilot-navigator.

I was then commissioned and posted to Old Sarum where I was on army co-operation command, where I was flying Lysanders and Hectors. Well, I didn't join the air force to fly with or for the army, and I couldn't stand what we were doing – gas-spraying and aerial photography and so on – so after about nine days I couldn't cope with this, so I went to ask for a posting.

I'd only been commissioned about ten days so that didn't go down very well. I went out with my tail between my legs, but another three or four days went by and I went again and asked for a posting. It so happened that morning they'd been notified of two vacancies in Fighter Command. One on Spitfires at Aston Down, and one on Hurricanes at Sutton Bridge. I said I still wanted a posting, so the CO said, 'Take one and clear off.' So I took Hurricanes and I went to Sutton Bridge.

Flying Officer Al Deere
(NEW ZEALANDER) 54 SQUADRON

I came to Britain from New Zealand to join the air force in 1937. The air force had started to expand, and they advertised in the national press in the then Dominions for young men. I applied and was one of the first eighteen to be selected.

Twelve of us went to White Waltham near Maidenhead, where we learned to fly in a Tiger Moth. I went from the initial training to No. 6 Flying Training School at Netheravon to train on Hawker Harts and Furies. I was always keen to be a fighter pilot and kept saying so. Eventually I was posted to 54 Squadron at Hornchurch, which was equipped with Gladiators. I did a year in 1938 flying Gladiators, but thank God we didn't have to fight in them! It was a lovely aircraft, but it was so outdated. We were disappointed then, but fortunately Munich kept the war off for about a year, and by that time we'd gone on to Spitfires.

Flying Officer Michael Wainwright
64 SQUADRON

I went into the air force and got my short service commission – in 1938 I was flying Magisters – I started on Tiger Moths. I never told them, when I went to my first school, that I'd already learned to fly, because if I'd said that, they'd say, 'You think you know everything,' and they'd shoot me down. So they thought I was reasonably apt.

Flying Officer Al Deere, 54 Squadron.

When I did my test for solo a chap called George Lodell was chief instructor, and he failed me because he said I was a bit too slow coming in to land. So I had to go and do a bit of practising. I did my solo flight after eight hours' dual instruction, and I went solo after that. My first solo was 6 October 1937. Then I went to Number Three Flying Training School at South Cerney, and my instructor, Sergeant Miles there, had to call me 'sir' on the ground. He didn't call me 'sir' in the air! I started off on Hawker Harts – biplane.

You do right up to night flying at the FT. After you'd finished your first term, you went on to flying the Hawker Audax, which is a similar sort of plane to the Hawker Hart, and then we went on to Hawker Furies – that was a little biplane fighter with a Rolls-Royce Kestrel engine in it, and you did all your stuff – air firing. We used to go and do air firing at a place called Chesil Bank, and that was where the swannery was, so they used to say, when we were doing our diving and air firing at Chesil Bank, firing at targets on the ground, we were not to disturb the swans.

The Hawker Fury had twin Vickers machine guns which were always getting jammed, and you had a thing to unjam them. From there they sent me to Number One Air Armament School in a place called Eastchurch on the Isle of Sheppey – a miserable place. I did my air armaments course and then they moved the whole thing to a place called Manby in Lincolnshire. Then they sent me to one of these air armament schools where they trained rear-gunners for the Bomber Command at Acklingon. There I was flying a variety of aircraft – and I flew aeroplanes like the Hawker Hind, and two old twin-engined bombers – one was called a Sidestrand, which had an open cockpit, and its successor was called the Overstrand which had a glasshouse cockpit – and I flew a Fairey Seal. I got a lot of experience. Then I got posted in early September '39.

Pilot Officer Glen Niven

(Canadian) 602 and 601 Squadrons

My name went through to the CO at Abbotsinch – and I was asked to go for an interview. I was ushered in to his office, and he said, 'Ah, young Niven. I understand you want to join the squadron.'

'Yes, sir. Please, sir. If that's all right, sir.'

'Yes, that's fine,' he said, picking up the phone. 'Is there a pilot down there not doing anything at the moment?'

Yes – there was – Donald Jack.

'Will you show this young chap around?'

That was the sum total of my interview to join 602 Squadron. Donald Jack showed me around. He said, 'Have you ever seen an aircraft before?' and I said, 'No, sir.' He pointed to a Magister – a little two-seater training aircraft – and he said, 'They're not very good. You put them in a spin and they're liable to give you trouble.' And that's all I can remember him saying.

He took me around and showed me the aircraft they had, which were Gauntlets – not much different from First World War fighter aircraft. I was introduced to the crew – the people who had joined and were flying every Thursday night.

I think he then went to the CO and said I seemed to be a decent enough chap. In those days if you were a gentleman and spoke English, you were all right. A few weeks later I was told to report for a medical, which I did, and when it came to test my eyesight the sod covered up my left eye and asked me to read the letters on the card – and I didn't do very well. With the other eye I got them right, down to the bottom line. He told me my eyesight wasn't up to standard, so I told him the biggest lie and said I'd been going to a lot of films recently and it must have upset my eyes. They were very decent in those days – they wanted pilots – and they took me.

I was told to come back in three months to see if things had improved, so I went to six different opticians and had my eyes tested, and the first five said that my left eye was not up to the standard for the air force. The sixth one I saw was a nice chap and he said the same – but he added, 'But are you quite keen to join the air force?' and I said, 'Yes, sir,' so he said, 'I'll tell you what to do. You cheat. When they show you this chart, for God's sake remember the last two lines – because with two eyes you can read them – memorise the last two lines – the other ones you'll get away with.'

After three months I went for the medical and I managed to cheat enough, so when he tested my left eye, I reeled off the letters. I waited on tenterhooks for two months and nothing happened. I thought that was it, so I phoned up 602 Squadron adjutant – I was too young to drink at the time, so I don't know how I got the courage, but I said who I was, and that I'd undergone a medical two months before but hadn't heard anything.

'Haven't you?' he said. 'Well, you'd better come along on Sunday.' And that was me in the air force. And they didn't give a damn about my sight. They just assumed I'd passed the medical.

Our instructor was a Canadian – and he must have been a very good pilot, because only the good ones became instructors – so we went through all our training not being too good, because if you were too good you were made a bloody instructor. So you made a hash of some things . . .

Flight Lieutenant Johnny Kent

303 AND 92 SQUADRONS

On my return from leave in Canada I found that I had been posted to the Experimental Section of the Royal Aircraft Establishment at Farnborough for test pilot duties. To say I was overjoyed would be a decided understatement. To be chosen as a test pilot was a very great honour indeed, indicating that my skills were held in high regard in the right quarters.

Throughout 1938 and '39 I had been busy studying for my Specialisation Examination in the hopes of getting a permanent commission. Shortly after the Munich crisis I sat the exam at Odiham. When the results of the examination were announced I was gratified to find that I had been selected for appointment to a Non-Specialist Permanent Commission – just what I wanted.

I was still faced with the prospect of taking Promotion Examination 'B' for promotion to flight lieutenant in September. Despite the continuing threat of war during all the summer preparing for the exam, which was scheduled to take place on 5 October, I was saved from the ordeal by Mr Chamberlain's announcement a few days before.

Pilot Officer Tom Neil

249 SQUADRON

I was born in Liverpool and my parents used to bring me to London every now and again. They took me to Croydon and they'd got these great four-engine Leviathans that were flying between London and Paris. I was always entranced – there were ladies at Croydon Airport that had plantpot hats and smoked cigarettes in long holders – this was the place where money was – how the rich lived. And I was fascinated by that. Then I was interested in aeroplanes – I used to be in the Christchurch choir in Liverpool and we used to sit in the choir stalls eating our Mars bars and talking about aeroplanes. I knew all about Bristol Bulldogs and Bristol Fighters and the First World War Sopwith Camels and Sopwith Snipes. I had this fascination with aircraft, right from the word go – I used to build models. There were three magazines – there was *Aeroplane*, edited by C.G. Grey, and there was *Flight*, and a thing called *Air Stories*, which was largely fiction.

I hadn't flown before joining the air force – in fact, I lied when I was interviewed. I said I'd done this and that – but I hadn't. I first tried to join the Auxiliary Air Force – in those days you could join when you were seventeen and three-quarters – and I was still at school. I tried to join 611 Squadron, which was my local squadron in Liverpool. In the meantime my parents had moved to Manchester, so they deemed I was too far away from Liverpool, and they were a squadron rather than a training establishment, so they turned me down – which absolutely flattened me. But they did recommend that I try to join up in Manchester – which I did.

Until I joined the Volunteer Reserve on my birthday in 1938, I'd never been near an aeroplane – in fact, the Neil family were outrageously ignorant about anything to do with it – although I knew all about the First World War. My bedroom was covered in photographs of Sopwith Camels and Bristol Fighters. I was an expert on that sort of thing. This stood me – and many others – in good stead during the Battle of Britain, because we knew all about the First World War, which was only twenty years before, and very much part of our recent history. Our station commander and some of our flight and squadron commanders had been in the First World War. The AOCs, Leigh-Mallory and the rest, had been majors in the First World War, so they knew all about it – but they were in their forties and we were kids aged 19 or thereabouts.

When I first got to No. 17 Elementary and Reserve Flying Training School we had Gipsy 1 Moths. The first aeroplane that I flew was K1900, and I remember thinking at the time, 'My God, this was when it was made.' Then we re-equipped with Tiger Moths about nine months later – which came as a great thrill – the new aircraft. They were the only aircraft I flew until the war started, when I was just about to go on to bigger types – Hawker Harts, Hawker Audaxes and Hawker Furies – which I didn't succeed in doing until I went to flying training school.

The Tiger Moth was a hot ship – all of 140 horsepower engine – and it was a lovely aeroplane. It was the trainer right throughout the war, principally – and it was absolutely vice-free. Once you'd gone solo – which took me quite a time, because I was only turning up at the weekend, and particularly during winter, sometimes you didn't fly for two months, and you went on making the same errors you'd made two months before. It took me sixteen hours to go solo, and thereafter my instructors left me alone. I had no more instruction after that, so my idea of aerobatics was what I'd read in books, and I'd taught myself, virtually – and they weren't very good.

Even when the war broke out, I was still only half taught, and although I'd done sixty hours total I didn't know much about flying. The engine was just a black mass up front which operated when you pushed the lever backwards and forwards, but I didn't know very much about the aeroplane. When you're eighteen or nineteen as I was then, it's rather like a car – you don't really know very much about it; it just goes or doesn't go, according to whether it's unserviceable or not – and the same thing with our Tiger Moths, except that they were new and they kept going.

Pilot Officer Nigel Rose
602 SQUADRON

I was sent to 602 Squadron which was at Drem near Edinburgh – City of Glasgow Auxiliary Squadron – and there my adventures began. I suppose you could say my experience of the Battle of Britain started there, because it was already 21 June 1940 or somewhere around there. We had no influence over where we were posted – all I knew was that it was going to be a fighter squadron and I didn't realise what my luck was in that respect.

Because I got a good standard thing out of flying training school – one was supposed to be respectable material – but some of the chaps got posted to bomber squadrons where you were trundling along and had to be much braver and have a much more prolonged set of nerves. With fighters you were up and down fairly quickly, and what you did was in fairly hot blood – whereas the bomber boys had to stick to their mission plan – I have so much admiration for them. You didn't really have much influence over where you went – certainly not specifically to a particular squadron. They were just filling in the holes.

I went up to 602 Squadron – I was received extraordinarily well. I rather expected to be looked down on – maybe I didn't know what to expect. They were very friendly and when you consider that 602 was an auxiliary squadron, very much like a young gentlemen's club – most of them were sons of the fairly comfortably off or professionals.

They were the nicest possible crowd. They'd been flying together – some of them for six or seven years before that – in all sorts of types of aircraft. Things like Gladiators and biplanes, Hawker Harts and Hinds too. They'd received their Spitfires in December '39, so they had been flying them for about six months when I joined them. They were some of the first off the factory floor, with pump undercarriages – you had to pull a lever to get the oil to flow around and bring the legs up. This was new to us because the Harvard had an automatic undercarriage. But when we were sent south there were automatic undercarriages by then.

There we were – there were three or four of us from my flying training school sent to the same squadron. Two of us had commissions and two were sergeant pilots – which left a slight embarrassment on our part, because heaven knows why there was the division of the sheep from the goats, because we were great friends and we remained so in the squadron. But one was bound to feel a slight division. I think even at flying training school you could see the difference between the officers and the sergeants – but not really unpleasantly. On the squadron on the whole there was very much a chummy sort of feeling except there was an officers' mess and a sergeants' mess.

For the first few days we flew a Magister – a little two-seater monoplane – and that was running in double harness with the Tiger

Moth. I was taken round the countryside in a Magister and shown the landmarks – the Forth Bridge and Edinburgh and the islands out at sea – to get an idea of the lie of the land and also the bad areas of mud on the airfield, especially as a Spitfire could turn over fairly easily on its nose if you went into a boggy bit. Then came the great moment after eight or nine days – my first solo.

Off I went, pretty nervous about it. I'd been shown round the cockpit quite often by old sweats who had been there several years, and given some tips on take-off and landing, but it was never quite the same as opening the throttle of a 1000-horsepower motor and trundling along and finding yourself airborne. You throttled back through revs and selected 'up' on the undercarriage and start pumping with one hand, the other hand on the throttle is doing rather the same thing, and for the people on the ground it was even more scary as you were doing this as you were taking off and suddenly the block of hangars shot past your wing, and you'd think, 'Oh Christ! I wonder how much I missed that by!'

Pilot Officer Glen Niven

(CANADIAN) 602 AND 601 SQUADRONS

On my second solo, the squadron had just been equipped with Spitfires, which frightened them all to death, because it could do 300 mph, and the Gauntlet, flat out, could only do 150 mph. I got halfway across the aerodrome and I saw six Spitfires coming towards me. The chaps all said that the one thing with a bloody Spitfire is that you can't see where you're going landing because of the ruddy great nose with a huge engine – you have to look sideways. I saw them coming in to land and thought they couldn't see me. So I opened the throttle and went like a bomb towards the hedge.

Up to then the aircraft had a handle like a brake in a car, and you pulled it up to slow it down. Some bugger had fixed it – I moved it one inch and the wheels jammed. So I went straight on to my nose. I thought that was me finished. I stopped the engine – I was not going all that fast but I just wanted to get out of their way because I thought they couldn't see me. I was walking back from the far side of the aerodrome and I saw someone with a car.

'Problem, young Niven?'

I thought I was going to get thrown out, but maybe because the chief instructor, Sharratt, was a Canadian, he said, 'Don't worry. We'll get a new propeller.'

Flying Officer Geoffrey Page

56 SQUADRON

They were like the bulldog and the greyhound – the Hurricane being the bulldog, and the greyhound being the Spitfire, one being a tough working animal, the other a sleek, fast dog. I think their characteristics were comparable to the dog world. If anything, the Hurricane was slightly easier, but wasn't as fast and didn't have the rate of climb – but during the Battle of Britain, what really evolved was that the Hurricanes would attack the German bomber formations, and the Spitfire, because of their extra climbing capability, would go up and fight the German fighter escort.

Pilot Officer Tom Neil

249 SQUADRON

A lot of our training was low flying, and being in Yorkshire we used to wander round the Yorkshire Dales at nought feet. I remember a wonderful occasion when I was leading a formation of three, in Spitfires, somewhere around Giggleswick in the Dales, and I came across a chap up a telephone pole mending the wire. We aimed ourselves at him, and he didn't know whether to jump or stay put. I remember going round in a circle and coming at him a second time, and as I passed over the top he decided to jump. All I remember was seeing him, arms spread-eagled, as he leapt from the top of the pole. He was obviously damaged, but that didn't worry us a scrap. A nineteen-year-old pilot doesn't worry.

After that we went down to near Leeds where there was a wood with a big lake. In the middle of the lake in a canoe was a courting couple, doing what courting couples do in canoes. I remember going down, leading my trio of aeroplanes, and nearly knocking the chap out of the boat. I looked back into the mirror we had above our heads and saw the boat – it was not exactly upturned, but not going the way it should have gone – with nobody in it. I thought, 'My God, they've jumped overboard!' and I was dead keen to get away from this as quickly as I possibly could. I climbed up and took my motley crew of three away and circled for half an hour until we began to run out of fuel before going home. We exchanged glances on the ground and decided we wouldn't tell anybody what we'd just done.

Pilot Officer Ludwik Martel

(POLISH) 54 AND 603 SQUADRONS

In November 1939 we heard that we could get transferred to England and I came to England in March 1940 by boat. We were all very happy that at last we had managed to get here – there were about a hundred of us on the ferry who had been waiting to come to England. We'd heard so much about England, and this was the only country that was going to fight the Germans. I left Poland very angry. We were all hoping we would get back to flying sooner or later and that was the object of our coming to England.

We were attached to Eastchurch where there were quite a few Poles and there we started to learn English. We had special lessons – we had plenty of time and we felt we should make the maximum effort to learn English so we could fly again.

We were welcomed with open arms. The British people were so friendly to us – they were happy to have us there in 1940.

There were differences in the construction of Polish and English aircraft so we had to learn that. I'd had about 250 hours' flying in Poland, and I just looked forward to continuing in England. The first aircraft I trained on in England was the Tiger Moth – very pleasant, but quite a demanding aircraft to fly. I just enjoyed it, hoping we could go in stages to something better. The next aircraft was another trainer – a Magister.

During this time we got some time on the Link trainer – it gave us experience and it was a chance to get a good look at the instrumentation and remind us of what was coming. We tried to learn as much as possible on the practical side, but it was a dream when we were posted to an OTU to try the new aircraft.

From the OTU we did all the training we needed to fly the Spitfire and Hurricane and were there nearly a month before we were posted to squadrons. The Hurricane, for a fighter aircraft, was a huge big cow, but it was a good experience. The dream was to fly the Spitfire, and when I was in the 7 OTU there was a moment when news came to the flight commander that they wanted two pilots to fly Spitfires in a Spitfire squadron. I had about forty minutes' flying in a Spitfire and a friend of mine the same, and we were sent to a Spitfire squadron at Hornchurch – 54 Squadron. I stayed there for about a month then 54 Squadron was posted away from Hornchurch for rest and I was transferred to 603 Squadron – City of Edinburgh. I was with that squadron for a very long time, and I was very happy with it.

Flying a Spitfire is just a dream come true. I thought there was nothing nicer than to be able to fly a Spitfire.

The authorities decided that you had to have a similar aircraft – dual aircraft – before you got to fly a Hurricane or Spitfire, and the choice was a dual Fairey Battle – which was used as a bomber, but being a dual-control, we had two or three flights in it, landing and taking off. Provided you could cope with that, the instructor would decide if you could fly a Hurricane or Spitfire. At that time I was lucky that I got posted to a Spitfire squadron because they had big losses during the Battle of Britain and they wanted replacements.

The training was very pleasant because I was doing something I'd been dreaming of for months. The transfer from 54 to 603 was a very happy one because 603 was an auxiliary squadron and the pilots were very nice people who were flying because they loved to fly and wanted to form an auxiliary squadron. 603 was special because the people came from Edinburgh and they always remembered they were Scots. I came to it as a Pole and I was very proud to be a Pole flying in this Scottish squadron – it was an experience that doesn't come very often.

There was Gilroy – one of the aces – and Uncle George, who was the CO. There were about a dozen people – all very nice. Al Deere was my first CO in 54 Squadron and I was very proud to be in his flight. Al Deere was very charming – he was a Catholic and I am a Catholic, and he said, 'You don't have to worry, Ludwik. God is taking care of us.' He was a very strong believer, and I felt that too.

We were very aware that although we were fighting in England, we were fighting for Poland too. In Poland food rationing was very bad and to try to get extra was an offence, and you would be heavily punished. People tried to grow food and it was an advantage to do this if possible, but there wasn't much available. My brother was taken to the camp by the Germans and was working in an aircraft factory. My sisters were put on a farm. One brother managed to stay home to look after my stepmother because she wasn't well. Otherwise everyone was distributed according to the Germans' needs. Some people said they were treated well and some badly – it depended on the people. There were some decent people among the Germans.

At Drem we didn't do much for recreation – we would only meet people when there were parties – we were invited to private houses for meals, which was very nice, but we all had our own way of living and it wasn't that easy. At the beginning it was embarrassing because of language difficulties. You couldn't express yourself and sometimes you said something and you looked funny. We met one or two women – the wives of pilots – but we didn't meet local girls. Sometimes we would go to Berwick to the cinema, but you had to have transport and that was a problem.

Pilot Officer Tom Neil

249 SQUADRON

The life of the Merlin engine in fighter aircraft during the war was 240 hours and you had them inspected every thirty or forty hours. At the end of 240 hours the aeroplane was taken away. This amounted to about nine months' flying – and then it went away to maintenance units. The engine was taken out and replaced and a lot of other modifications were done. Then the engine that was put in was known as a 'second life engine'. In its original 240 hours you could trust the Merlin absolutely implicitly. The second life engine was not quite so good. This was mainly because all the ancillary parts, like the generator, were not changed, and used to give us trouble, so if you had a squadron with second life engines you really ran into problems.

The Hurricane came to us as a tried and trusted aeroplane because it had been over in France during the Phoney War and had done very well. We'd heard strange tales about Hurricanes flying from Glasgow to London from the bloke in the London Squadron, at four hundred and something miles an hour. Well, what he did was to get up into the jetstream and fly downwind, so obviously he went very fast. It was a bigger aircraft than the Spitfire, but it wasn't as well developed. And the Spitfire was all metal and

Pilot Officer Tom Neil, 249 Squadron.

the Hurricane was very largely a fabric-covered steel frame – so the Hurricane was developed over a period of years but with only one or two different developments.

The Spitfire finished the war with twenty-four different marks and fifty-six different variations. But both were designed as interceptor aircraft – they were designed to take off quickly, climb to altitude as quickly as possible and stay up for an hour and a half, shoot their guns – and you had about fifteen seconds' fire in your guns – come back, refuel and do the same thing again. The difference between the Hurricane and the Spitfire was that the Spitfire climbed at 180 mph – which meant that it climbed at that sort of angle – and the Hurricane had what they called a 'high lift wing' which was very thick, and it climbed like that, at 140 mph – which got you to a height quicker, but of course it got you to the scene of the battle at a speed you didn't really want to go into the fight at, because the best fighting speed was about 220 or 240 at, say, 17,000 feet.

When you arrived at the bomber formation you were much too slow, so very often we used to have to circle and work up a bit of speed in order to make our attack. The Hurricane didn't have the agility of a Spitfire, and you couldn't catch a 109 in a Hurricane – once the 109 saw you, it could dictate the terms of combat. It could dive away or climb away – and you really couldn't cope with it in a Hurricane.

Sergeant Pilot Iain Hutchinson

222 SQUADRON

The Spitfire was like a really powerful sports car. It was highly manoeuvrable, and it was nose heavy. It had a narrow track undercarriage and two pitch propellers, so you had to be careful taxiing and careful taking off, because with its powerful engine there was an enormous amount of torque. While the propeller was trying to turn round the aircraft, the aircraft was trying to turn round the propeller. That meant it put a lot of weight on one wheel and that wheel therefore tended to drag, so you had a tendency to swing to one side. You had to counter that carefully. When you opened up the throttle, you had to open it up gently. You also had to make sure that you were in fine pitch, because if you didn't, the airfield runway wasn't long enough to take off in.

Pilot Officer Nigel Rose

602 SQUADRON

The brakes were pedals on the Spit – through the rudder there were pedals for the brakes and you gradually applied those – not too firmly because it was not too dry an airfield and you came to a standstill – haaaaa. The first time, everybody admits, was a little bit scary. It was a lovely sensation, even to begin with – the feeling of this beautiful aeroplane which answered so neatly to the controls, with a lot of power, and speed. A little side thing – a year later after we'd been down to Tangmere through the Battle of Britain, one of the aircraft towards the end of the time at Tangmere had been shot up and the pilot got it back, and had to bring it back in a very poor condition. He must have been wounded, and he got the aircraft back, but it was sent off to the maintenance unit for considerable repair.

When they were taking this aircraft to pieces, in the exhaust manifolds they found two little sticks of dynamite, and this was not the first bit of sabotage that had been discovered. We don't know anything about that but the reason I mention it is that this was the aircraft I did my first solo in. We don't know whether those sticks of dynamite had been placed in it by somebody on the ground staff who had perhaps a connection with the Communists in Clydeside – we couldn't tell. I don't think they ever discovered. I can't see it being put there while we were in the thick of it down south – or it might have been somebody who was still part of the rather nasty organisation who were trying to do their part for the Russians, who weren't on our side in those days. I think the Russians then had a treaty with the Germans, but in June 1941 the Germans attacked them.

Our CO didn't find out about this until after we left – somebody in the CID or Air Ministry or brother organisation had been notified by the maintenance unit who'd disassembled this bit and found the sticks of dynamite, and probably got the bomb people to come and dispose of them. Fortunately they hadn't been ignited and the whole story was most extraordinary. I wondered if I'd been carrying them around for a month or two . . .

The idea was that it would almost certainly be detonated by the heat of the exhaust. It needed a detonator – it wasn't just something you could set fire to casually, but even so.

Pilot Officer Tim Vigors

222 SQUADRON

Following my training at Cranwell and Aston Down, I was posted to 222 Squadron at Duxford. Shortly after I'd arrived with my dog, Snipe, I was talking with some of the other new arrivals when a broad-shouldered, dark-haired, determined-looking flight lieutenant, much older than any of us, entered the door at the far end of the room. 'Marvellous how he can get along without 'em,' remarked one of my companions.

'Without what?' I queried. The man in question looked to me to have just about everything he needed. 'Without his legs, of course.' This was my first sight of Flight Lieutenant Bader. My informant said that Bader had lost both his legs when he crashed a Bristol Bulldog, doing a slow roll straight off the ground some ten years before. He was out of the service for a long time but managed to get back in just before war was declared.

Bader strode across the room towards us, moving with only the slightest of stiffness apparent. 'Are you Vigors?' he said, his piercing blue eyes looking straight into mine.

'That's me,' I replied, holding his gaze. 'You've been put in my flight. Come on over to my office. I want to talk to you.'

I followed him out of the door. We walked down the side of the hangar at a brisk pace and I just couldn't believe that the man striding out beside me had no legs. He must have guessed what I was thinking, for as we turned into his office Bader said, 'Yes, it is a bloody nuisance having no legs.' He lowered himself into his chair, motioning me to sit also. 'But it has its compensations. One of these days a Hun may shoot me through the legs and then who will be laughing?'

Sergeant Pilot Iain Hutchinson

222 SQUADRON

After I'd flown for a while in the Volunteer Reserve, I applied for a short service commission and, not unsurprisingly, I was rejected because they already had me as a trained pilot, so why should they pay more money to me to do the same thing? I then applied for a commission in the navy and on 31 August 1939 I got a letter saying, 'You have been accepted for a short service commission in the Fleet Air Arm, joining instructions will be sent,' but that was a bit late, because the next day we were called up.

I was sent to No. 12 Service Flying Training School at Grantham, where we were split up into single-engined pilots, destined to go to fighters, and multi-engined, and I was put in the multi-engined group where we flew Ansons – and a more pedestrian aircraft you can't imagine. It wasn't until March 1940 that I came back from leave to find a Christmas present – a whole squadron of Spitfires!

We converted to these and you were really on front-line aircraft of the first class, equal to anything the opposition might have.

Pilot Officer Nigel Rose

602 SQUADRON

The whole flying school at Kinloss was upended and moved to Cranfield in Bedfordshire – it's now the University of the Air. We got our wings there because by then we'd had all our tests and we were taken up by the chief flying instructor – and you had to sit written tests.

We then waited – and this was while Dunkirk was on and the battle for France was in full flight. Most of us on single engines were posted to OTUs – but as Dunkirk was more or less over, Churchill told Dowding (or the other way round) that fighter squadrons must not be sent to France any more, but the chaps posted to OTUs must be posted straight to squadrons because they were getting a bit short of pilots. I had been posted to Sutton Bridge which was an OTU, and when I got there – I'd just got my commission, and I looked forward to a life of comfort – the chap said that a cable had come in that morning saying that my posting there had been cancelled and I was to go to a squadron – and he said he'd try to find out which one it was.

Everything was very vague about postings. I didn't do any gunnery training or advanced operational training – which was a great pity because the instructors in those places had already had some experience in France and were there to teach us what was needed in real life – in real fighter operations, to get in there close behind and don't squirt into the air or all over the countryside and think the enemy was going to fall out of the sky – because they weren't.

Pilot Officer Tom Neil

249 SQUADRON

War broke out on 3 September, but in the meantime I had left school when I was eighteen and my father insisted that I go into a bank, because he said that I ought to know something about money – which couldn't have been less true. I used to go over there two or three nights a week, learning how to do navigation and other things like that, and on 3 September we all appeared at our headquarters in Manchester and somebody said, 'We are now at war, chaps,' and they had a radio which gave the Prime Minister's speech. I remember it virtually word for word.

We all waited to be thrown in at the breach, expecting to be bombed out of existence almost immediately – instead of which nothing happened, and we were all sent home. We wandered around for a few weeks at home, drawing the princely sum of £12 every fortnight – the like of which I'd never received in my life before. In those days the pound meant a lot of money.

Then I was sent to flying training school. I'd hoped to go to Zeeland which was not too far away from where I lived, but not a bit of it. I was sent up to the north of Scotland to No. 8 FTS Montrose. There we were introduced to Hawker Harts, Hawker Furies and Hawker Audaxes – it was a wonderful period. I was there until early May 1940, by which time I'd done 156 hours and 15 minutes, and I was posted straight to a squadron, there being very few operational training units in those days. I got to a newly forming squadron at Church Fenton. I had no idea where Church Fenton was – I had to look at my school atlas to find out – and it was in Yorkshire.

I turned up there by train, because that was the only way of travelling around in those days – cars were pretty thin on the ground and nobody had any petrol anyway. It just so happened that I was the first officer to arrive at 249 Squadron – so I had a rather spurious element of seniority because of being first to arrive – Acting Pilot Officer T.F. Neil. I found that we had no aeroplanes and that we were designated as a Hurricane squadron, because it said so on my posting notice. So it was no surprise to us when eight Spitfires turned up, and we flew Spitfires straight from biplanes. None of us (most of us were volunteer reservists) had ever flown monoplanes before and suddenly we were faced with these fearsome Spitfires.

The bloke said to me, 'This is a Spitfire. Get in and fly it.' All the training you had was to sit in the hangar with the blindfold round your eyes – the Spitfire was up on trestles – and you felt around the cockpit trying to identify all the tits and bits, pulling the wheels up and you put the flaps down, etc. – half a day.

Then you were introduced to your aeroplane and told to get on with it – and that was that. We flew incessantly, because we were told we'd been given five weeks to become operational – that is, fit to take on the enemy. So on 15 May I started flying Spitfires, and I did a hundred hours in four weeks – about five hours a day – because you had to do other duties in those days, being a pilot was only part of your life in the Royal Air Force. You had to do the duty pilot, you had to do orderly officer – you had to do all sorts of things as well, so sometimes you couldn't fly during the day.

The squadron did more flying on Spitfires than anyone had achieved before – 1,010 hours in four weeks – which is a lot of flying. Then suddenly one day we were told that our Spitfires were going to be taken away from us and we were going to be given Hurricanes – and the Hurricanes turned up the next day. We climbed out of one aircraft into another and flew Hurricanes, just as hard as we'd flown Spitfires.

First Combat and the Battle for France

For the people of Britain there was a brief – but hopelessly optimistic – respite from the conviction that war was unavoidable when Prime Minister Chamberlain returned from talks with the German Chancellor Hitler in September 1938 with a promise of 'Peace for our time'. Air Marshal Sir Hugh Dowding, however, continued to pursue his goals of building the strength of the RAF, increasing the production of new fighter aircraft and setting up the radar defence chain around the south coast.

The nation's optimism was shattered when Hitler invaded and annexed Czechoslovakia in March 1939 – and went on to invade Poland on 1 September. Two days later, Chamberlain addressed the nation:

This morning the British Ambassador in Berlin handed the German Government a final note stating that unless we heard from them by 11 am that they were prepared at once to withdraw their troops from Poland, a state of war would exist between us. I have to tell you that no such undertaking has been received, and that consequently this country is at war with Germany.

At once preparations were made to send troops and the Advanced Air Striking Force across the Channel to stand against any encroachment Hitler chose to make beyond the Belgian border and into France. Dowding once more found himself at odds with the wishes of senior air staff. He resisted all demands that Spitfire squadrons be sent abroad – the new elite aircraft were too crucial to his defence plans for Britain to sacrifice them in a bid to protect other nations.

For the first nine months of the war the presence – or otherwise – of Spitfires in France and Belgium was immaterial. The 'Phoney War' lulled the nation into a sense of false security – which was broken when on 10 May 1940 German troops parachuted into Belgium as a prelude to the full-scale invasion of Belgium, Holland, France and Luxembourg – Blitzkrieg. Tanks and motorised troops and guns smashed through the Belgian and French defences in a relentless and irresistible wave – and the RAF squadrons who had been rusticating comfortably at their adopted airfields, making only standing patrols and reconnaissance flights, were suddenly in action.

For the first time the German Luftwaffe showed its strength, bombing strategic targets, devastating civilian dwellings – and strafing the streams of defenceless refugees who took to the roads to flee the advancing enemy. Dowding's fighter boys now met the new adversary – the Me 109 fighter – and as they were unprepared for its speed and agility, losses were high. In his plan, Dowding had set at fifty-two the number of squadrons essential to defend Britain. A full-strength squadron would be twenty aircraft and two reserves, plus sixteen operational pilots. The squadron would be expected to fly twelve aircraft as either four flights of three, or three flights of four. For him the 'security of base' overrode all other considerations – but by 13 May his reserve of home squadrons was down to just thirty-six. This parlous state strengthened Dowding's resolve not to jeopardise more vital fighters in a bid to remedy the situation in France.

As the German advance beat the British Expeditionary Force back to the beaches of Dunkirk, RAF fighters flew from bases in France and from forward airfields in England – Hawkinge and Manston. The troops on the ground, taking cover from German strafing and bombing over Dunkirk, unfairly accused the RAF of failing to protect them – but the fighters were there. If they were not seen it was often because they were far inland, trying to prevent German bombers from getting near to the beaches, or were so high above Dunkirk that they were out of sight. The RAF knew they were in a battle, and by the time all British forces were evacuated from France on 18 June, the Luftwaffe had lost 150 aircraft shot down – but the RAF had lost 25 per cent of its strength – 100 precious fighter aircraft, and 80 irreplaceable pilots.

To: Air Council
   Air Ministry
16th May 1940

Sir,

I have the honour to refer to the very serious calls which have recently been made upon the Home Defence Fighter Units in an attempt to stem the German invasion on the Continent.

2. I hope and believe that our Armies may yet be victorious in France and Belgium, but we have to face the possibility that they may be defeated.

3. In this case I presume that there is no one who will deny that England should fight on, even though the remainder of the Continent of Europe is dominated by the Germans.

4. For this purpose it is necessary to retain some minimum fighter strength in this country and I must request that the Air Council will inform me what they consider this minimum strength to be, in order that I may make my dispositions accordingly.

5. I would remind the Air Council that the last estimate which they made as to the force necessary to defend this country was 52 Squadrons, and my strength has now been reduced to the equivalent of 36 Squadrons.

6. Once a decision has been reached as to the limit on which the Air Council and the Cabinet are prepared to stake the existence of the country, it should be made clear to the Allied Commanders on the Continent that not a single aeroplane from Fighter Command beyond the limit will be sent across the Channel, no matter how desperate the situation may become.

7. It will, of course, be remembered that the estimate of fifty-two squadrons was based on the assumption that the attack would come from the eastwards except in so far as the defences might be outflanked in flight. We have now to face the possibility that attacks may come from Spain or even from the North coast of France. The result is that our line is very much extended at the same time as our resources are reduced.

8. I must point out that within the last few days the equivalent of ten squadrons have been sent to France, that the Hurricane squadrons remaining in this country are seriously depleted, and that the more squadrons which are sent to France the higher will be the wastage and the more insistent the demand for reinforcements.

9. I must therefore request that as a matter of paramount urgency the Air Ministry will consider and decide what level of strength is to be left to the Fighter Command for the defence of this country, and will assure me that when this level has been reached, not one fighter will be sent across the Channel however urgent and insistent the appeals for help may be.

10. I believe that, if an adequate fighter force is kept in this country, if the fleet remains in being, and if Home Forces are suitably organised to resist invasion, we should be able to carry on the war single-handed for some time, if not indefinitely. But, if the Home Defence Force is drained away in desperate attempts to remedy the situation in France, defeat in France will involve the final, complete and irremediable defeat of this country.

I have the honour to be,

Sir,

Your obedient Servant

Air Chief Marshal

Air Chief Marshal Sir Hugh Dowding. 'It was Germany's objective to win the war by an invasion, and it was my job to prevent such an invasion from taking place.'

Pilot Officer Frank Carey

43 SQUADRON

I was a fully trained pilot when war broke out. I had joined the RAF in 1927, and had four years' flying experience and even one year on Hurricanes before anything started. In November 1939 I was sent to a North Sea station from Tangmere with 43 Squadron.

It was a very, very cold winter. We were in a sort of hutted camp in Acklington, which is not the warmest place at the best of times! Our first important task there was to find a way to cope with the Germans who used to come over with an individual He III when the cloud base was at about 1,000 feet. They'd pick out small fishing boats and coastal shipping and bomb and strafe them. Our job was really to clobber these chaps. This was very difficult because, if they spotted us, they went up in cloud and hid for a while and came back down again, for as long as they had fuel. I don't know how we thought of it, but one day the idea came that we should keep right on the deck – because you can't be seen nearly as well if you're skating across the sea at nought feet. The moment we did that we started to have success. We hit them before they could clamber up and get away. It made all the difference.

Squadron Leader Sandy Johnstone

602 SQUADRON

Together with pilots of 603 (City of Edinburgh) Squadron, I took part in the first historical fighter engagement over the United Kingdom on 16 October 1939, when German bombers attacked naval units moored near the Forth Bridge. My first victory was at night when I attacked a Heinkel bomber caught in the searchlights – it crashed into the sea and the crew were taken prisoner.

People went about their everyday business with little idea of what was taking place high in the sky. Usually all they saw was the ever-changing patterns of our white vapour trails, but sometimes they would see us as a number of tiny specks scintillating like diamonds in the strong sunlight of those cloudless days.

Flight Lieutenant Peter Brothers
32 AND 257 SQUADRONS

The first hint of war came into my life with the Munich crisis, when I began to think, yes, this is deadly serious. Then came the so-called Phoney War, convoy patrols and constant scrambles, but you never saw the enemy. When we went into action for the first time, on 10 May 1940, we were told to ground-strafe an airfield in Holland which had been captured by the Germans.

I was leading the squadron because the commanding officer was new, and flying number two to me. We left 'A' Flight up above to protect us whilst we went down to ground-strafe, but to my surprise the airfield was covered with Junkers 52s, troop transport aircraft. They were all burned out in the middle, but the nose, tail and wing tips were still there. We thought this was very odd, so we didn't fire at them because it was a waste of time. Then we found one undamaged aircraft parked between some hangars. We set that on fire and came back to base. It was some months later before we discovered that the Dutch had recaptured the airfield just before our arrival. They'd destroyed those aircraft on the ground, leaving one in which to escape to England. And that was the one we'd set on fire.

We then started doing the usual thing, going to France for the day. We started in Belgium, at a place called Mooresele. It was only a little flying club airfield, and when we arrived, the chaps there, 615 Squadron, were rather jumpy because refugees were streaming down the road, and that morning one of their sergeant pilots had been found with a knife in his chest. We operated from there during the day, but it was all very chaotic. We received no instructions, and not only did we have to refuel the aircraft ourselves, but we also had to hand-start them. We'd start mine, then I'd get out and wind somebody else's, and so on, until we'd got them all started.

We received no assistance whatsoever from the French. In fact, on one occasion, we were refuelling when a Do 17 flew over us at about 8,000 feet. We thought he was going to bomb us on the ground, but he carried on his way. Meanwhile, there was a French fighter aircraft doing aerobatics over the airfield. When we shouted to the Colonel and pointed to the aircraft, he said, 'Oh, today he is only authorised for aerobatics, not combat.'

It was a very tiring business, because we were getting up at about three o'clock in the morning, having breakfast, getting airborne in the dark, flying inland across the French coast and arriving at first light. We'd spend the day operating there with no assistance, begging food from a local farmer or something, then come out at Le Havre and back across the Channel, reaching Biggin Hill at 9.30 or 10 at night, having a meal and going to bed. Then being called up in the morning again. Very wearing. It all seemed rather pointless too, because we didn't feel we were achieving very much. We had several engagements in France but not enough, I would have said, to justify our presence there.

The bombing of UK ports started next, as well as attacks on our airfield at Biggin Hill. I had got married in 1939, and one night I went to see my wife, in Westerham, and discovered that she'd been sitting at her dressing-table one evening, and a bomb splinter had come through the open window and smashed her mirror while she'd been sitting there. I decided these people needed to be taught a sharp lesson.

Prior to the evacuation of Dunkirk in 1940, we had several combats while we were operating in places like Merville. The first chap we lost was my great chum, Johnny Milner. He baled out and became a prisoner of war. Interestingly, all the fatal casualties were new boys. Chaps got shot down, they got burned and were wounded, but they survived. The only ones who were killed were the replacements coming in. Of course, most of the chaps had been in the squadron for a couple of years, so they knew the aircraft, they knew the tactics. They knew what they were doing.

Taking on the enemy was a game to start off with. It was fun and you didn't wish to hurt anybody. You wanted to shoot an aircraft down, but when you'd actually hit a cockpit . . . well, it was a bit sick-making to see that you'd killed a chap. That was only in the early days. Later on, you couldn't give a damn whether you'd killed someone or not – you thought, 'So much the better!'

I vividly remember shooting a 109 down and seeing him crash in Kent. He went straight into the ground, and I flew over it, thinking, 'Jolly good, that's one. Now, where are the rest?' The object really was to shoot the bombers down as the fighters weren't doing any damage to anybody, apart from ourselves. The trouble was that, when you attacked the bombers, you got jumped by their fighter escort. That often used to happen to me, probably because I was flight commander leading 'B' Flight. 'A' Flight would go in after the bombers first, followed by us, by which time the fighter escort was coming down, and so we'd be the ones who'd break away to fight them off.

Bringing down a bomber was really satisfying, particularly if you got it before it dropped its bombs. Getting them when they were on their way home was better than nothing, but if you'd caught them before they'd made their drop, it was a real success. You usually went for the engines, but one of the best ways to attack them was head-on. The He III, for example, had a glazed nose, and they could see you coming, but they'd got no protection head-on; all their guns were firing backwards. Our machine guns were arranged to fire a pattern at 250 yards, although some of us decided to have our guns turned in to concentrate at a point. Usually, we tried to get much closer than 250 yards. In head-on attacks the question was whether you went over the top of the aircraft or underneath it after the firing. I always used to go down, because I thought the bomber would pull up instinctively.

I was hit once in those early operations. I got shot up and the controls were broken, shot away. I was halfway out of the cockpit before I realised the aircraft was still controllable, and climbed back in again.

Stukas were pretty easy meat because you could shoot straight into the top of them as they pulled out of their dive and they were slower than we were. That awful screaming sound they made had been built into them to terrify people. Once they had started the dive, you could follow them down, and hit them if you were lucky. If you were too close, of course, you'd overtake.

Pilot Officer Nigel Rose
602 SQUADRON

At Drem the only actual enemy action I saw was at night where they were still trying to bomb Clydeside and the Forth Bridge. Our squadron was sent up every now and then because there was a warning of something approaching by stations in Yorkshire. We were put up in the air quite a bit but never saw a German by day – but the squadron had had a number of episodes before I arrived there – famously some months before I arrived one of the first raids the Germans put across to try to get the Forth Bridge, a Heinkel came over and the squadron was under the command of Squadron Leader Farquhar – a Scot – and they got up in time to shoot this Heinkel down. He evidently couldn't continue his flight so he jettisoned his bombs in the Forth and found a lovely large field and put down in it on his belly.

Farquhar sent the chaps that had been with him back to base and said, 'I know I've expended my ammunition on this thing, and we don't want this chap to set fire to it and there may be important things in the aircraft – I'd better make sure I get hold of the chaps before they set fire to the thing. It's a big enough field so I'll put down too.' But he failed to notice that there was a ditch across the middle of the field so in due course he turned over and landed – he was running along still doing 20–30 mph – in this ditch. There he was, on his back up above the ground, which would be sufficient to break his neck if he pulled his straps – because there was no way of dropping yourself gently on the ground if you were upside down in a Spitfire.

The Germans meanwhile had climbed out of their aircraft, and having seen this Spit doing this curious exercise they scratched their heads as it was strange for a chap to immolate himself right in front of them. They went over and gently eased him out of his aircraft and put him on his feet. Whereupon – I think he was a bit puzzled by all this too – they were chatting for a while and Farquhar noticed that there was a body of men with what looked like pitchforks arriving on the horizon.

In fact, this was the Land Army with all the weapons they could muster. I don't know if they had First World War rifles with a round or two up the spout – it's possible. But he drew his captors' attention to this, 'In no way had I better leave you to this lot – you'd better surrender your Lugers. It would be better for you.' Two or three of them had revolvers and they handed them over to him – obviously a gentleman. When these chaps came nearer they reckoned they'd got the lot, and they surrounded them all, including Farquhar – especially as he was carrying German revolvers which he had to hand over to the Land Army.

The whole lot were marched up the hill – and Farquhar was now a POW – and the Land Army marched them up to the local farmhouse where the farmer's wife provided them with a cup of tea, while they awaited the arrival of somebody from the army who came up with their rifles, and the whole thing was explained. They sent somebody down to confirm that it was a Spitfire and that they could verify that Farquhar was a Brit. He was in flying kit because in those days you wouldn't put on anything that would identify you. His trousers might have been air force blue – but they wouldn't have taken any notice. The upper part would have been a Sutton suit from flying up a little higher.

So he got back to base and raised hell and was much commended – and also slightly in the doghouse for ruining one Spitfire. But they got the Heinkel intact, and everything that was in it.

Flying Officer Michael Wainwright

64 SQUADRON

One of our first flights on 19 May we had to patrol Calais and Boulogne, and I had my section – Red Section – but Yellow Section got shot at by some Germans, and they had some slight damage but nothing serious.

On one very bad day we had four sections of three stepped down – because you couldn't see in front of you in a Spitfire so you flew below the section in front of you so you could see them to keep in formation. In the afternoon we made the landfall of Calais and made a left-hand turn to go to Dunkirk, and we might have been doing a fly-past for the Queen's birthday – perfect formation – and we got bounced by Me 110s and we lost a whole front section with the CO and two others, and some others from another section.

I said to my section, 'Let's get into a turn and see what we're doing and one of you starts to do lookout.'

I said to my number two, 'Do the lookout. Number one, keep in formation with me.'

So I started going round, looking to see what was happening, in a right-hand turn, because in a Spitfire, if you wanted to sort things out, it was best to go into a right-hand turn. I saw an Me 109 and a Do 17 go past me and I thought, 'Oh my God, what's next?'

My number two said, 'I think you're going to get somebody on your tail,' so I told number one to break away – every man for himself. I went into a steep right hand turn and then a 109 spun in while chasing me round in the right-hand bend. I was going quite slowly and he tried to get in front of me to shoot and he spun in. He pulled it too hard and he spun in so I put him down. I couldn't claim him because I didn't shoot him. We'd started off from Gravesend, so we went back there – we knew that three had gone, but we didn't know what the others had done. I think they went back and landed somewhere else – but there were only five of us at Gravesend, and Keith Park who was the AOC of 11 Group came to see what was happening.

My flight commander survived – then I said, 'Excuse me; I've got something to say. We were flying in perfect formation and got bounced. It's crazy. If we're going to survive we can't go up that way.'

It was Keith Park who went back and said that we should fly in looser formation so that somebody could keep an eye on things. Then they decided to put on little mirrors so you could see what was behind you – but you couldn't see much as there wasn't much field of view. Thereafter they kept our squadron on the front line and they used to try to replace our losses one at a time, so we never got back to a full twelve-aeroplane squadron for some little time.

Flying Officer Gerry Edge

605 SQUADRON

On 23 May we were ordered to take off at 4.50 hrs, and I led 2 Squadron of Spitfires with 605 Squadron of Hurricanes to rendezvous over the coast. I had not been to bed for five nights and had difficulty keeping my eyes open. The trouble seemed to be that the evening shift of controllers kept telling us we would not be called before midday, and the next shift brought us to readiness at dawn. However, I thought I could manage one more patrol – but I did not know if there had been any other wings patrolling and thought this might be the first, and I was sorry not to be in better condition.

We joined the Spitfires at 6,000 feet over the coast and climbed to 20,000, crossing into France just south of Boulogne, and set course for Bethune. My eyes closed and I was asleep; waking with a start, I looked to starboard and saw what for a moment I took to be a formation of enemy aircraft – and I thought I had let my wing be jumped. I then realised that my port wing was pointing at the ground and that the aircraft I had just seen were those I was meant to be leading. I climbed back and took over the lead again, and we carried out the sweep without seeing any enemy aircraft.

On landing, I turned off the petrol and then switched off the magnetos before my plane stopped rolling and as the propeller stopped I was asleep again. My crew thought I had been wounded and had brought a stretcher for me, and were trying to lift me out of the cockpit when I woke.

Flight Lieutenant Robert Stanford Tuck

92 AND 257 SQUADRONS

When war broke out, I'd been in the RAF for some four years and was delighted when I was posted as a flight commander to a new Spitfire squadron that had just been formed. We put in some pretty intensive training and long before the spring of 1940 arrived, we were right up to the mark and ready to go. Our first combat chanced to be with a large formation of Me 109s. It took place over the coast of north Belgium in May, and the first thing I noticed after we had closed with them was that the air seemed to be full of planes milling around. I singled one out, and was lucky enough to shoot him down in a wood near St Omer. On that first meeting, the squadron shot down eleven Huns for the loss of one of our pilots, who had crash-landed on the beach. That beach near St Omer shall be one of the first places I will visit when we have won the war – because while out on our second patrol that same afternoon, I shot down two Me 110s right beside it.

I had picked the first one out of a large bunch covering a bunch of Ju 87s which were dive-bombing the harbour, and I forced him to crash-land beside the wreckage of my morning Me 109. Incidentally, the pilot of that Me 110 very nearly made an early end to my fighting career with nothing more than a pistol. I had circled him very low to make sure that he'd crashed when he stepped out of the cockpit, apparently unhurt, and took a pot shot at me with his pistol. It was either wizard shooting or the world's biggest fluke – for that shot went through my windscreen within an inch or two of my head.

I turned quickly and dealt with him, and as I did so, I saw that another 110 had been snooping along behind me over the treetops. He opened up with cannon-fire and put a shell through my fuselage. I did a tight turn, squirted at him with what ammunition I had left, and he went down and crashed alongside his two friends. As you can imagine, I was pretty bucked with that bag of three from my first day in action.

There were a couple of Do 17s the next day, and another of the same type on the third day. The second three were bagged over the Dunkirk, Calais, Boulogne area, and the last affair was a regular shooting match. I arrived back at base with no oil, no glycol and the sliding hood and side door of my Spitfire shot away. I had a cannon shot through the tail which left only two inches' play on the elevators with which to land – and I had no flaps, no brakes and a flat tyre. I did somehow manage to put it down all right, and as I finished my landing run, the engine seized up. That Spitfire was too shot up and damaged to fly again, but I was lucky enough to escape with only a slight wound in the thigh, caused by a piece of metal flying off the rudder bar.

Pilot Officer Frank Carey

43 SQUADRON

We went from Acklington up to Wick in Scotland. By that time the weather was getting a little warmer; it was March. We thought that we would be even further away from the action, but suddenly we had a raid on Scapa Flow. So we even had fun up there.

I was then commissioned, and went straight to France with 3 Squadron from Kenley. We patrolled the front line, wherever it happened to be at the time. The Hun aircraft were all over the place – you just took off and there they were. If you flew anywhere in the Pas de Calais or east over Belgium, there were lashings of them, absolutely asking for it. And they had very few fighters about at that time. Over the first four days after my arrival, I must have had about twenty engagements. I shot down what I think was about six aircraft in that period. I didn't get out of my clothes because we had nowhere except the floor to sleep. We had nowhere to eat. We used to ask the ground crew to get bits and pieces from the local village and bring them out to us. On my fourth day there, I was finally given a billet. So I picked up my kit – which was still on a big pile at the edge of the airfield – and took it to this place. I was on the dawn shift the next morning, so I couldn't sleep there, and I thought, 'Tomorrow night I'll have a bath and I'll have a sleep.' And then I was shot down.

I was attacking a Do 17 and it did a snap half-roll – which was an extraordinary thing for a kite of that size to do. I did the same and followed it closely down. It was nearly vertical; in fact, the pilot was dead, I think, because it just went straight on in. But before I'd realised that, the rear-gunner fired and hit me well and truly. Stupidly, perhaps, I'd been following it rather closely – because it was such a fast aircraft and I knew it could get away from me. If I'd known the pilot was dead, of course, I wouldn't have bothered. Then I was busy getting down myself.

First of all, I was on fire. So I thought, 'Right, I must get out.' I thought what I had to do in my mind, pulled the thing up into nearly a stall, and stood up. Of course with a 100 mph draught over me I got thrown back, and my parachute pack got caught up in the hood. The aircraft slowly got itself into a dive, and the faster it went, the harder it was for me to get out. Eventually, I climbed up on to my own legs to get back into the cockpit. My ticker was going at a fairly fast rate; but at least the fire seemed to have gone out and I was able to select a big ploughed field and had no difficulty in getting it down.

When I stood up in the cockpit I heard a little clink – it was the core of an armour-piercing bullet which had come straight through the engine and finished up in my parachute! I knew I'd been hit in the leg, but didn't know how lucky I'd been until I examined the bullet holes in my trousers: I could have finished up with a very different category of voice! I was very lucky because I was in what they would have called, in the First World War, No-Man's-Land. The British ground forces had retired to a river a few miles back just the night before.

Being ignorant of the changed circumstances on the ground, I started walking due east, which was quite the wrong way. I'd gone quite a distance when I heard two motorcycles coming. I pulled out my revolver to sell myself dearly and greeted these two chaps by shouting at them to halt. I didn't know who they were. When they started to talk it was even more confusing because they were Belgian motorcyclists who had been on a morning patrol and had met some German tanks up the road. They'd seen me come down and they jolly bravely went across a lot of ploughed fields to where I was – and they were greeted by a revolver!

I got on the back of one of these motorbikes and they rushed me back. But all the time, of course, they were pretty worried about being caught themselves. They left me with four or five British sappers who were blowing up a bridge we had just come over, which saved me a swim across the river.

I then took up walking with the refugees along the roads; we were regularly strafed by He IIIs. Then a British Army truck came along and took me to a village somewhere south of Brussels. I had a slight leg wound, and they said there was an army medical officer in one of the houses. I went along to see him, and he gave me some brandy and cleaned up my leg quite painlessly.

I was put on another truck for a while and joined up with a bloke who had the best part of a long-nosed Blenheim front end in his eyes, and his bomb-aimer, who had only one hand. They'd been shot down a few miles from where I was. They were strafing one of the German columns and ran into a solid block of anti-aircraft guns, which threw an awful lot of stuff at them. It blew the nose off his Blenheim straight into his face and took a hand off the front bomb-aimer. The pilot only had very imperfect sight through all the bits of Perspex in his face and eyes; he crash-landed it with what little he could see, plus the directions of the one-armed bomb-aimer. They had done their best to bury the rear-gunner who had been killed outright, and collected the contents of his pockets for his next of kin.

They not only brought back their parachutes, they had disconnected the gun and brought it with them too. And they'd crossed a river with that lot! I thought they were fantastic. It sort of pulls you back and makes you think how proud you are of them. There was I, limping along, thinking I was badly wounded! It took all the limp away from me, I can tell you.

We then got into a 1914 Crossley ambulance, where they asked us if we would hold down a poor chap who was badly shattered in the pelvis with a bit of shrapnel. We were taken to a casualty clearance station which was just over the French border. That took an hour or two and it was a very bumpy trip; the poor devil was screaming his head off. On arrival, I sat on a bench in a tented camp with a lot of other people, delighted to sit down stationary at last. Then I don't remember any more, and they said that, by the time it was my turn to be dealt with, I was fast asleep. I'd had four nights with almost no sleep and no clean clothes – I must have smelt to high heaven. They dressed my wounds – they didn't bother about any anaesthetic, put me into a bed, and I woke up late the following day.

I was taken out of this casualty clearing station to a Dieppe hospital; I finished up in a ward where there were only four of us. There was the Blenheim pilot, a chap with meningitis, me and the Duke of Norfolk – a very nice fellow, very shamefaced because he was in with gout! We played rummy for two or three days.

But the Hun was moving along fast and getting closer, and eventually the commander of the hospital decided to evacuate everybody. He arranged for a hospital train, and we had just settled into our seats when a couple of dozen Heinkels came and unloaded everything they had on us. They hit the train. That was when the boat *Maid of Kent* was sunk in Dieppe harbour: it was alongside the train. The interesting thing was that, when the bombing started, there was I with the leg, limping again, and His Grace with gout, and it was touch and go who was beating whom! We did about a hundred yards in four seconds.

We felt rather sheepish because we could see all the fire and damage behind us, so we sort of tottered back and did what we could to save the seriously wounded and move them into the part of the train that wasn't burning. The walking wounded then disconnected the burning part of the train. The French driver had already unhooked his engine and disappeared. Then we pushed the train out. It was very flat there, and once we got it moving it was all right to keep it going. We pushed it out of the danger area – probably about a mile or so. Those that were able to just leaned against it. It staggered me that we were able to do it, but we did.

We were left with a very limited number of medical supplies and no medical officer that I could remember seeing, but several medical orderlies did a wonderful job. We also got our driver and engine back once the bombs had stopped. After two or three days we finished up in La Baule, a well-known resort town right on the Atlantic coast. There The Hermitage, an immensely posh hotel, was the officers' hospital.

Suddenly it was impossible to believe that there was any war going on at all. All the lights were on, we had strawberries and cream – we were in totally new surroundings! And very thankful we were for it too. The next thing was that they were going to evacuate that hospital back to England. Much to our disgust, the chap with the damaged eyes and I were discharged back to the nearest Royal Air Force unit, which was an aircraft stores depot not too far away from Nantes. I was still in the same uniform; it was full of bullet holes, but at least the shirt had been washed. There we joined up with two similar RAF derelicts. None of us knew where our units were, so we were stuck.

In the second week of June we got a message that there was a British aircraft on an adjacent airfield that somebody had left several days previously. It was a Bristol Bombay – a bright-yellow transport plane. We checked it over and filled it up with some petrol we got from a small French Air Force contingent there. The next morning at dawn we left, all four of us. They put me in the back at the rear gun, as I was the only one who had fired a gun. All the way back I was trying to find out how to work the thing. We felt very naked, I can tell you – a bright-yellow plane, clear blue sky and doing about 120 mph!

We were not sure where the front line was: the whole place was a mass of rumours. Even the Forces broadcasts didn't seem to know where anybody was. We had to take our chance. We didn't see a thing until we got just off the English coast, where the British fighters intercepted us. There were all sorts of funny-looking aircraft coming from the Continent over those days; nobody took a pot at us. Everybody knew what we were – bright yellow, 120 mph – complete lunatics! They could have hit us with rocks.

We landed at Hendon, and then I had to find out where my unit was. It turned out that my squadron had left France only two days after I was shot down! They had nothing much left, so they were sent up to Wick to relieve 43 Squadron, who came back to Tangmere. Well, 43 was my old squadron, and I wanted to get back into action. I asked the Air Ministry if I might rejoin them. They said they'd have a word with the CO, Squadron Leader George Lott. Two days before, he had taken twelve aircraft on a Dunkirk patrol, and arrived back with just two – one flight commander and himself. They didn't all get killed – some of them were shot down over the water and were picked up by boat. Others fell on land the other side and scrambled out; they were coming back in broken condition for quite a few weeks. So I was very lucky because the CO was dying to get some pilots, and I started flying again with 43 squadron in late June.

Flying Officer Gerry Edge

605 SQUADRON

On patrol in the Calais–Dunkirk area, south of Gravelines, we engaged a formation of twenty-plus Ju 87s heading for the coast. I closed with one which went on fire after a short burst and I began looking for another. I saw my number two, Pilot Officer Mike Cooper-Slipper, firing at one, which went on fire. I closed right up with a third, which went down on fire with a short burst. The sky seemed to have cleared and, for a short time, I could see no other aircraft.

I had climbed to about 8,000 feet when I saw a large formation of about 30 to 40 Ju 87s in the south-east, some 2,000 to 3,000 feet above. I did not climb away from them in case I should lose sight of them, so I opened up to full boost and climbed towards them. As they came closer, the range between us diminished very rapidly and I realised that their leader was almost overhead, so I pulled up into vertical climb. My speed dropped very quickly and I thought I would crash into the middle of them. I realised a Ju 87 was about to pass over me. I fired and my plane came to a stop, but I was hitting the Stuka from about twenty feet. Pieces of it fell past me as my aircraft was reversing away. I had never done a tailspin before, but I had been told that if I ever found myself in that position, to hold the controls against a stop, as if they were loose, the reversed airflow might smash them across and break them. I pushed my right foot hard forward and pulled the stick hard back and to the right and saw the flames below me on the starboard side.

My plane fell into a dive very smoothly, but the engine kept running and I lost a great deal of height, so I was down to a little over 1,000 feet. I turned for home and saw, about half a mile north of me, a Ju 87 flying east at 3,000 to 4,000 feet, just south of the coast road, which was packed with refugees. The rear-gunner was standing up and well out of the rear-gun cockpit, firing at the refugees. I had a good look round while diving towards him.

Overtaking too fast, I throttled right back, but to keep out of his slipstream, as I knew I could only have very little ammunition, I kept a small distance above him. The gunner suddenly started to swing his gun towards me. Easing the guns down on to target about fifty yards away, I fired and, after about one second, ran out of ammunition – but it was enough. The Stuka rolled over to port and dived into the field and burst into flames some 100–150 yards south of the coast road. Feeling naked without any ammunition, I returned to base, but being low, I ran into very heavy ack-ack, which damaged my starboard wing spar.

The aircraft had to go back to MU for repair and I asked my fitter to put my parachute – which I always left in the cockpit of my plane – into another aircraft. When he moved my chute, it revealed that the back of my aluminium seat was all dented from the rear. A shell which had hit on my previous patrol had burst on the armour plate behind my seat, but did not penetrate, the shrapnel ricocheting into the back of the seat. Further search revealed that the shell had hit the plywood cowling just forward of the throttle controls. The plywood had sprung shut, leaving only a black line about 1.5 inches long which was not easy to see, and then made a small rip in my leather glove, from where it passed through the ripcord handle, making a hole in my Irvin jacket and a tear in my uniform. It also grazed the ripcord handle on the other side. It went on to make a quarter-inch groove in the side of the seat before bursting on the armour plate.

As my crew apologised to me amidst laughter, I said, 'So you did think I was going nutty!'

They answered, 'Oh no, sir, we are sorry we didn't find the damage.'

I was really sorry to lose No. 2557, which I had been using for quite a while, and which so far had carried me safely through several tight spots over France.

Sergeant Pilot Iain Hutchinson

222 SQUADRON

We weren't taught to think about tactics, at our level – you did what you could, but you were not really thinking objectively about the whole thing, otherwise we would have done something different. But another thing I would have liked to have known about earlier is that some of our aces harmonised their guns at 50 yards, while we were harmonising ours at 250 yards – because we were being harmonised for attacking bombers. In fact, however, Spitfires were designated to tackle the enemy fighters, and you didn't tackle the enemy fighters from 250 yards. You tackled them from close up – which meant that a lot of your bullets were just zizzing off into empty air. You went up as close as you could but you weren't really being as effective as you could in destroying the other aircraft.

I only found that out after the war, when I was talking to Johnny Johnson and he was telling me that's what he did – but he was an officer and so he had the right to do that. As a sergeant pilot I would have been rapped over the knuckles if I'd tried to tell the armaments sergeant how to harmonise my guns. But it was simply a question of survival at that time.

Sergeant Fred Roberts

ARMOURER, 19 SQUADRON

We used to take the Spitfire down to the firing range at Duxford, put it up on trestles, level it fore and aft, and laterally, then sight the guns on the target in front of the firing range. The gunsight was harmonised with the guns, and then we got the pilot along. We had a little microscope that we put on the breach of the guns to sight them, and the pilot went along, on the wing, to make certain that the guns were sighted on the target to his satisfaction, and the same with the gunsight. Then we locked all the guns and wired them up. But that changed after Dunkirk, when a lot of the pilots disagreed with this method of sighting, and they had their guns harmonised on a target like a dartboard. Then all eight guns were harmonised on this one central point about 300 yards in front of the aircraft.

We didn't fire the guns – that was a pilot's job. When they wanted to fire the guns, three or four of us went and hung on to the tail of the plane while it was up on trestles, and a couple more of us were on each wing, to keep it steady while they fired the eight guns.

Flight Lieutenant Billy Drake

1 SQUADRON

We first met the Luftwaffe in France, 1939. We were standing by, but we had no early warning, and it was literally a question of looking up and if you saw a con trail you asked permission to take off and to investigate. My first sight of an enemy aircraft was when I chased one of these condensation trails until eventually I found what was causing it – which was a 109 going back to Germany.

I caught up with him and he dived away. I did my best to catch him, which I couldn't, as the 109 was a good deal faster than the

Flight Lieutenant Billy Drake, 1 Squadron, seen here later in the war.

Hurricane – however, he got down to ground level and went under some high tension cables. He pulled up to see whether he'd forced me to crash – which I hadn't – and by pulling up he lost his speed advantage and I was able to get a shot in at him and he crash-landed. He was not in flames, he just crash-landed.

It was exciting, no doubt about it. It was exciting – but what was much more exciting was that I was running out of fuel so I had to find out where I was and get back to base. I was proud of this first success, but there was nothing euphoric about it – it was just a job that I'd done for which I'd been preparing for three or four years.

Flight Lieutenant Johnny Kent

303 AND 92 SQUADRONS

About two weeks after my first sortie I flew over to France in a Hudson to visit our sole remaining base at Meaux, some forty miles east of Paris. On the way over I could see the long lines of refugees as they made their way south, away from the invading Germans; it was a horrible sight and one that made my blood boil.

On arriving at Meaux I was welcomed by Bob Niven, who declared that I was just the chap they wanted, and I had better stay. I pointed out that I had no kit of any kind and I would have to go back and get some – which I did – and returned to France the next day.

Early in June and shortly after landing from a sortie, the sirens sounded and the low hum of approaching aircraft could be heard. It turned out to be the first mass raid of the war and some 250 German aircraft took part. Their targets were various factories on the outskirts of Paris but, just for the hell of it, they dropped a number of visiting cards on us at Meaux, both on their way to Paris and on their way back.

In the middle of the attendant hullabaloo, I managed to get some of the airmen into shelters, but several were unaccounted for, so I set out to find them in case they had been wounded. By this time there was quite a fight going on overhead and jettisoned bombs, spent bullets and cartridge cases were exploding and spattering around all over the place. It was sickening to be stuck on the ground and unable to do anything about it.

The Germans were advancing more and more rapidly and it was not long before we were ordered to clear out and go south to the airfield at Bricy near Orléans. Two of us remained behind after the main party had gone to finish clearing up and then, on 9 June, we departed in the sole remaining aircraft – two Tiger Moths.

Although operating from Bricy, most of us were accommodated in Orléans, and the city was filled with refugees, all desperately trying to keep ahead of the advancing Germans. Some of the sights were so pathetic that it was impossible to avoid a moist eye – one old lady I recall particularly apparently had all her possessions piled into a pram, and swinging from the handle was a parrot cage with her pet cat inside it. She herself just wandered on as though she was unaware of the crush of people around her, all moving south.

Sergeant Pilot Paul Farnes

501 SQUADRON

My first combat was over France, before Dunkirk. I remember shooting at this and that, but I have no clear memory of most of the things I did. I can remember one or two – the pilot baling out and me waving to him – and another one I went and landed where the pilot had come down, and I met him. There was a 109 that I shot down, and the pilot baled out, and I flew around him and followed him down – I waved to him halfway back. He was all right and I saw a farmer come out to him.

Pilot Officer Frank Carey, 43 Squadron, seen here later in the war in the Far East.

Pilot Officer Frank Carey

43 SQUADRON

In early May 1940, the air over northern France and Belgium fairly teemed with German aircraft – mostly without fighter escort. With this backing, my luckiest sorties began promisingly enough when I saw a He III with one engine feathered. A short burst at the working elastic abruptly terminated its flight. Minutes later a great gaggle of some sixty-odd Ju 87 Stukas hove into view. The Stuka had the rather obliging habit of bursting into flames almost as soon as one opened fire. Two of these performed predictably and hit the ground and two others were following suit on their way down when I saw a beautiful bright-silver Do 17 float across my bows. Giving it the remainder of my ammunition in one long burst, it slewed violently with much smoke pouring out, but, being very short of fuel, I turned hurriedly for base. The conspicuous Do 17 was confirmed by a fellow pilot who saw it crash.

Flying Officer Geoffrey Page

56 SQUADRON

Our operations over Dunkirk fell into two main categories. One was that we would do a fighter sweep. We would sweep all the way round, behind the beaches and try and intercept any German aircraft coming up to attack the soldiers on the ground. In the other role, we would escort a bomber called the Blenheim, and be their fighter escort when they went to bomb targets that were related to the evacuation from Dunkirk.

I think our ground crews were the people who got into more fisticuffs in local pubs, because after a few beers, the soldiers would say, 'Where were you?' and our ground crews knew very well that we'd gone over there.

Flying Officer Geoffrey Page, 56 Squadron.

Flight Lieutenant Robert Stanford Tuck
92 AND 257 SQUADRONS

At 1045 on 23 May 1940, No. 92 (F) Squadron took off from Hornchurch, led by Squadron Leader Roger Bushell, and headed for a patrol line of Dunkirk, Calais, Boulogne. At 1145 hours a large number of Me 109s dropped on us in a steep diving attack. Pat Learmond's Spitfire immediately went down in a ball of flame – sadly 92 Squadron's first casualty of the war. As the Me 109s pulled up, using full throttle, I was able to get in behind one which had turned for home. Skimming the top of some cloud, I closed on him, knowing that he hadn't seen me. After some tense moments I had him centrally in my gunsight. At 300 yards I pushed the firing button and the Me 109 performed a violent upward manoeuvre followed by three flick-rolls, and went over on its back into a vertical dive, shedding debris.

At near maximum speed I followed him through a thin layer of cloud at 16,000 feet, but he made no attempt to pull out and hit the deck with an almighty explosion just outside St Omer. This was my first victory.

Sergeant Pilot Paul Farnes
501 SQUADRON

In France our radios were terrible. We used to get lost in France – and the maps we had were not much better than kids' geography maps. We could communicate between aircraft, but once we got away from the ground base we were out of touch. I remember that twice one of the six of us had to do a forced landing as it was getting dark. We didn't know where we were and couldn't get anything on the RT. We all got away with it and twice we had to come down – we ran out of petrol and didn't know where we were over France. At that stage the Germans hadn't reached the coast.

I never flew over Dunkirk, as we were further into France. We were trying to stop the German fighters from getting to Dunkirk, and protecting the chaps on the beach that way. We eventually got out through Le Havre through Jersey, and three of us were detailed to go on to Guernsey and see to the evacuation there. Nothing much happened and we hung around for a couple of days so we flew back to Tangmere.

Flight Lieutenant Brian Lane

19 SQUADRON

There we were smoking, talking, fourteen pilots assembled on the tarmac, wondering who would be the unlucky two who would have to stay behind on this first patrol over Dunkirk. We had brought twelve aircraft with us, and two extra pilots had come down by road the previous night. The section leaders alone looked quite happy, for they knew they were definitely starters. For fairness we drew names out of a hat and face after face lit up as its owner's name was called. In my flight the unlucky one was Flight Sergeant Unwin, and he stood looking at me with a hurt expression on his face, for all the world like a dog that has been told he can't come for a walk. I went over to try and console him, but he just shook his head sadly and said, 'Well I'm damned, sir!'

I couldn't help it – I burst out laughing, while the other pilots shot humorous remarks at him. 'Go on, Grumpy, you'll live to fight another day! Don't get too drunk while we're away!' And that was why, from that time on, one flight sergeant was called Grumpy.

On 26th May we flew over to France. Ahead rose up a great black pall of smoke from Calais, drifting out in a long trail across the water. To the left, another inky column showed the position of Dunkirk. There was something infinitely sad and terrible about that towering mass of smoke. I cannot describe just how I felt as I gazed, fascinated, on the dreadful scene, but I know that a surge of hatred for the Hun and all his filthy doings swept over me, and I felt that no mercy must be shown to a people who are a disgrace to humanity.

Flight Lieutenant Brian Lane, 19 Squadron.

As these thoughts were racing through my mind, the CO turned and we flew up the coast towards Dunkirk. We were at 18,000 just below the layer of high cloud, and turning at the other end of the patrol line we gradually lost height towards Calais. Suddenly from behind a bank of cloud appeared twenty-one Ju 87 dive-bombers, heading out to sea over Calais and looking like some sort of strange bird with their big spotted undercarriages and upswept wings. We turned in behind them and closed to the attack.

The Huns flew on unheeding, apparently suffering from the delusion that we were their own fighter escort, until the leading section of Spitfires opened fire. Panic then swept the enemy formation. They split up in all directions, hotly pursued by nine Spitfires, while Eric and Co. kept watch behind us. I picked out one dive-bomber and got on his tail, staying there as he twisted and turned this way and that, trying to avoid the eight streaks of tracer from my guns. Finally he pulled up and stalled, rolled over and then plunged headlong towards the sea out of control.

I felt happy! I had often wondered what it would feel like really to shoot at an aircraft and bring it down. Now I knew, and it was definitely exhilarating!

Flight Lieutenant Billy Drake

1 SQUADRON

When I got up to 14–15,000 feet I realised that I hadn't got any oxygen. I called up my leader and said I had no oxygen and I was going home. I looked around and I saw three or four Do 17s, and decided to have a go at them. They were quite low at about 10,000 feet, so I got behind one of them and shot at him. I realised I had inflicted damage on that one, so changed my sights on to another one – and then there was an almighty bang. An Me 110, the twin-engined fighter, had got behind me and was doing the same damage to me that I'd been doing to his chum. He was a good shot because

I was in flames and I decided the best thing was to get out. But being inexperienced in getting out of a burning aeroplane, I undid everything, but forgot to release the hood – so I didn't get out that way. But this probably saved me from getting very badly burned, as all the flames were going upwards, but by the time I'd released the hood I was upside down and all the flames were going in the right direction and not towards me. I popped out and landed in – in a field.

When I landed I'd been wounded and I thought my leg had been shot off. It was hurting like hell and my back was hurting too. The French farmers thought I was German because I was very blond in those days, so they walked towards me very cautiously with scythes and pitchforks. Fortunately I was able to speak French and I was able to persuade them that I was not a German but an Allied airman, and when they realised that and I was able to show them my wings, they couldn't have been nicer.

They took me to the local field hospital which was being evacuated at the time, so when I arrived there was no doctor – but some nurses said, 'We've got to get all this stuff out of your back – but we have no anaesthetic.' I asked what they were going to do, and the nurse said, 'We'll give you some morphine . . .' It was a very unpleasant ten minutes while they took all the cloth and stuff out of my back and made certain that my leg was still all right – that it hadn't disappeared. Then eventually they got me to the local hospital.

Bernt Engelman
LUFTWAFFE PILOT

On the beaches and in the dunes north of Dunkirk, thousands of light and heavy weapons lay in the sands, along with munitions crates, field kitchens, scattered cans of rations and innumerable wrecks of British Army trucks.

'Damn!' I exclaimed to Erwin. 'The entire British Army went under here!' Erwin shook his head vigorously. 'On the contrary! A miracle took place here! If the German tanks and Stukas and navy had managed to surround the British here, shooting most of them, and taking the rest prisoner, then England wouldn't have any trained soldiers left. Instead, the British seem to have rescued them all – and a lot of Frenchmen too. Adolf can say goodbye to his Blitzkrieg against England.'

Flying Officer Al Deere
(NEW ZEALANDER) 54 SQUADRON

The three squadrons at Hornchurch – 54, 65 and 74 – were the first Spitfire squadrons to be sent over to Dunkirk to try and protect the evacuation. I was then operational on Spitfires. Not all the squadron were but we had a hard core of experienced pilots. Unfortunately, we lost most of them at Dunkirk. There were seventeen pilots in the squadron and twelve aircraft at Dunkirk – I crashed, one or two chaps baled out and got back, but we lost quite a few.

The first time that we knew we were going to be involved on the Continent was when the station commander, 'Boy' Bouchier, assembled all the pilots in the billiard room in the officers' mess to tell us we had been assigned to take part in the protection of British troops over Dunkirk. For fourteen days we went non-stop: I did something like thirty-seven hours in ten days. We just kept flying. We had no reserve pilots.

For the first week or so we went across and cruised around in an old 'Vic' formation – which was already outdated. We didn't see anything and thought this was a piece of cake. One morning 74 Squadron's CO, 'Drogo' White, got shot down and crash-landed at Calais/Marck airfield, which was still in French hands. It was decided that our CO would fly a Master – a twin-seat training aircraft – to pick him up, and I and a chap named Johnny Allen went along to protect the Master. That's when I got into the first dogfight with an Me 109; the battle was observed by the CO, who was on the ground hiding in a ditch.

Johnny Allen, my number two, was above the cloud, and he shouted when the 109 arrived. It came through the cloud right in front of me. It was a sitting duck. I wasn't all that good a shot, but I was close to him. I turned behind him and he saw me and pulled up, which was the worst thing he could have done, because he slowed his plane and I shot him, and down he went. Johnny Allen got one too. We got three altogether. The Master picked up Drogo and brought him back.

That afternoon we went out again and were jumped by some 109s. I shot a lot of ammunition – not in the right direction. Then I got behind one and in range, had a couple of bursts, and then ran out of ammunition. I thought I would stay with this guy; in retrospect it was a bit stupid, but I did it; and I found that I could stay with him in every manoeuvre except when he dived. When I got back, I made my report to the powers that be that I'd flown with this chap and was convinced that the Spitfire could do anything the 109 could do and in some cases better: it could turn better, it could climb better, but it couldn't dive quite so well. They laughed at me and said that didn't match up with their figures. But they hadn't accounted for the fact that 54 Squadron was equipped with the Rotol constant speed propeller. All other Spitfires were two-speed. It gave me a lot of confidence.

The next time I went up I got tangled with an Me 110. A few days later I was coming back and I saw two strange aircraft and wondered what the hell they were. They were 110s. They didn't see me – it was cloudy – and I managed to shoot one down. I had no difficulty because it didn't know what to do. The other one pulled into cloud.

On 31 May No. 54 Squadron flew one last patrol before 41 Squadron came to relieve us. I was leading the squadron, and just as we arrived over Dunkirk, a Do 17 came flying up the coast. We went after it and, being the leader, I was first there. I was lining up behind to shoot it when the rear-gunner fired; he hit my engine and the glycol header tank, which is the cooling system. I had to break off and I crash-landed north of Dunkirk.

The tide was out and I got down on the beach, but I knocked myself out on the edge of the windscreen. When I came to, I got out and was looked after by a girl who stitched me up with an ordinary needle and put a plaster on me. Then I headed for Dunkirk, where I knew the British Expeditionary Force was intending to evacuate. We had been reading in the British newspapers that the British Army was retreating 'according to plan'. Somewhere en route to Dunkirk, I went into a small café where I saw two Tommies.

'Am I heading for Dunkirk?' I asked. 'I understand the British Army are going to be evacuated.'

They looked at me and said something to the effect of 'What British Army? There's no retreat, chum, there's bloody chaos.'

Dunkirk was a complete shambles – burning buildings, abandoned vehicles, falling masonry. On the beach were thousands and thousands of troops. They were swimming out to the boats.

I could see a destroyer coming in. I think it was the last destroyer to get into Dunkirk harbour. I managed to force my way on to this against the wishes of the army: the troops were all down the side of the pier for protection from the bombing, but I ran along the top, and a major jumped up at me and said, 'Get down there!' And I said, 'Not bloody likely.'

Anyhow, I got on a destroyer and the army aboard weren't very impressed at all – where the hell had the RAF been? All I could say was, we've been over here: I wouldn't be here if we hadn't been over here. They weren't friendly at all. We were bombed quite badly, and about halfway across the Channel a harassed army captain came to me and asked if I'd come up on the deck because they didn't recognise the aircraft and didn't know which to shoot at. So I finished up on deck identifying aircraft for the gunners.

When we got to Dover they had an orderly disembarkation. Again, I wasn't going to be held up, so I climbed up one of the mooring ropes and got off that way. I went to Dover Station and on to the train. I was looking a bit of a mess by this time: I was bleeding, dirty and unshaven, and had a filthy bandage wrapped around my head. I got into a carriage with an army general. The ticket chap came round, and I said, 'I haven't got a ticket; I've just come back from Dunkirk, and I'm going back to my base in Essex, and you'll have to charge it up to His Majesty the King or something because I haven't got any money. We don't carry money.' He wanted me to get off the train, but the general stood up for me. I went through to London, took the tube and got all the way back without a ticket. I walked into the mess at Hornchurch, much to everyone's surprise.

My squadron had moved north to Catterick to re-equip and refurbish. I went up to rejoin them. It was only when I arrived there that I realised what losses we'd had. I think we were down to eight or ten aircraft. We'd lost a lot of pilots – a lot of friends. We lost two flight commanders, and I became a flight commander because of that. We had lost the experienced ones. That's always the way: they were leading. I'd gone out to fight full of excitement, but after a few days of that I realised war wasn't all that much fun.

Pilot Officer Bob Doe

234 AND 238 SQUADRONS

I fell in love with the Spitfire the first time I saw it. We had been flying Blenheims and Battles with a bomber squadron at Leconfield when a Spitfire landed. This marvellous thing taxied over to our hangar and we swarmed around it. It was an early model; the wings had a coating on them, so the rivets were flush. It was absolutely smooth, almost hand-made. We walked around it, we sat in it, we stroked it, oh it was so beautiful. It really was beautiful.

The next day fifteen more turned up, which was a dream we never thought would happen. When you closed the cockpit of the Spitfire, you just felt part of it. You were out of the world, you were on your own. You were your own boss, you were everything you wanted to be. The first time I took off in a Spitfire was, I think, the greatest joy I have known. The joy of this thing that rocketed up into the air and was so easy to fly, so smooth! And in spite of its looks, how easy it was to land!

By June 1940 the war had begun in earnest and we were moved to St Eval in Cornwall as 234 Fighter Squadron and assigned to convoy patrols. I know of nothing more boring in life than convoy patrols! You take off and meet a convoy, you circle that convoy for an hour, and then come back. The most boring thing I have ever done. We also had to do night patrols over Plymouth. There were only four of us that were deemed night operational, so we had to do all of the night patrols, as well as the day patrols.

In Cornwall you get odd weather conditions where the weather will suddenly clamp without any notice at all. Once when I'd gone on patrol down off the Plymouth area somewhere the weather clamped. I was entirely on my own, and I found that there was a gap in the cloud cover around the coast between the top of the cliffs and the sea. So I went from Plymouth right the way round the coast. I hadn't realised how far it was until I got back to St Eval – I had been up two hours and twenty minutes, which is more than maximum endurance of a Spitfire. In that time, the rest of the squadron had started to auction my gear; they had sold quite a lot of it. I had trouble getting it back.

I suppose we were developing a callous sharpness – it was our way of dealing with death.

Operations Room at Fighter Command at Bentley Priory.

3

The Battle of Britain Phase I

The Channel Battles
1 July to 11 August

Following the withdrawal of troops from France, Prime Minister Winston Churchill pulled no punches: 'The Battle of France is over. The Battle of Britain is about to begin.' As Hitler massed his forces facing Britain across the Channel, an invasion attempt looked imminent – but before troops could be landed Hitler recognised that Germany would need air supremacy. He instructed Reichsmarschall Hermann Goering, Commander in Chief of the Luftwaffe, to destroy the RAF's bases and aircraft, and take out the radar stations around Britain's coast. This was a task Goering felt he could achieve in as little as a month before autumn weather made the Channel too rough to allow a seaborne landing of 125,000 troops. The first move would be to attack British convoys in the Channel and draw the RAF out – where they would fall prey to the German fighters. Goering had some 2,600 bombers and fighters at his disposal and felt assured that this would easily overcome whatever the RAF could put up – and unknown to him, this at the start of July, was just 640 fighters.

In 1936 Dowding had structured the RAF Fighter Command to defend against likely attacks from across the North Sea and the Channel, creating two main areas. London and the South East would be protected by 11 Group, and 12 Group would defend the Midlands and the North; later he would create 10 Group to cover the West Country and South Wales, and 13 Group for the north of England and Northern Ireland. Crucially, Dowding had a major ally, Air Vice Marshal Sir Keith Park, who took over the command of 11 Group in April 1940. He did not see eye to eye as well with Air Vice Marshal Sir Trafford Leigh-Mallory, Air Officer Commanding of 12 Group, and their views on tactics remained at odds throughout the battle.

As German bombers and their fighter escorts took off from airfields across the Channel, the newly serviceable radar system began to play its part in Dowding's defence plan. The chain of 350-foot masts would feed back details of the incoming aircraft to the underground filter room at Stanmore, and from there to the Command Operations Room and the appropriate sector controllers. This relay of information took just four minutes – then it was the responsibility of the sector controllers to direct squadrons to take off and intercept the enemy – and to assess how many aircraft to commit to any action.

At the start of the battle Dowding could muster forty-two squadrons – twelve of which were auxiliary – and these were all that stood to prevent the Luftwaffe gaining air superiority – and ultimately invasion.

Winston Churchill had only recently become Prime Minister when he made this speech on 18 June 1940:

I look forward confidently to the exploits of our fighter pilots – these splendid men, this brilliant youth – who will have the glory of saving their native land, their island home, and all they love, from the most deadly of all attacks . . . What General Weygand has called the Battle of France is over: the Battle of Britain is about to begin. Upon this battle depends the survival of Christian civilisation. Upon it depends our own British life, and the long continuity of our institutions and our Empire. The whole fury and might of the enemy must very soon be turned on us. Hitler knows that he will have to break us in this island or lose the war. If we can stand up to him, all Europe may be freed and the life of the world may move forward into broad, sunlit uplands. But if we fail, then the whole world, including the United States, including all that we have known and cared for, will sink into the abyss of a new Dark Age made more sinister, and perhaps more protracted, by the lights of perverted science. Let us therefore brace ourselves to our duty and so bear ourselves that, if the British Empire and its Commonwealth last for a thousand years, men will still say: "This was their finest hour".

Frederick Winterbotham
AIR STAFF DEPARTMENT, SECRET INTELLIGENCE SERVICE

I think the most important signal we had through ULTRA, right at the beginning of the Battle of Britain, was Goering establishing his strategy with his commanders. He told them that they were to fly over Britain and bring the whole of the Royal Air Force up to battle, because only in that way could it be destroyed in the time they had.

That was the key for Dowding – to fight the battle with very small units every time they came over – gradually wearing them down and always having aeroplanes to send up. It became evident that Hitler and his generals wouldn't contemplate invasion unless they had absolute control of the air over the Channel.

Myrtle Ariege Solomon
CIVILIAN, SOUTH OF ENGLAND

At the time of the fall of France there was a good deal of British joking going on – if they come here we'll do this and that – and people were making the most comic preparations. My mother reckoned that she'd be able to keep them off with a huge log fork – a fork for sort of stirring logs – that we had at the open fire. It was a most vicious-looking instrument, it's perfectly true. There was a very patriotic woman in the village who never went about in her car without a row of pepper pots on the front. She thought she could blind the Germans when they arrived. We were told that the Germans might arrive dressed up as nuns, so every poor nun in the country went about being observed, and being looked at in a suspicious way. I remember, myself, I went on a walking holiday for a while, in Cornwall. I had a haversack on. I thought everybody was looking at me and thinking I had parachuted in. So you were a bit twitchy.

The preparations that were made by the nation you really didn't think would keep anybody away. I mean, a bit of barbed wire on a beach – or the erection of what appeared to be sort of small concrete pyramids each side of a line – you just couldn't see how they could stop anything.

Flight Lieutenant Peter Brothers
32 SQUADRON

Before the battle I realised that if the Luftwaffe gained air superiority then, of course, the whole country was open to them. However, one didn't have time to consider the background; you were worrying about your own chaps, your own aircraft, and your own ground crew. It was day to day, minute to minute. I realised that they were going to come in greater masses. The going then got heavier as I think everybody realised, and one was tired, inevitably. I am a fairly

92

equitable person but occasionally used to lose my temper. Having got engaged one day, I pressed the gun button and nothing happened at all, because the guns hadn't been reloaded. On landing back, I had the armourer in the office, drew my pistol, and said, 'I'll shoot you if you ever do that again.' But I was tired.

Our tactics didn't change, apart from the fact that we'd thrown away the idea of Fighter Command Attack number 1, number 2, number 3, different formations and so on, because they didn't fit in with what the enemy was doing. We were often compelled to attack from the stern, because we were usually scrambled late in the day. The controllers, quite rightly, didn't wish to launch us off too soon and find that it was a spoof raid. Then we'd have to turn back to base and refuel and be caught on the ground. So inevitably, they would delay as long as possible before sending us off.

The result was that we'd be struggling for height to try and get up, not only to the height of the raiding bombers, at about 18,000 feet, but above them to launch our own attack. I mean, ideally you wanted to be up-sun, but it rarely worked out like that. You just had to keep away until you'd got the height, otherwise they flew over the top of your head, and you were cat's-meat for their escorting fighters.

It was quite impressive, meeting this black cloud of aircraft, all piled up like – as somebody described it – 'the moving staircase at Piccadilly Circus'. They would be up in their hundreds, with the bottom squadron leading. They'd be stacked up behind, as well, with the fighters sitting up on top. One thing I remember from those early heavy raids was the density of the rear-gunners' fire. They'd put up a sort of a barrage that you had to go through if you wanted to get in close – to about fifty or a hundred yards – which was vital. The aim was to get that rear-gunner out of the way. There was nothing you could do to avoid it – you'd collect a few holes and just hope for the best.

Pilot Officer Tom Neil

249 SQUADRON

Our first air vice marshal in 11 Group was Park – a tall, spare rangy-looking New Zealander – and he used to arrive at the airfield flying his own Hurricane. He was an approachable man and a fighting man's man – then we suddenly found that he'd been moved sideways and he was superseded by Leigh-Mallory, who was altogether different. He was frighteningly stiff and rather stuffy – hat straight on his head. He used to come round and talk to us, and he talked to me once at North Weald. He rather appealed to me because he sat on the bed, calling me by my nickname.

'Hello, Ginger,' he said, 'we're thinking of repainting our aircraft, what do you think about the spinners? Do you think we ought to change them?' The significance of that is when you look around and you see an aircraft behind you, usually you can see by the spinner what sort of aeroplane it is. We used to all have black spinners in the RAF.

I said, 'If I look round and I see a gaudy spinner behind me, that's not one of ours, and I'd get out of the way. So what you don't need is to change the spinners to something gaudy.'

He said, 'Yes, yes,' and he disappeared and changed the spinners to duck-egg blue!

Pilot Officer David Crook

609 SQUADRON

All through July and early August we regularly used to get the unpopular task of escorting convoys up and down the Channel.

The Germans at that time were concentrating mainly on attacking shipping rather than land objectives, and some very fierce fights used to occur when they bombed the ships. We all disliked this work – the weather was brilliant and the Huns

94

invariably used to attack out of the sun, and sometimes took us completely by surprise.

Also we were always outnumbered, sometimes by ridiculous odds, and a lot of pilots were lost. Some of these were drowned, without doubt, when their machine was hit and they descended in the water 10 or 15 miles from land, and were not found despite all the searching that took place afterwards.

Sergeant Pilot Cyril Bamberger

610 AND 41 SQUADRONS

Probably the most ridiculous tactic that came in was the idea that someone should fly above the squadron weaving backwards and forwards to protect the squadron. But that person was a sitting duck for the 109s. If you turned to starboard as part of your weave and the squadron turned to port, you then had to turn round and catch them up, flying straight and level. Which made you even more of a sitting duck.

Flying Officer Brian Kingcome

92 SQUADRON

When you were sent off in time, you could climb to your height ahead of the enemy bombers and then turn round and attack them head-on. A head-on attack did far more to destroy the morale of approaching bombers than anything else. It upset the poor old pilot so much that he was the chap who turned tail. When he was sitting and couldn't see the attack and was protected by a nice sheet of metal behind him and he had gunners and he could hear them firing away, he was in a much more relaxed state of mind than when we were coming straight at him and he had nothing between himself and the guns.

Flying Officer Brian Kingcome, 92 Squadron.

Flying Officer Harold Bird-Wilson

17 Squadron

We had a squadron commander who believed in the head-on attack. 'The next raid we go up to intercept, we will do a head-on attack,' he said. It turned out to be a head-on attack into an Me 110 and I'm afraid Jerry got the better of him and all we found of him was his shirt.

Flying Officer Al Deere

(New Zealander) 54 Squadron

We used to try and get up above them and come in from out of the sun if we could. But it didn't always work that way. Sometimes you didn't see them. They were somewhere up in the sun. And when you became engaged with a German formation it was every man for himself. One minute there were Spitfires and 109s going round in circles, the next minute you were all by yourself, it seemed. That was if you were still there.

Flight Lieutenant Billy Drake

1 Squadron

What you did depended on your rank. A squadron commander had to see the threat in front of him, decide what to do and then to detail members of his formation of twelve or twenty-four aeroplanes, depending on the size of the formation involved in the battle. You decided who was to do what – whether part of your formation was to go for the fighters, or whether you, with the whole of your formation, were going to go in for the bombers and perhaps leave the Spitfires to deal with the fighter threat.

Once you'd decided what to do and you'd done it, suddenly, without any warning, it was all over. You'd done your stuff, the

LAST OF THE FEW

Germans had done their stuff – and they wanted to go home because they would be running out of fuel or they're running out of protection. Most of these fights, no matter what time in the war you're talking about, were all over in a matter of minutes – and then everything was empty. You just said, 'Thank Christ for that,' and went home.

If someone got shot down and lost his aeroplane, it was just bad luck and provided you weren't being attacked yourself, you watched to see whether he got out or whether he crashed in flames. You'd know who it was and you'd report as soon as you got home what you thought had happened to that particular aeroplane and pilot. Depending on your seniority, you either had your own particular aeroplane that you flew practically every time, or if you were a very new boy and had just joined the squadron you probably shared an aeroplane with somebody else.

Pilot Officer Nigel Rose

609 SQUADRON

The squadrons used to take off and climb in threes in four sections of the twelve. Red, yellow, blue and green. I was in 'A' Flight, which was red and yellow, and I used to fly Red Three – I was the junior bloke in the Red Section. Later on we learned chiefly from the Germans that it was much better to fly in twos than threes, as with twos you had the second chap guarding the first chap's tail. This was a much more sensible way of flying.

In the early days when we were told to go down after these great swarms of bombers, you would break off one by one and go down after them and if, on the other hand, we were attacked from above, there was usually a call, 'For Christ's sake watch out, Red Three – somebody coming down after you!' and you'd go into a steep turn straight away and to hell with any formation flying with anyone else. You'd do your best to get out of it. If you saw one of your own chaps in a convenient position where you could help, you did, but that wasn't very often. In these big brawls we had with so many aircraft flying around, at one moment there's a mass of them and the next, clear air.

I used to go home – I didn't look around for trouble. I think in later days, flying over France, quite a lot did look around but it was dangerous work because there we had the enemy up in the sun most of the time and looking out for us, whereas here they were mostly escorting and usually split up from the bombers by the time they'd been attacked, so it was every chap for himself.

We had an old-fashioned TR-9 push-pull radio, which meant you were normally listening to base control but you could also put it on speak and talk to other people in the squadron – but you were duty bound not to do that during any action or going up to an action because you could give your place to the enemy who were wanting to hear comment on tactics. Nevertheless, quite a lot was recorded and people were heard by the girls back at control at sector HQ, and using fairly fruity language to each other – particularly to warn other people of who was around. Several of the girls said that they were able to hear chaps screaming as they went down in flames. There was a certain amount of that, but we were not supposed to use the air unless you had to.

The Spitfire, although similar to the Hurricane, had a tank of about forty-five gallons in front of you, and you were separated by a sheet of armour plating – quite a nice chunk of thick armour – and behind you had the protection of another sheet of armour plating. When I got shot up, one or two armour-piercing bullets came through it, but mostly they dented themselves on it and if it was an ordinary bullet, they did. That was quite good protection. Incendiaries going into the petrol tank was the thing we dreaded – that could be nasty.

Pilot Officer Tim Vigors

222 SQUADRON

Pilots on night readiness always slept down at dispersal. There was a lot of rivalry between different sections concerning who could get all three aircraft off the ground in the shortest space of time from the sounding of the alarm bell. Characteristically, Bader was determined to prove that his section was the fastest. This led to many hours of rehearsal.

Our three camp beds were placed close to the door of the dispersal hut. Douglas's Spitfire was positioned slap bang outside the door with Hilary's and mine nearby. In order to sleep better, Douglas liked to remove his false legs before retiring. Lowering himself on to his bed, he would hand his right leg to me and I would place it at the foot of my bed. Hilary's responsibility was the left leg. Wherever we were, Snipe liked to sleep on my bed and somehow or another he managed to squeeze himself beside me on the narrow mattress.

On the sound of the alarm bell, my first responsibility was to seize Douglas's leg and place it on to the stump of his thigh, which he would be sticking over the end of the bed. Hilary would be helping him with his left leg. At the same time, his fitter and rigger, the two mechanics who were responsible for the maintenance of the engine and airframe of his aircraft, would have rushed through the door. Seizing him under the arms they would carry him bodily out of the door and down the steps on to the grass. Lifted by them on to the rear edge of the wing, he would grab the sides of the cockpit and lever himself into his seat. Hilary and I would run to our Spitfires and hit the starting buttons as our bottoms touched the parachutes, already positioned on the metal seats. The three engines would splutter and roar into life and, with Douglas taxiing fast in front, we would head for the big floodlight which marked the end of the take-off area. Opening the throttles, we would roar off the ground in loose formation, about twenty yards apart.

Spurred on by Douglas's unswerving determination, we managed to reduce the interval between the sound of the alarm bell and all three Spitfires being off the ground to two minutes and fifty seconds – at least thirty seconds better than the time achieved by any other section.

Pilot Officer Tom Neil

249 SQUADRON

I first went operational on 2 July 1940, and, the day after, I intercepted my first German aeroplane, out to sea off the Yorkshire coast. It was a Do 17 reconnaissance aircraft, and it was a wonderful feeling, for the first time, seeing a German aircraft you hadn't seen before. And if you were not careful you'd spend all your time looking at it instead of doing anything about it. It was about 25 miles out to sea and at about 20,000 feet – a wonderful position to be attacked. In the process of attacking it, it saw us and, being an experienced chap, instead of turning and running – in which case we would have had him – he turned towards us and dived between our legs, so to speak.

We used to be drilled in those days into doing what is known as 'Standard Fighter Command Attacks'. The bloke in front, who was the leader, would say, 'Number one attack, number one attack. Go!' and everybody used to get in a line astern. I was behind one chap praying that he'd get out of the way so I could shoot this aeroplane which was in front. We were rapidly overtaking it – but he didn't, and eventually we hadn't quite caught it when it disappeared into cloud. My first interception was unsuccessful in as much as it got away from us and disappeared, and we rushed round, the three of us, like Jack Russells round a haystack looking for rats, but he didn't look there again, and that was that.

Sergeant James A. Goodson

(AMERICAN) 43 SQUADRON

Even the Germans got to respect the Spitfire. I remember Peter Townsend went to see one of the German pilots which he had shot down, close to the base. The German pilot said to him, 'I'm very glad to meet the Spitfire pilot who shot me down.'

And Peter said, 'No, no – I was flying a Hurricane. I'm a Hurricane pilot.'

The German kept arguing with him, and Peter kept saying, 'No – you were shot down by a Hurricane.'

The German pilot said, 'Would you do me a favour? If you ever talk to any other Luftwaffe pilots, please tell them I was shot down by a Spitfire?'

Pilot Officer Frank Carey

43 SQUADRON

I had arrived back ready for the Battle of Britain with lots of experience. In the battle sometimes, you would see enormous formations of Germans – a terrific stretch of them. Once we were taking off from Tangmere to look after a convoy called, I think, 'Peewit'. It got badly battered from the Dover Straits right down; it was almost eliminated. And we were taking over to do our stint.

There were six of us on this patrol. As we arrived, we could see planes stretched out in great lumps all the way from the Isle of Wight to Cherbourg. At the bottom, Ju 87 dive-bombers; above those, Me 109s in great big oval sweeps covering the distance; and above them Me 110s. The flight commander had told three of us to do the fighter protection at the back, and we got up into them. The situation was absolutely ludicrous – three of us to take on that mob! The others went straight into the dive-bombers. Within seconds we were split up all over the place. The only advantage was that it was a hundred to one against hitting your own side; you could fire at anything.

I took a tremendous amount of damage that day. In the odd way that air fighting has, one minute you're in a mass, and you do three or four turns, and everything has disappeared. Where the devil have they all gone? And they can return just as fast. After this first kerfuffle I looked around for my two and I saw a formation and went to join them. And of course they were Me 109s, but they hadn't seen me. They were in a very curious long echelon line.

I got hooked on to the tail of the last and started firing away quite merrily. Then I had an awful wallop: it was an Me 110 with his four cannons sitting just behind me. I got one in the port block of guns and ammunition; there was a big bang, and there, in the wing, was a hole a man could have crawled through. It threw me over on my back and by the time I'd straightened up again, I thought I'd better find someone friendlier to join. I had a slight wound from one of their explosive bullets. They used to explode almost into powder. Suddenly my arm was perforated just as though someone had stuck a lot of pins in it all the way down. For a few seconds an immense amount of blood came out and I thought, God, my arm's coming off – but it was all right.

By that time I was nearly in Cherbourg. As I was on my way back, I came up behind some more 109s who hadn't seen me. And again a 110 was looking after the 109s and it blew off the whole of my rudder – one whole elevator on one side and a lot of the canvas skin covering the other elevator. Really, I shouldn't have been able to control the aircraft, and I thought I'd better get back to Tangmere. When I arrived in the circuit the ack-ack opened up on me! The little bit of rudder and tail I had looked very peculiar, I suppose. I'd no idea of the extent of the damage at the back end! A rudder didn't matter so much, but the elevators were very important, particularly at the lower speeds. But somehow it flew. It was a great tribute to the Hurricane.

Flying Officer Al Deere

(NEW ZEALANDER) 54 SQUADRON

We were frightened. On the way out there was an awful gut fear. When you sighted them it really was quite a frightening sight. But once you got into combat there wasn't time to be frightened. But we were frightened – of course we were – the whole bloody time. But if you're in combat, you're so keen to get the other guy and, if you like, save your own skin, that your adrenalin's pumping and there's no room for fright.

I've often wondered why there weren't more collisions. There were probably more than we knew about, because if somebody collided, you didn't know about it. There was, in the initial engagement, a danger of collision.

They started bombing the airfields. 54 Squadron's forward base was Manston, in Kent, which was the most forward airfield in England – we could see Calais from Manston. We operated from there. We used to go off from Hornchurch about half an hour before first light, land at Manston, and stay there all day. We did sometimes four sorties a day, sometimes five, not always making combat, but being shot at and shot down. We very rarely arrived back with the number of chaps we went out with.

One morning, after we'd had a bit of a fight over a convoy, we were sent off to intercept a raid coming across the Channel at 3,000–4,000 feet. We went off south of Manston, and found some 109s at between 3,000 and 5,000 feet. And down in the water I could see a seaplane. I didn't know it at the time, but it was a German air-sea rescue plane, which had come in to try and pick up one of their pilots. I told Johnny Allen, who was in my sub-section, to go down and get the seaplane, and I'd look after the 109s.

Just at that moment the 109s saw us. They started to turn around just as we did, and I found myself in a circle going head-on towards a 109 coming from the opposite direction. I pressed my gun-button more in hope than anything else, and I think we must have done the same thing. I felt the bullets hit, and the next thing I knew we had collided. It was all very quick. I hit underneath him. My engine seized straight away, and the cockpit filled with smoke, and flames appeared from the engine. I reached to open the hood in order to bale out, only to discover that his propeller had struck the front of my windscreen and the whole fixture was so twisted that I could not move the hood. I could not see for smoke, but managed to ascertain that I was headed inland.

Nearly blinded and choked, I succeeded in keeping the airspeed at about 100 mph. The engine had now seized and I just waited to hit the ground. Suddenly there was a terrific jerk and I was tossed left, then right, and finally pitched hard forward on my straps, which fortunately held fast. I'd hit the ground in an open area where they had put a lot of anti-invasion posts against enemy gliders. Of course I ploughed through these, and finally came to a halt. The remains of my ammunition were going off in a series of pops and the flames were getting very near the cockpit. I managed to break my way out of the cockpit. We had a little thing inside, a little jemmy thing, and I managed to smash my way out with that and my bare hands, and got clear of the aircraft and ran to a safe distance. I was pretty shaken and my eyebrows were singed, both my knees were bruised, but otherwise I was uninjured. The Spitfire was blazing furiously in the middle of a cornfield and had left a trail of broken posts and pieces of wing, plus the complete tail unit, extending for 200 yards.

A woman came out from a house nearby, and asked if I'd like a cup of tea. All I remember saying was, did she have anything stronger? She rang Manston and within a fairly quick time the ambulance was up, and took me back. Of course when I got back, inevitably the whole squadron had gone back to Rochford. I was all right for flying the next day. I'd have preferred to take a breather, but we were just too short of pilots.

Flying Officer Hugh Dundas

616 SQUADRON

A fighter pilot's most significant and most important combat experience is when, for the first time, he is comprehensively shot down and manages to survive. He learns from that, as from nothing else.

Sergeant Pilot Leslie Batt

338 SQUADRON

I saw a 109 coming down vertically from above me. He was going at a phenomenal rate of knots and suddenly his wings came off and they appeared to shoot upwards. He must have made such a hole in the ground that I thought, 'That's saved somebody from digging a grave.'

Flight Lieutenant Tom Morgan

43 SQUADRON

I joined the squadron at the beginning of June and then in July we lost four commanding officers in battle and I was made CO.

We had been receiving young replacements – I was about twenty-two at the time, but we'd get eighteen-year-olds, so my flight commander, Kelly, or I would take them off whenever operations would allow us, and give them some combat training. When they first came to us they could just fly the aeroplane. The overall spirit in the squadron was good, but Fighter Command decided to get us out and let us rebuild. I got mostly trained Czechoslovak, Norwegian and American pilots – the Americans were volunteers. I had fourteen nationalities in my squadron at one time, including Hindus – and this built us up quite well.

Then instead of sending us back – which we all would have liked – they started to post these chaps out to their national squadrons in the air force. We were able to keep a core to train up for our own use as the squadron had to maintain an operational state while at the same time getting any new boys up to operational standard.

I certainly felt not only for the friends I lost, but for the youngsters that really didn't have a chance. We had to commit them to battle before they were really ready to cope with it. It wasn't their lack of keenness – they just lacked operational training, particularly in using their guns.

Sergeant Pilot Iain Hutchinson
222 SQUADRON

Any replacements that came into the squadron were totally inexperienced. They were not battle hardened and they didn't know what to expect. There was one particular friend of mine who was a wonderful pilot and by halfway through the battle there were numbers of experienced sergeant pilots who had been cut down, so I was the most senior sergeant pilot in my flight. Basically I was taking charge of who flew and who didn't. I flew every time until one day he came up to me when the scramble was given, and said, 'Could I not fly this time? You're hogging the flights.' So I said, 'Yes, OK, on you go,' and he was shot down and killed. He just didn't have the fighting experience. Even the experienced pilots got shot down. The problem was that you couldn't take anybody under your wing – you couldn't defend another fighter pilot, so everybody had to take their chance.

Virtually every time we went out there were one or two casualties. I remember one day we were at cockpit. The first six of us in the squadron went off, and the other six would come up later. The radar had reported a raid of 500-plus coming in and when I sighted this great mass of aircraft, I thought I'd better calm things down a bit. I said that it was at least 250-plus – there was no means of counting them, so Squadron Leader Badger said he'd go in with his flight of six. Behind us were other squadrons but they were 20 or 30 miles behind. He said he'd take on some of the bombers, and I was to take on the fighters if they came down. He went into the bombers, and I looked around and I could see the fighters up there but none of them came down, so I went in with my two chaps and had a go at another flight of the bombers. We only lost two chaps but they would have lost some people too. Their fighters stayed up there – I don't know why they didn't come down, but I think that there were so few of us that they never really saw us. We got lost in among this mass of German aeroplanes.

Flight Lieutenant Bob Stanford Tuck
92 AND 257 SQUADRONS

Holland and Eyles were a little slow in turning, but Titch stayed right up with me. The 88s were in a fairly wide line abreast, and honestly you couldn't see anything between them and their own shadows on the surface. I managed to get up behind the port one and hit him hard. He started to lose speed immediately and streamed black oil and muck. I gave him another bash. He went splat into the water, and as I flashed over him I could see him ploughing along like a bloody great speedboat in the middle of a tremendous cloud of white spray.

All this time Titch was banging away at the starboard one. I tried to get on to the leader, but by now we'd lost the extra speed from our dive, and it was all we could do to keep up. The Ju 88 was a wonderfully fast kite, especially when it had unloaded and the pilot was homeward-bound with a Spit up his backside.

I was at long range – I think about 900 yards – but I was managing to lob a bit on to him. This was one of the many times I cursed because I didn't have cannon. I was hitting him all right, but nothing was happening. We got well out over the Channel, and I remembered to take a quick check on fuel – we'd been bending

Flight Lieutenant Bob Stanford Tuck, 92 and 257 Squadrons.

our throttles on the end of the 'emergency' slots for minutes on end now. My gauge was reading a bit low, so I lined up very carefully and gave him a last, long burst. This time a few bits flew off him. Then I called up Titch and we broke off the attack. Titch left his Hun streaming a thick trail of oil.

Heading back for the land we saw Holland and Eyles, very low on the water, circling the wreckage of the one I'd shot down. The crew of three were huddled in their rubber dinghy, looking up at the Spits, obviously very worried. I think the poor sods were afraid we'd strafe them.

I climbed to 1,500 feet, called up base and let them get a good fix on the position so that the Air Sea Rescue boys could come out and collect. Then all four of us went down and once around the dinghy, we made V-signs and rude versions of the Nazi salute.

Flight Lieutenant Peter Brothers

32 SQUADRON

Once, I'd made an attack and everybody seemed to have vanished. I looked around and saw five 109s in a 'V' formation, heading for home all on their own. I thought, 'Well, this is splendid. I'll just climb up behind them and start picking them off, one by one.' The chap on the far right of the formation had obviously seen me coming and he eased away to the right, so I thought, 'Oh, I'll be content with this chap today, and not bother about the others.' An almost fatal mistake. As I was about to open fire, he opened the throttle wide and started climbing rapidly. I pulled the stick back to follow him, and at that moment all hell broke loose.

The other four came in behind and they all had a go at me, and filled me full of holes. I was so angry with myself for being so stupid! I was chattering with rage and frightened, I shot off fairly quickly and they all whizzed past, firing at me, and then they were gone. I didn't get anything other than a severe fright, but I never did that again. In fact, I used to warn chaps about it. I also used to warn them that, if we were jumped by escorting fighters and you saw tracer passing on your left, 'Turn into it, not away.' Instinctively you want to turn away, but the enemy, having seen he was firing to the left of you, was then correcting his aim to fire to the right. Well, if you turned left you threw his aim completely; you went through some of his fire, and took your chance on that.

It was all fairly intense, but the waiting around at base was the hardest part. We'd either sleep, play mah-jong or read. When we were 'scrambled', one of our chaps would run to his aircraft, be violently sick, and then jump into his aircraft and be off. Your adrenalin really got going once that bell went. We all swore we'd never have a telephone at home after the war because as soon as the telephone rang you'd all automatically be at the ready. Then you'd hear someone say, 'No, Corporal so-and-so has just gone to get his lunch,' and you'd all relax again. It would either be that or '32 Squadron scramble 18,000 feet over Ashford' and off you'd go.

After we returned from an operation, the intelligence officer would want all the details. We weren't all that interested, it was over, finished. But he needed the information. We'd give him the information and then perhaps we'd be off again. We could be scrambled in the middle of telling him something. During one of the raids on Dover, I'd shot down a Stuka and then gone into the airfield at Hawkinge to refuel and rearm. I didn't even get out of the aircraft. They were rearming the aircraft and there was a chap standing on the wing in front of me, pumping fuel into the tank.

The battle was still going on up above and, as we watched, a Spitfire shot down a 109, and the pilot baled out. The airman who was refuelling me said, 'Got him!' And then, when the pilot's parachute opened, he turned to me with a look of utter disgust on his face and said, 'Oh, the jammy bastard!' As soon as they'd finished I was off again, back into the battle. But it was rather amusing. I got a 109 later on that day.

Sergeant Pilot Paul Farnes
501 SQUADRON

It was damned cold in the air, even in the summer months – it was about –15. The sun was there but don't kid yourself that it was warm. You had an Irvin jacket and trousers, but they were so clumsy and bulky, and if you had to get out of the aircraft it was difficult. You wore them on the ground but you didn't need them there – but we seldom flew in them. You put on overalls and a thick pullover and battledress jacket – and a Mae West. It got jolly cold and some of the chaps used to pinch their mother's or girlfriend's silk stockings and put those on – I never tried that. The cold was a factor as there were no heaters in the cockpit. A little heat might come through from the engine, but not much at all.

We'd sit around in our Irvin jackets at dispersal – and we were in a tent – others might have been lucky enough to have a hut.

The most times I went up in a day was about six. We'd be at dispersal, at readiness, at about 4.30 am – but we were very lucky because we had two sergeant WAAFs who by the time we were up always had tea and toast and dripping for us – it was absolutely delicious at that time in the morning. They were great, those two: they always put sugar in the tea – it was always sweet, and I didn't take sugar, but it was fine at that time of the morning. We had a better ration than civilians did, but we still didn't get many eggs – maybe just two a week.

Pilot Officer David Crook
609 SQUADRON

One evening in July at about 6.30, we were ordered to patrol Weymouth, so Peter, Michael and I took off, Peter leading.

We circled round for about three-quarters of an hour, and saw nothing at all. We were told, however, to continue our patrol and

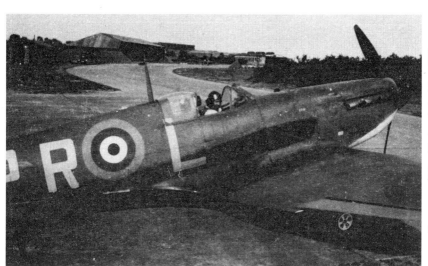

Pilot Officer David Crook, 609 Squadron.

turned out again over Weymouth at about 7,000 feet. A moment later, looking out towards the left, I saw an aircraft dive into a layer of cloud about 2 miles away and then reappear. I immediately called up Peter on the RT, and he swung us into line astern, and turned left towards the enemy.

A moment later I saw one or two more Huns appear, and recognised them as Ju 87s. I immediately turned on my reflector sights, put my gun button on to 'fire' and settled down to enjoy a little slaughter of a few Ju 87s, as they are rather helpless machines.

I was flying last on the line, and we were now travelling at high speed and rapidly approaching the enemy, when I happened to look round behind. To my intense surprise and dismay, I saw at least nine Me 110s about 2,000 feet above us. They were just starting to dive on us when I saw them, and as they were diving, they were overtaking us rapidly.

This completely altered the situation. We were now hopelessly outnumbered, and in a very dangerous position, and altogether I began to see that if we were not jolly quick, we should all be dead in a few seconds.

I immediately called up Peter and Michael and shouted desperately, 'Look out behind, Messerschmitts behind!' All the time I was looking over my shoulder at the leading enemy fighter, who was now almost in range. I kept shouting, but both Peter and Michael continued straight on at the bombers ahead, and they were now almost in range and about to open fire.

I have never felt so desperate or so helpless in my life as when, in spite of my warnings, these two flew steadily on, apparently quite oblivious of the fact that they were going to be struck down from the rear in a few seconds.

At that moment the leading Messerschmitt opened fire at me and I saw his shells and tracer bullets going past just above my head. They were jolly close too. I did a very violent turn to the left and dived through a layer of cloud just below.

I emerged from the cloud going at very high speed – probably over 400 mph, and saw a Ju 87 just ahead of me. I opened fire (my first real shot of the war), and he seemed to fly right through my tracer bullets, but when I turned round to follow him, he had disappeared.

I climbed from the cloud again to try to rejoin the others, and saw an Me 110 some distance above me. I pulled into a steep climb and fired at him – but without result. He turned away immediately and I lost him.

At that moment I saw dimly a machine moving in the cloud on my left and flying parallel to me. I stalked him through the cloud and when he emerged into a patch of clear sky, I saw that it was a Ju 87.

I was in an ideal position to attack and opened fire and put the remainder of my ammunition – about 2,000 rounds – into him at very close range. Even in the heat of the moment I remember my amazement at the shattering effect of my fire. Pieces flew off his fuselage and cockpit covering, a stream of smoke appeared from the engine, and a moment later a great sheet of flame licked out from the engine cowling and he dived down vertically. The flames enveloped the whole machine and he went straight down, apparently quite slowly, for about 5,000 feet, till he was just a shapeless burning mass of wreckage.

Absolutely fascinated by the sight, I followed him down, and saw him hit the sea with a great burst of white foam. He disappeared immediately, and apart from a green patch in the water there was no sign that anything had happened. The crew made no attempt to get out, and they were obviously killed by my first burst of fire.

I had often wondered what would be my feelings when killing somebody like this, and especially when seeing them go down in flames. I was rather surprised to reflect afterwards that my only feeling had been one of considerable elation – and a sort of bewildered surprise because it had all been so easy.

Flight Lieutenant Myles Duke-Woolley

23 AND 253 SQUADRONS

I lost many friends during the battle but none more courageous than Squadron Leader 'Spike' O'Brien. Spike and I had our first combats on the night of 6 June 1940, and Spike's saga started then.

It was a gin-clear night with a full moon, and Spike took a new pilot up with him in a Blenheim I to show him the Sector that night. After take-off he was diverted and intercepted a He III that was returning after bombing Birmingham. In the gunfight the Heinkel went down and Spike's Blenheim went out of control in a spin. At that time no pilot ever had got out of a spinning Blenheim alive, because the only way out was through the top sliding hatch and you then fell through the airscrew. The new boy probably didn't know that but nevertheless he froze, and Spike had to get him out.

He undid his seat belt, unplugged his oxygen, and threw him bodily out of the top hatch while holding his parachute ripcord. He told me afterwards that he felt sick when the lad fell through the airscrew. Spike then had to get out himself. He grasped the wireless aerial behind the hatch, pulled himself up it and then turned round so that his feet were on the side of the fuselage. Then he kicked outwards as hard as he could. He felt the tip of an airscrew blade 'pat' him on the earpiece of his helmet.

He landed on the outskirts of a village and went to the nearest pub to ring base and ask for transport home. He got himself a pint and sat down at a table to chat with another chap who was sitting there in uniform. After some time, thinking the chap's dress was a bit unusual, Spike asked him if he was a Pole or Czech.

'Oh, no,' said his companion in impeccable English, 'I'm a German pilot actually. Just been shot down by one of your blokes.'

At this, Spike sprang to his feet and said, 'I arrest you in the name of the King. And anyway, where did you learn English?'

The German said, 'That's all right. I won't try to get away. In fact I studied at Cambridge for three years, just down the way.' Then he said, 'I shall be out of here anyway in a week or two's time, you know.'

'Like bloody hell you will!' said Spike.

'Let's agree to disagree,' said the German.

'My shout, what's yours?' said Spike. 'Hey, you can't go buying me a drink.'

'Why not?' said the German. 'I've got plenty of English money and it's no more your pub than mine.'

So that's what they did, sat and had a drink.

A few days later Spike was posted for a rest to a controller's course in the West Country. One morning, when strolling along the tarmac of the airfield, he was surprised to see a Do 17 overhead at 2,000 feet. Alongside the perimeter track was a visiting Spitfire. Spike leapt in, started up, and took off in pursuit. No helmet, no parachute, he caught the Dornier and shot it down. When the AOC 10 Group heard the story he was immediately promoted to command a Spitfire squadron at Middle Wallop.

In late August his squadron reinforced 11 Group on one sortie against a raid by Me 110s on Hawker's Weybridge factory. Spike was seen to be engaging an Me 110, believed destroyed, whilst being himself attacked by another. Some fifteen minutes later he appeared in the circuit at Biggin Hill. He lowered the undercarriage and flaps and was turning on to finals at around 600 feet when his aircraft caught fire. Probably an incendiary bullet had lodged in his petrol tanks, and then sparked off the petrol vapour above the fuel when its level fell. He was seen to bale out, but his parachute was not fully deployed when he hit the ground and he was dead when the ambulance reached him.

I spoke later to the doctor who was in the ambulance. When he examined Spike's body, he found that his left arm had been shot off at the shoulder, and his left eye shot out of his head. Yet he had flown that Spit right down to approach for a normal landing! It was almost unbelievable that he had done that with one arm. Throttle control, airscrew pitch, control column, undercarriage control, flap control, elevator trim – that's what you needed to juggle. Opening the roof is one-handed – if you let go of the stick – but then to have climbed out with those injuries and pulled the ripcord must have required almost superhuman will power and guts. But then that was Spike.

Pilot Officer David Crook

609 SQUADRON

We took off just before dusk to return to base. We got back and I went up to my room in the mess. Everything was just the same as Peter and I had left it only eighteen hours before; his towel was still in the window where he had thrown it during our hurried dressing. But he was dead now. I simply could not get used to such sudden and unexpected death, and there flashed across my mind the arrangements we had made to go up to London together the following day. It all seemed so ironical, so tragic, so futile. I felt that I could not sleep in that room again, so I took my things and went into Gordon's bed next door and slept there.

I could not get out of my head the thought of Peter, with whom we had been talking and laughing that day, now lying in the cockpit of his wrecked Spitfire at the bottom of the English Channel.

The next day, at lunch, Pip was called to the telephone, and a few minutes later I went out into the hall and found him standing there looking very worried and unhappy. Peter's wife had just been ringing up, wondering why he had not telephoned her about his trip to London that afternoon. The telegram had not yet reached her, and so Pip had to tell her the news. It all

Dornier shot down over the south coast, 26 July 1940.

seemed so awful; I was seeing for the first time at very close quarters all the distress and unhappiness that casualties cause. I walked out of the mess and drove to the station, very thankful to be doing something that took my mind on to other subjects. I never saw Pip again either.

Pilot Officer Douglas Hamilton Grice
32 SQUADRON

On 4 July I was shot down for the second time. We were in the air, somewhere near Ashford in Kent. We were told over the RT that there were Me 109s beating up Manston Aerodrome, so our leader turned and made towards Manston – and I realised that this probably wasn't a good idea.

There must have been a delay between the shooting happening on the ground, and our hearing about it in the air – and therefore the enemy would be on their way home. So, I took my section off towards Deal. It was a very cloudy day – there we were, flying along at about 7,000 feet, I suppose, looking mostly downwards through the gaps in the clouds. I took one glance behind, and there were three 109s – I suppose about 400 yards away – diving on to us. For the very first time in my operational life, I froze. A most extraordinary feeling. I couldn't move, except that my hand was shaking on the stick. Of course, the inevitable happened. There was one very large bang, my engine stopped, I suddenly realised that I had no rudder control and also that I had no left-hand aileron control. So my first thought was 'I must bale out.' But by this time, I was over the sea – and the idea of baling out over the sea didn't appeal.

Meanwhile, I was looking around madly – once again, there wasn't an aircraft to be seen. So I managed to get the aircraft pointing towards the land, and I was losing height. I did my second belly landing in a field not very far from Sandwich golf course. I started to get out of my aircraft, when the hedgerows erupted with brown jobs – the army, headed by an officer, who came running. Stopped two paces away – looked at me (I had taken my helmet off by then) and said, 'Hello, Douglas – how are you?' And I looked at him and said, 'Hello, Bill! How nice to see you.'

We'd known each other as territorial soldiers three years beforehand, in the Artists Rifles – and here he was, guarding Britain with a few soldiers and a few rifles. And there was I, a stricken fighter pilot. I was quite unhurt. His troops were very impressed to find that their officer knew the pilot.

Pilot Officer David Crook
609 SQUADRON

It is an odd thing when you are being fired at by a rear-gunner that the stream of bullets seems to leave the machine very slowly and in a great outward curve. You chuckle to yourself, 'Ha, the fool's missing me by miles!' Then, suddenly, the bullets accelerate madly and curl in towards you again and flick just past your head. You thereupon bend your head a little lower, mutter, 'My God,' or some other suitable expression, and try to kill the rear-gunner before he makes any more nuisance of himself.

Charles Gardner (BBC War Correspondent)
BROADCASTING LIVE AT DOVER; RECORDED 14 JULY 1940 – X003-1795

Well now, the Germans are dive-bombing a convoy out to sea in the Channel. There are one, two, three, four, five, six, *seven* German dive-bombers – Ju 87s. There's one going down on its target now! Bomb! No! It hasn't hit a single ship. There are about ten ships in the convoy, but he hasn't hit a single one! [*Sound of guns firing*] There! You can hear anti-aircraft going at them now! Now the British fighters are coming up! Here they [the dive-bombers] come in an absolute steep dive, and you can see their bombs actually leave the machines and come into the water. You can hear our own guns going like anything now! Oh, here's a Spitfire coming down now! There's one coming down in flames! Someone's hit a German, and he's coming down completely out of control! There's a long streak of smoke! The pilot's baled out by parachute! He's a Ju 87 and he's going slap into the sea! There he goes! *Smash!* Terrific funnel of water! Only one man came out by parachute – so presumably there was only a crew of one in it.

There's a terrific mix-up now over the Channel. It's impossible to tell which are our machines and which are the Germans'. There's a fight going on, and you can hear the little rattles of machine-gun bullets. Here comes a Spitfire! There's a little burst! There's another bomb dropping! It missed the convoy! They haven't hit the convoy in all of this! The sky is absolutely patterned now with bursts of anti-aircraft fire, and the sea is covered with smoke where the bombs have burst, but as far as I can see, there's not one single ship hit, and there's definitely one German machine down.

Looking across the sea, I can see the little white dot of the parachute as the German pilot is floating down to the spot where his machine crashed with such a big fountain of water. Everything is peaceful again for the moment. The Germans delivered their attack on the convoy, and I think they've made off as quickly as they came. I can see the Germans haring back towards France as quick as they can go. And here are the Spitfires coming after them! There's going to be a big fight – but it will be too far away for us to see.

There are two layers of German machines, and I think they're all Ju 87s. Are those two more parachutes? No . . . I think they're seagulls. Well, that was a really hot little engagement while it lasted! No damage done except for the Germans who lost one machine and a pilot who's still on the end of his parachute – but appreciably nearer the sea than he was. I can see no boat going out to pick him up – so he'll probably have a long swim ashore! So that was a very unsuccessful attack on the convoy, I must say . . .

There's another fight going on way up, 25,000 even 30,000 feet above our heads – and we can't see a thing of it. The anti-aircraft guns have just put up six bursts. There we go again! Oh! We've just hit a Messerschmitt! Oh that was beautiful! He's coming right down now! That burst definitely got him! Yes, he's coming down like a rocket now! Absolute steep dive! Let's move round so I can watch him a bit more. Here he comes! I'm looking for the parachute . . . no . . . no . . . the pilot's not getting out of that one! That man is finished! He's come down from about 20,000 to about 2,000 feet and he's not stopping . . .

There are five fighters fighting right over our heads now. There's a Spitfire coming right down on the tail of a Messerschmitt! Oh, darn, they've turned away! I can't see! You can't watch these fights very coherently for long! You just see swirling machines, and you hear little bursts of machine guns and by the time you've picked up the machines, they've gone! Oh whoops! There's a dogfight up there! Six machines wheeling and turning, and hark at the machine guns! They're being chased home! And *how* they're being chased home! There are three Spitfires chasing three Messerschmitts.

Oh boy! Look at them going! That is really grand! There's a Spitfire just behind them – and he'll get them! Oh boy! I've never seen anything so good as this! The RAF fighters have really got these boys! Our machine is catching up the Messerschmitt. It's got the legs of it. Come on, George, you've got him! No . . . no . . . the distance is a bit deceptive from here, you can't tell . . . But I think something dangerous is going to happen to that first Messerschmitt . . . Just a moment . . . I think he's got him . . . no . . . no . . . they've chased him right out to sea . . . but the odds are really on that first Messerschmitt catching it . . . [voice off – *Look! Look! He's got him down!*] Yes, he's pulled away from him . . . that first Messerschmitt's been crashed on the coast of France, all right!

Unknown pilot
616 Squadron

I'd done about five hours on Spitfires – I, and another trainee with an operational pilot, was doing a battle climb to 1,500 or 1,000 feet and flying around. We climbed up – it was a beautiful day and the sun was shining and I was flying a Spitfire and everything was at peace with the world, when suddenly we received a message on the radio to say that there was a bandit in the area. The operational pilot was not going to say, 'I've got two trainees with me,' so we were vectored on to this thing.

I was flying the Mark I – which was the only Mark I they had – and the others were in Mark IIs, and they hared off, leaving me far behind. By the time I arrived I realised (a) I had never fired a gun on a Spitfire, and (b) nobody had explained to me how to use the gunsight – I knew nothing and I hadn't realised that a training battle climb might be going into action.

I arrived and they had gone, so I closed on what happened to be a Dornier. I turned the firing button to on – I thought this was a good thing to do – and pressed the thing. I closed on the Dornier and there were tracer bullets hitting him which caught fire and he went down and crashed in the North Sea. I flew back full of elation, thinking I had only done five hours' flying and I'd got my first Hun. I was being debriefed by the intelligence officer and I'd just got to the bit where it caught fire when the flight sergeant came in and said, 'Excuse me, sir, but did you know that your guns weren't loaded?' The other two had gone in and shot at it, but the fire didn't start until I got there. The tracer bullets I could see was the Germans firing at me!

Flight Lieutenant James Brindley Nicolson
249 Squadron

16 July was a glorious day. The sun was shining from a cloudless

sky and there was hardly a breath of wind anywhere. Our squadron was going towards Southampton on patrol at 15,000 feet when I saw three Ju 88 bombers about 4 miles away, flying across our bows. I reported this to our squadron leader and he replied, 'Go after them with your section!' So I led my section of aircraft round towards the bombers. We chased hard after them, but when we were about a mile behind, we saw the 88s fly straight into a squadron of Spitfires.

I used to fly a Spitfire myself, and I guessed it was curtains for the three Junkers. I was right – and they were all shot down in quick time with no pickings for us. I must confess I was very disappointed for I'd never fired at a Hun in my life and I was longing to have a crack at them, so we swung round again and started to climb up to 18,000 feet over Southampton to rejoin our squadron. I was still a long way from the squadron, when suddenly, very close, in rapid succession, I heard four big bangs. They were the loudest noises I'd ever heard – and they had been made by four cannon shells from an Me 110 hitting my machine.

The first shell tore through the hood over my cockpit and sent splinters into my left eye. One splinter, I discovered later, nearly severed my eyelid. I couldn't see through that eye for blood. The second cannon shell struck my spare petrol tank and set it on fire. The third shell crashed into the cockpit and tore off my left trouser leg. The fourth shell struck the back of my left shoe, and shattered the heel of it, and made quite a mess of my left foot. But I didn't know anything about that either until later. Anyway, the effect of these four shells was to make me dive away to the right to avoid further shells. Then I started cursing myself for my carelessness. What a fool I'd been, I thought. What a fool . . .

I was just thinking of jumping out when suddenly an Me 110 whizzed underneath me and got right in my gunsights. Fortunately, no damage had been done to my windscreen or sights and when I was chasing the Junkers, I had switched everything on, so everything was set for a fight. I pressed the gun button when the Messerschmitt was in nice range. He was going like mad, twisting and turning as he tried to get away from my fire, so I pushed the throttle right open. Both of us must have been doing about 400 as we went down together in the dive. First he turned left, then right, then left and right again. He did three turns to the right, and finally a fourth turn to the left.

I remember shouting out loud at him, when I first saw him, 'I'll teach you some manners, you Hun!' And I shouted other things as well! I knew I was getting him nearly all the time I was firing. By this time, it was pretty hot inside my machine from the burst petrol tank. I couldn't see much flame but I reckoned it was there, all right. I remember looking once at my left hand which was keeping the throttle open. It seemed to be in the fire itself, and I could see the skin peeling off – yet I had little pain. Unconsciously, too, I had drawn my feet up under my parachute on the seat: to escape the heat, I suppose.

Well, I gave the Hun all I had, and the last I saw of him was when he was going down with his right wing lower than the left wing. I gave him a parting burst, and as he disappeared, I started thinking about saving myself. I decided it was about time I left the aircraft and baled out, so I jumped up from my seat. But first of all, I hit my head against the framework of the hood – which was all that was left. I cursed myself for a fool, and pulled the hood back. Wasn't I relieved when it slid back beautifully? I jumped up again. Once again, I bounced back into my seat. For I'd forgotten to undo the straps holding me in. One of them snapped, so I had only three to undo. Then I left the machine.

I suppose I was about 12–15,000 feet when I baled out. Immediately, I started somersaulting downwards. After a few turns like that, I found myself diving head first for the ground. After a second or two of this, I decided to pull the ripcord. The result was that I immediately straightened up and started to float down. Then an aircraft – a Messerschmitt I heard afterwards – came tearing past me. I decided to pretend that I was dead, and hung limply by the parachute straps. The Messerschmitt came back once, and I

Flight Lieutenant James Brindley Nicolson of 249 Squadron, the only Fighter Command pilot to be awarded a Victoria Cross.

kept my eyes closed, but I didn't get the bullets I was half expecting. I don't know if he fired at me. The main thing is that I wasn't hit.

While I was coming down like that, I had a look at myself. I could see the bones of my left hand showing through the knuckles. Then for the first time, I discovered I'd been wounded in the foot. Blood was oozing out of the lace holes of my left shoe. My right hand was pretty badly burned too. So I hung down a bit longer, and then decided to try my limbs just to see if they would work. Thank goodness – they did. I still had my oxygen mask over my face, but my hands were in too bad a state to take it off. I tried to but I couldn't manage it. I found, too, that I had lost one trouser leg, and the other was badly torn, and my tunic was just like a lot of torn rags. I wasn't looking very smart.

After a bit more of this dangling down business, I began to ache all over, and my arms and legs began to hurt a lot. When I got lower, I saw I was in danger of coming down in the sea. I knew I didn't stand an earthly if I did, because I wouldn't have been able to swim a stroke with my hands like that – but I managed to float inland. Then I saw a high-tension cable below me, and thought it would finish me if I hit that. Fortunately, I was travelling towards a nice open field.

When I was about 100 feet from the ground, I saw a cyclist and heard him ring his bell. I was surprised to hear the bicycle bell, and I realised I'd been coming down in absolute silence. I bellowed to the cyclist but I don't suppose he heard me. Finally, I touched down in the field, and fell over. Fortunately, it was a very calm day. My parachute just floated down, and stayed down without dragging me along as they sometimes do. I had a piece of good news almost immediately. One of the people who came along, and who had watched the combat, said they had seen the Me 110 dive straight into the sea. So it hadn't been such a bad day after all . . .

Flight Lieutenant Nicolson was the only member of Fighter Command to receive the award of the Victoria Cross.

Pilot Officer Tom Neil

249 SQUADRON

We suffered our first major casualty when Nicolson got his Victoria Cross. He was hideously burned around his face and hands. Naturally we followed his career thereafter, because he went down to the hospital in East Grinstead where McIndoe was evolving his organisation to deal with pilots who were burned. There were quite a few people in the squadron – Lewis and Wells, for example – who were very badly burned. We certainly knew all about it and we just prayed it didn't happen to us because you can put up with wounds. If you're wounded you tend not to feel it until later – but if you're burned, you know about it very quickly.

Then there was LMF – lack of moral fibre. In the First World War a lot of people who flew Sopwith Camels and SC5s found they couldn't continue, and it was termed 'flying sickness D'. The D stood for debility. It meant that people just couldn't go on. Lack of moral fibre means you shirked combat – and you could shirk combat by not showing willing. The same people could well be very good night-fighter pilots – or do jolly well on bombers. It required a different type of courage. I wouldn't have been very good on bombers – I don't have that type of courage. I was perfectly happy to fight on my own, but not with a lot of people around me. LMF could be interpreted in many ways – the sheer out-and-out cowards – there were very few of them. The shirkers – well, there were always one or two shirkers.

If a person didn't measure up, they suddenly disappeared. There was no acrimony, because if you didn't measure up, you didn't stay in the unit.

Gunther Rall

LUFTWAFFE FIGHTER PILOT

I had never met the RAF before. We were not very successful – we were not very experienced at all. I had only had one experience of a dogfight with a French plane on 12 May. We had to escort the 287, which was an obsolete aircraft, against the British Spitfires and Hurricanes. We got the order for flying direct escort – in most cases we met over Boulogne at 4,000 or 5,000 metres, and then we escorted this heavily loaded 287 across the Channel to Margate or Ramsgate – about three times a day. It was very difficult to stay with them at speed, so we had heavy losses. Right after the first missions, we lost our group commander and then my squadron commander – he was shot down. The weather was not very good, and the Spitfires just waited for us upstairs, and came out of the clouds at high speeds and dashed on us – and pulled up again. So we lost a lot of aeroplanes.

Squadron Leader Jack Satchell

302 SQUADRON

On 16 July, Flight Lieutenant Donald spoke to me as he got out of his aircraft – 'You have been posted, sir, to Leconfield, to a Polish squadron.' There was considerable mirth and polite leg-pulling and I frankly didn't believe it. Then he produced a signal confirming that it was so, and that I had been posted to form and command No. 302 (Polish) Squadron with effect from 13 July – three days previously.

My joy at getting my first command was very great, but I was, I'll admit, a trifle shaken at the word 'Polish' in the signal. To the best of my belief, I had never met a Pole in my life and what lay in store for me I could not guess.

The next morning I said goodbye to my friends in 141 Squadron with many good wishes and wisecracks, most of which had a lot of 'vitches' and 'skis' about them. My heart was very full of joy during that drive and I was full of hopes and building wild castles in the air, all the way.

On the 18th or 19th the first two Poles arrived at Leconfield – they were Lapka and Pilch, and two of the nicest blokes one could meet anywhere. I liked them immediately. They had come to us from the OTU at Sutton Bridge and had each done about thirty hours' flying in Hurricanes. They both transpired to be well 'above average' pilots and both could speak quite a lot of English. Having these two right at the beginning was a very great help, particularly in helping us out with the language when the others arrived.

On the morning of the 23rd I got a call to say that about eighty Poles would be arriving at Leconfield that day – and from that night onwards, the conversation in the mess sounded like the Tower of Babel. I remember standing in the centre of the crowd that first night and hearing all the following languages being spoken at once: Polish, German, Russian, Czech, French and pidgin English. I'm afraid that there were times that evening when I had an awful empty feeling in the pit of my stomach, and I wondered how on earth I should ever run this mob.

As far as I can remember there were about sixteen Polish officers who arrived that night. We all seemed to get on friendly terms quite quickly – perhaps under the friendly influence of a few drinks – but conversation was terribly difficult. It transpired that they had only been in the country about three weeks, having come straight from the South of France. They had, it appeared, escaped from Poland when the country fell, and gone on foot into Romania and Yugoslavia, and had embarked on ships in Greece.

They landed at Marseilles and joined the French Air Force, with whom they fought until France capitulated. The French then burned their aircraft and ordered them to lay down their arms, but the Poles refused, and as a result, they had to fight their way back to Marseilles – fighting the French! They arrived at Marseilles with absolutely nothing but what they stood up in – not even a toothbrush – *but* every one of them, even those with no footwear and consequently bleeding feet – and there were many of these – had a rifle or machine gun and many revolvers also and a quantity of ammunition. A very fine show indeed and a very good illustration of just how much guts they had.

There was a fiendish amount to be done for the pilots alone – to say nothing of the airmen. They all had to be taught the British methods of aircraft maintenance, which they did not take to very easily, probably because they had been working with the French for some months . . . then the translations. Every maintenance order and instruction had to be translated into Polish, and it was a huge undertaking. But we got it all done in time and sent copies of most of our work to 303 Squadron at Northolt, and later to 306 and 308 Squadrons.

Sergeant David Evans
INSTRUCTOR, 12 OPERATIONS TRAINING UNIT, RAF BENSON

Very few of the Poles could speak English so what we used to do was buy up all the newspapers with cartoons and we'd show them Jane, the blonde that used to be in the *Daily Mirror*. We'd point out all her attractive features in English. That gave them a smattering of English.

Flight Lieutenant John Simpson
43 SQUADRON

I had my first parachute descent on 19 July, during a battle off the south coast. I'd had the pleasure of sending two Messerschmitts into the sea, and then two others attacked me. I twisted and turned but they were too accurate. I could hear the deafening thud of their bullets. Pieces of my aircraft seemed to be flying off in all directions. My engine was damaged and I couldn't climb back to the cloud where I might have lost them. Then came a cold, stinging pain in my left foot. One of their bullets had found its mark. I was about to dive to the sea and make my escape low down – when the control column became useless in my hand. Black smoke poured into the cockpit and I couldn't see. I knew that the time had come for me to depart.

Everything after this was perfectly calm. I was at about 10,000 feet, some miles out to sea. I lifted my seat, undid my straps and opened the hood. The wind became my ally and the slipstream caught under my helmet. It seemed to lift me out of the cockpit which was a pleasant sensation. I was in mid-air, floating down so peacefully in the cool breeze. I had to remind myself to pull the ripcord and open my parachute. When the first jerk was over, I swung like a pendulum. This was not so pleasant, but I soon settled down and I was able to enjoy a full view of the world below, and of the beach some miles away with soldiers and long lines of villas in a coastal town. There was no sensation of speed but the ripples on the water became bigger and the soldiers became nearer.

I had one minute of anxiety as I floated down; one of the Messerschmitts appeared and the pilot circled round me, and I was just a little alarmed. Would he shoot? Well, he didn't. He behaved quite well. He opened his hood, waved to me, and then dived towards the sea and made off towards France.

The wind was still friendly. It was carrying me in towards the beach, so I took out my cigarettes and lit one with my lighter – without any difficulty. Ages seemed to pass. I threw away my cigarette and I came nearer to the coast. I could hear the 'all clear' sirens and as I was passing over the houses on the seafront, I could see the people coming out of their shelters. People were looking up at me. I descended to about 1,000 feet. I began to sway a little. I could hear my parachute chaffing like the sound of a sail on a small boat. Soldiers' faces were quite clear and I must have looked English, even at 1,000 feet – which is comforting. For the first time since the enemy circled around me, I became anxious. Was I to end my escapade by being banged against a seaside villa? It didn't seem possible that I could reach the field beyond.

Well, the journey ended in a cucumber frame after I'd pushed myself clear of a house with my foot. It was the first time I'd ever baled out – and really one of the most enjoyable experiences of my life.

Flying Officer Roland Beamont

87 SQUADRON

On 24 July, we were in the area of Purbeck, near Wombwell airfield, and I rolled over to see this 109 going towards the sea. He was trying to get the hell out of it, but as he came out of his roll, I was back on his tail, ready for another burst. It was then that I could see that he had his undercarriage coming down, and that he was streaming coolant. He started to sideslip fairly violently, and he did another roll – this time with his wheels down, and then a diving turn towards the ground. I thought either he was going to go in, or he was aiming for a forced landing. Obviously he was a very capable pilot.

Eventually he went in rather hard, to land in a field, buckling his undercarriage. He slid on his belly across the field and ended up at the far end, near a hedge. I dived around after him and saw him lift his canopy sideways, opening the cockpit. He jumped out, off the wing and lay flat on the ground. I wondered if he thought his aeroplane was going to blow up – and then I realised he might think I was going to strafe him on the ground. Of course the thought hadn't occurred to me.

Hans-Ekkehard Bob

LUFTWAFFE FIGHTER PILOT

Goering ordered us to adapt to the bombers' speed and we were supposed to fly alongside them, and this meant throwing away the fighters' advantage. The whole point of a fighter's advantage is the fact that it's fast. Now we were ordered to give up our speed and to fly alongside the bombers. And in doing so we were totally inferior.

Flying Officer Roland Beamont, 87 Squadron.

Pilot Officer George Herman Bennions

41 SQUADRON

On 29 July, the first aircraft that shot at me, I ducked out of the way, but unfortunately it had hit my port wing and damaged the flaps and the undercarriage and all the guns. Then I broke away and attempted to attack another 109. I managed to get back to Manston, and as I was coming in to land, the aircraft seemed perfectly all right as far as I was concerned. When I got near the ground, I put my flaps down, but only one flap went down, which was rather disastrous, because the aircraft slewed all over the place. Fortunately I'd left it until I was almost on the ground anyway. I'd pumped my undercarriage down, but what I didn't know was that one tyre had been blown off, and one leg damaged, and the flaps damaged – so when I hit the ground, the aircraft just spun like a top across the aerodrome, like a Catherine wheel. I came to rest completely bewildered, not having the faintest idea what had happened – but very relieved to find I was still in one piece.

Flight Lieutenant Tom Morgan

43 SQUADRON

On 8 August I had to bale out. I'd just shot down a couple of bombers and I turned to get another in that flight. They fired at me as I was coming in. They hit my aircraft in the gravity tank which is just in front of the windscreen on a Hurricane – and it caught fire. I sideslipped both ways to try and put it out. I did this manoeuvre until I got down to about 3,000 feet and then I realised I'd have to bale out. I turned my aircraft to make sure it would fly on into open country, then I disconnected the oxygen and the radio, opened the emergency hatch and got out and jumped off the wing.

My parachute opened and eventually I landed on the side of a hill not far from Midhurst. I was gathering up my parachute when a voice behind me said, 'Have you got any – any identification?' I turned round and there was a uniformed policeman. I said I hadn't but explained who I was and that I was from Tangmere.

'I think you'd better come to the police station with me,' he said.

'All right,' I said. The police had lovely little MG open sports cars in those days, in British racing green, and we got in it and off we went down to Midhurst.

We went to see the sergeant and the policeman gave his version and I gave mine. He asked me again if I had any identification, I said, 'No, but my station is Tangmere – ring my adjutant and ask him to come and collect me.'

They told me I was under suspicion so they put me in the cell with four Germans. One of them could speak English fluently, and one could speak it fairly well so I just sat chatting with them, exchanging things about our aircraft. I had a suspicion they were crew of one of the aircraft I'd shot down that morning, since they were already in the police station and the policeman who picked me up was wandering around in the area.

After I'd been there a couple of hours a constable came in and said, 'You come outside with me.' When I got outside and they locked the cell, across the desk I could see my adjutant. He had been a fighter pilot in the First World War. He looked across at me and it seemed that he had a smile on his face. The sergeant said to him, 'Can you identify this man?' And he said, 'Never seen him before in my life.'

So they put me back in the cell while, I presume, he and the sergeant and Tangmere sorted that one out. About two hours later out I came and the sergeant offered me a cup of tea. He said to the adjutant, 'Be very careful where you try on your little jokes in future.' And to me he said, 'You see that you carry some identification.' That was the only time I was shot down.

Pilot Officer Peter Stevenson

74 SQUADRON

On 11 August an attack came in over Dover, and I climbed up to attack a 109. He must have thought I was an Me 109, but when he suddenly dived away, I followed him and gave him a two-second deflection burst. The Me 109 lurched slightly and went into a vertical dive. I kept my height at 15,000 feet and watched. I saw the aircraft dive straight into the sea 15 miles south-east of Dover and disappear in a big splash.

I then climbed to 23,000 feet up-sun and saw a formation of twelve Me 109s, 2,000 feet beneath me, proceeding north of Dover. It was my intention to attach myself to the back of this formation from out of the sun, and spray the whole formation. As I was diving for them, a really large volume of cannon and machine-gun fire came from behind. There were about another twelve Me 109s diving at me from the sun and at least half of them must have been firing deflection shots at me. There was a popping noise and my control column became useless. I found myself doing a vertical dive, getting faster and faster.

I pulled the hood back, I got my head out of the cockpit and the slipstream tore the rest of me clean out of the machine. My trouser leg and both shoes were torn off. I saw my machine crash into the sea a mile off Deal. It took me twenty minutes to come down; I had been drifting 11 miles out to sea. One string of my parachute did not come undone, and I was dragged along by my left leg at 10 miles an hour with my head underneath the water. After three minutes, I was almost unconscious, when the string came undone. I got my breath back and started swimming. There was a heavy sea running.

After one and a half hours an MTB came to look for me. I fired my revolver at it. It went out of sight but came back. I changed magazines and fired all my shots over it. It heard my shots and I kicked up a foam in the water – and it saw me and took me to Dover.

Pilot Officer David Crook

609 SQUADRON

On 11 August there occurred our first really big action of the war. We were again down at advanced base, and about 11.30 am we were ordered to patrol over Weymouth Bay. Several other squadrons soon joined us, and altogether it looked as though it was going to be a big show.

Shortly afterwards we saw a big enemy fighter formation out to sea, and went out to attack it, climbing the whole time, as they were flying at about 24,000 feet. Some Hurricanes were already attacking the Messerschmitts and the latter had formed their usual defensive circle, going round and round on each other's tails. This makes an attack rather difficult, as if you attack one Hun, there is always another one behind you. We were now about 1,000 feet above the Me's at 25,000 feet, and the whole of 609 went down to attack.

We came down right on top of the enemy formation, going at terrific speed, and as we approached them we split up slightly, each pilot selecting his own target.

I saw an Me 110 ahead of me going across in front. I fired at him but did not allow enough deflection, and my bullets passed behind and fired a good burst at practically point-blank range. Some black smoke poured from his port engine and he turned up and stalled. I could not see what happened after this as I narrowly missed hitting his port wing. It flashed past so close that instinctively I ducked my head.

Newspaper seller watching a dog fight alongside a scoreboard on which the day's tally was somewhat optimistically chalked.

4

The Battle of Britain Phase II

Eagle Attack: Assault against the Coastal Airfields
12 to 23 August

By early August the RAF had the upper hand in protecting Channel shipping and destroying enemy aircraft. In terms of numbers the Luftwaffe had lost 248 aircraft to the RAF's 148. But even though aircraft production was keeping up with demand, Dowding was losing irreplaceable pilots, and knew this battle of attrition could not be sustained indefinitely. And Hitler was planning for more intense strikes against the radar chain on 'Adlertag' – Eagle Day – then a mass attack against Fighter Command bases.

On 12 August the Luftwaffe succeeded in taking down a significant section of the radar system – but this was quickly back in action. Strikes on the same day against fighter bases were deemed a success with claims that they had destroyed eighty-four fighters and eight air bases – but with the benefit of radar's early warning the defending fighters shot down fourty-six German aircraft for the loss of only thirteen, and similar German losses were inflicted in the ensuing three days.

The day elected for Goering's Luftwaffe to make the 'Adlerangriff' – the Eagle Attack – was Tuesday, 13 August, but bad weather thwarted the mission in the morning. Due to confused communications, seventy-four bombers of Kampfgeschwader 2 continued unescorted towards their target of the Isle of Sheppey naval base and Eastchurch airfield, and suffered significant losses. Other Ju 88s reached the skies over Hampshire before receiving the recall signal, and came under attack from the Hurricanes of 43 and 601 Squadrons. However, by mid-afternoon weather conditions had improved enough for the main Eagle attack to be launched and the skies over southern England were suddenly filled with huge formations of escorted bombers. It was fortunate that German intelligence had failed to grasp how the radar chain worked or that some of their chosen targets were Coastal and not Fighter Command bases – and consequently a number of sites less crucial to Fighter Command's survival bore the brunt of some of the attacks.

By the end of the day, the Luftwaffe had suffered fourty-four aircraft destroyed and thirteen damaged, to Fighter Command's thirteen aircraft lost and three pilots killed. Furthermore, of the fourty-seven aircraft destroyed on the ground by bombing, only one was a fighter. But even though the next day's attacks were less numerous and concentrated, the pressure was by no means off. The overall battle was becoming more intense, with the squadrons of 11 Group taking on most of the raids. The pilots of 12 Group felt acutely the frustration of their southern colleagues handling most of the action, but it was always Dowding's plan that they should be in reserve to defend London and the airfields of 11 Group in the event of their fighters taking on the enemy further forward.

The intensity of the battle increased through August, as Goering came under increasing pressure to deliver air superiority in time for

Operation Sealion. So far all his massed attacks had proved indecisive – now he harangued his pilots to greater efforts to destroy aircraft factories, take out radar stations and, most of all, finish Fighter Command once and for all.

Flying Officer Geoffrey Page

52 SQUADRON

We were all sitting around, having tea on the grass alongside a tent, which had a field telephone connected to Sector Operations. At about five o'clock, they phoned through and said there were 90 bandits approaching from the south at about 15,000 feet. There were only ten of us, but we took off. We could see the usual swarm of what looked like little insects taking shape – it was a large formation of Do 217s, escorted by 109 fighters. I was in the leading group of three, then I could see the tracer coming towards me from the whole formation – they had obviously singled me out as a target.

All these things which looked like lethal electric light bulbs kept flashing by, then finally there was a big bang and the aircraft exploded. The scientists reckon the temperature goes up from a cool room temperature at 15,000 feet to 3,000 degrees Centigrade in 10 seconds. So, when you consider water boils at 100 degrees, that's quite a temperature change. If you don't get out immediately, you're never going to get out. The beauty of the Royal Air Force training came to my rescue and I instinctively reached for the harness and slid the hood back. I rolled the aircraft on to its back, kicked back the control column so the aircraft pointed its nose upwards, but as I was upside down, I popped out like a cork out of a toy gun.

I stupidly wasn't wearing any gloves, so my hands got a terrible burning, and face as well. My mouth and nose were saved by my gasmask. I found myself tumbling head over heels through space. I remember seeing my right arm and extending it, making myself pull the metal ring of the ripcord on my parachute – and that was agony. It was like an electric shock through my burned hand. Again, you don't have a choice, because, if you don't, the parachute won't open.

Fortunately, my parachute wasn't on fire. One then took stock of the situation, and I noticed a funny thing had happened. My left shoe and my trousers had been blown off completely by the explosion. I was almost naked from the waist downwards – my legs were slightly burned. Then I could hear the fight all around me, and it took me about ten minutes to float down into the water.

I had various problems to deal with. First of all, I had to get rid of my parachute, but you had to turn this metal disc on your stomach. You turn it through ninety degrees and then give it a hard thump – but it was difficult because my hands were badly burned. Then the parachute was on top of me, so I was really inside a tent with the cords trapping me like an octopus's tentacles. I knew I had to get it away quickly, otherwise I would sink. Again, desperation comes into the issue, so you do turn it, and you do thump it.

The next thing was to blow up my life jacket. I got hold of the rubber tube over my left shoulder, but when I blew into it, all I got was a lot of bubbles. It had been burned right through. My face was swelling up at this point, and my eyesight was bad because my swollen eyelids were closing up. The distant view of England, which I could see a few miles away was a bit blurred, but I started vaguely in the right direction.

Then a happy thought came to my mind, and I remembered that in my jacket pocket I had a brandy flask that my dear mother had given me – which I had filled with brandy just as an emergency measure. I thought that this probably qualified as an emergency, so I rolled on my back. This was a painful process, but I got it out and held it between my wrists and undid the screw cap with my teeth. I thought, 'Well, life is going to feel a bit better.' But as I lifted it up to take a swig, a dirty big wave came along and the whole lot went to the bottom of the Channel. I was a bit annoyed about that, but there was nothing else for it, so I continued swimming.

I heard rather than saw the boat. There were two men in it, and they kept asking me questions. By this time I had been swimming for half an hour, and I was fed up with the whole affair, so when they asked me if I was a Jerry, I'm afraid I let loose with every rude four-letter word that I could think of, and that immediately assured them that I was an RAF officer. They picked me out of the water, and took me to the big ship, where the captain dressed my burns and gave me a cup of tea. Then the Margate lifeboat came out and took me in to transfer me to Margate hospital.

For the first time for an hour or more, I was able to laugh, because waiting on the quayside was the Mayor, dressed in his top hat and tails, saying, 'Welcome to Margate.' When you'd been in an air fight an hour before, and then there's a chap in top and tails, it is two different worlds. As it happened, it was the beginning of grouse shooting that day, 12 August. There was a certain irony in that.

Flying Officer Barton 'Barry' Sutton
56 SQUADRON

On 12 August my section was led by a man called Jumbo Gracey – a most positive, cavalier character. He did not give a damn what he said. He was a dreadful pilot, but he was extremely brave. He was annoying – he had a horrible raucous laugh – he was an ugly fat chap, full of fun, full of life. To sum him up, he was the sort of character you would need to weld people together when things were going badly and that's exactly what Jumbo Gracey did. Unfortunately, Page and I got the fag end of his rather bad leadership – Page getting the worse of the deal.

I first landed at Manston with blanco in my face and I really didn't see the runway, which was just taped out by an army officer, who, when I landed, said, 'Did you see them?' to which I said, 'Why the hell do you think I'm here?' – but he meant did I see the line of flags. In fact I hadn't seen them, and had landed purely by chance down the only serviceable bit of runway which he had mapped out.

I was flying number three, which was on the left, and Page was either number two or in the centre. I can't remember – but I saw him blow up and catch alight and go down, but I never saw him get out. In fact, I was quite certain he wouldn't get out. It looked to me as if the whole thing was too final. The reason why he was shot down and I was shot up was, I think, that we had insufficient overtaking speed due to old Jumbo's rotten leadership. We were only flying Hurricanes, and you need height – if you haven't got height you need a lot of overtaking speed to get in a quick attack from the rear quarter, and we sort of lumbered up from line astern and just ran across a tremendous lot of cross-fire.

I remember seeing Taffy Higginson coming over from the right to shoot clean across us to the left – from then on I was just concerned with getting down because I knew I had been hit. I had been hit in the radiator and poor old Geoffrey was concerned with getting himself out of his aeroplane – which he managed to do, and it was as well for him that he landed in the sea, as the salt water, painful though it was, undoubtedly had a cooling effect on his very extensive burns.

Pilot Officer Frank Carey

43 SQUADRON

On one attack I was ably assisted by an Me 109. Going in to attack some Ju 88s one day, we could see the fighters above, but we thought we would get a nice burst in before they got near us. I got behind this Ju 88 and pressed the button, and to my utter amazement bits flew off and the damage was astonishing! Our .303 guns weren't heavy enough to do so much damage. Then I saw fire over my head. There was a 109 trying to hit *me* but shooting high and we were both knocking the hell out of this poor old Ju 88! It went down. Really I shouldn't claim that one, I should have given it to the 109!

The trouble with the .303 on the Hurricane was that one had to learn to conserve one's ammunition: we only had fifteen seconds of fire and then you were finished. Chaps used to put on long bursts, and then they would only have half a burst left and that was it. An unarmed fighter is pretty useless. It was always a worry, that shortage of ammunition. I don't think the Spitfire was much better. Altogether I did about a hundred sorties in the Battle of Britain – from early July until 18 August. The most I did was six sorties in a day; roughly about an hour to an hour and a half each one. On 18 August I was shot down again.

I crash-landed at Pulborough. I don't know what shot me down. I was leading the squadron for the first time and we had just refuelled and taken off in a bit of a hurry and gone in to attack a mixed bunch of fighters and Ju 87s. The fur was flying everywhere. Suddenly I was stitched right across the cockpit. I handed over the squadron to the number two, called base, and said I was going to return because I'd been hit – I could make it there, I thought.

They said, 'Don't come back here, they're just about to bomb us!' I slowly eased my way north over the Downs, did a circle, losing a bit of height all the time, and asked again. They said, 'No, no, they're still all around us!' So I dropped into a field which didn't look as though it had any anti-invasion holes or poles. I got cocky and stupidly put the wheels down – which I should never have done – and just as I settled the plane down I said to myself, 'God, Carey, you're a wonderful pilot!' I was suddenly thrown forward as the plane flipped over. I thought, 'That's it.'

The next thing I knew I was laid out in the field looking up at the blue sky and two women were slitting my trouser legs, looking for bullet holes. One said, 'I can't find any more of them.' She seemed quite disappointed. It turned out that the locals had dug a trench and covered it over with grass. Of course I really mucked up the trap. I was very lucky because a Hurricane flipping over like that at almost flying speed nearly always killed the bloke by breaking his neck. The other lucky thing was it didn't catch fire, as it took the rescuers quite a time to get me out.

Chaps used to get out of their aircraft far too quickly – new pilots especially. Once over the Sussex coast I spotted a Hurricane flying along quite perfectly upside down without a pilot. I went right up to it and looked at it and it seemed to be totally undamaged; I knew who the pilot was from the marking on it – it was a Sergeant Buck who had been flying it. It turned out he had a bad wound in the leg and he baled out a few miles off the coast of Bognor. But by the time they picked him up he had drowned, even though he was a strong swimmer. If he'd stayed in the aircraft he'd have got to land.

I nursed another plane back from out in the Channel one day. The pilot got a glycol (coolant) leak – it comes out in little white puffs that get more and more frequent. I flew alongside and said, 'You stay there as long as that thing will take you back to land. Don't worry, it's all right.' I don't know what he was suffering in the cockpit, mind you. His cockpit was open and it must have been pretty hot. When it was no longer a puff but a regular little stream, he couldn't stand it any longer and got out. I followed him down and spotted him in the sea. I circled and radioed for help until I ran out of fuel. He was never picked up. I can only suppose he got tangled up and pulled down by the parachute. When he went into the sea he was only about a mile and a half off Selsey Bill.

Pilot Officer Henryk Szczesny

(POLISH) 74 SQUADRON

On 5 August 1940 at RAF Hornchurch I joined 'Sailor' Malan's 74 Squadron. He was famous even then. He was South African and younger than me. He seemed to like me even though my English was nil. I was learning slowly, it was a very difficult language. But

I wanted to fly so I had to learn. Malan and all the pilots helped me. They were really very good. There were South Africans, New Zealanders, Australians – all sorts. They talked to me slowly, and I had a dictionary. And the mechanics, they helped me very much. There were two of us Poles in the squadron but no one could say our names so they called Brzezina 'Breezy' and me 'Sneezy', and sometimes just Henry the Pole.

I remember first thing on 13 August we were told that bandits were coming from the Belgium area very low, without fighter escort. This was the day the Germans called 'Eagle Day'. So Malan, he says, 'Tally-ho!' And we saw about twelve of them; they had come to bomb Eastchurch, where I knew there was a Polish settlement. I got one – I shot him down. But he also got me. My undercarriage was down so I took off to West Malling and landed on one wheel and crashed, but I was OK.

Every day we were always fighting and flying and shooting but I couldn't say whether we shot anything down. But Malan always seemed to do so. He used to say, 'Henry, keep my tail, don't miss it.' So I flew on his tail all the time. I learned so much from him. He was a very great fighter. He had good eyesight. If he saw somebody they were dead.

He taught us many lessons. He had 'ten commandments':

First: wait until you see the whites of their eyes before you fire. Then fire short bursts of about one or two seconds, but only when your sights are on.

Second: think of nothing else while you are shooting – concentrate your whole body.

Third: even when attacking keep a sharp lookout, especially after a breakaway. Don't watch your 'flamer' go down except out of the corner of your eye.

Fourth: if you have the advantage of height you have the initiative.

Fifth: always turn to face the attack. If you are attacked from above, wait until they are committed to their dive and within 1,500 feet of you, then turn suddenly towards him.

Sixth: make your decisions promptly and smartly.

Seventh: never fly straight and level for more than thirty seconds while in a combat area or at any time when enemy aircraft are likely to be near.

Eighth: when diving to attack always leave a part of your formation above to act as top guard.

Ninth: initiative; aggression; discipline in the air; teamwork; all mean something in combat.

Tenth: and finally: get in quickly, punch hard, get out smartly.

I remember once in the middle of a battle watching hard to see if I had got one, when Sailor came up in my ears and said, 'Henry, don't think numbers, kill!'

The money, my goodness! I got twelve pounds something a month. It lasted only for three or four days. I didn't want to keep it because I never thought for a moment I would stay alive. Every day someone was missing – so always I thought one day it will be me. So I used to get my money and spend it. We then lived on King and Country, the mess bill.

Always, though, I thought I might return to a free Poland.

Pilot Officer David Crook

609 SQUADRON

On 13 August we patrolled over Weymouth, and after a few minutes I began to hear a German voice talking on the RT, faintly at first and then growing in volume. By a curious chance this German raid had a wavelength almost identical with our own and the voice we heard was that of the German commander talking to his formation as they approached us across the Channel.

The bombers, with their fighter escort still circling above them, passed beneath us. We were up at almost 20,000 feet in the sun and I don't think they even saw us till the very last moment. The CO gave a terrific 'Tally-ho!' and led us round in a big semicircle so that we were now behind them, and we prepared to attack.

Mac, Novi and I were flying slightly behind and above the rest of the squadron, guarding their tails, and at this moment I saw about five Me 109s pass just underneath us. I immediately broke away from the formation, dived on to the last Me 109, and gave him a terrific burst of fire at very close range. He burst into flames and spun down for many thousands of feet into the clouds below, leaving behind him a long trail of black smoke.

I followed him down for some way and could not pull out of my dive in time to avoid going below the clouds myself. I found that I was about 5 miles north of Weymouth, and then I saw a great column of smoke rising from the ground a short distance away. I knew perfectly well what it was and went over to have a look. My Me 109 lay in a field, a tangled heap of wreckage burning fiercely, but with the black crosses on the wings still visible. I found out later that the pilot was still in the machine. He had made no attempt to get out while the aircraft was diving and he had obviously been killed by my first burst of fire. He crashed just outside a small village, and I could see everybody streaming out of their houses and rushing to the spot.

All the machines were now coming in to land and everybody's eyes were fixed on the wings. There was the usual anxious counting – only ten back – where are the others? They should be back by now. I hope to God everybody's OK. Good enough – here they come! Thank God, everybody's OK!

We all stood round in small groups talking excitedly, and exchanging experiences. It is very amusing to observe the exhilaration and excitement which everybody betrays after a successful action like this.

It soon became obvious that this had been our best effort yet. Thirteen enemy machines had been destroyed in about four minutes' glorious fighting. Six more were probably destroyed or damaged, while our only damage sustained was one bullet through somebody's wing. I think this was the record bag for one squadron in one fight during the whole of the Battle of Britain.

Day after day, battles of incredible ferocity were taking place, often at a height of 5 or 6 miles, and the great conflict raged and thundered through the summer skies of southern England.

Many hundreds of German bombers and fighters littered the fields and countryside, and yet each morning brought a fresh wave of enemy aircraft, manned by crews who generally showed a fine determination and doggedness in the face of such murderous losses.

The strain on everybody in Fighter Command was very heavy indeed during this period. There were so many attacks to meet and so few pilots to do it – only a few hundred of us in all, and on many occasions only about half that number were actually engaged. A number of these pilots had only just arrived in squadrons to replace the losses of the previous months. At the end of Dunkirk in June one quarter of the pilots in Fighter Command had been killed, and now, halfway through, there were not many left of those who had started the summer's fighting.

I think the death of one experienced pilot was a bigger loss to a squadron in those days than ten Spitfires or Hurricanes, because, however many fighters we lost or damaged, replacements always turned up immediately. This must have demanded the most terrific efforts from both the factories and the ground crews, and though we couldn't see the efforts we did appreciate the results. But experienced pilots could never be replaced. You could only train the new ones as best you could, keep them out of trouble as much as possible in the air, and hope they would live long enough to gain some experience. Sometimes they did.

Hans-Ekkehard Bob

LUFTWAFFE FIGHTER PILOT

In a case of escorting a particularly large German bomber formation we flew between two cloud layers. For that reason we felt relatively safe because there was close cloud cover above and beneath us. To our surprise we were suddenly attacked by a large Spitfire formation exactly in our rear. At first it was incomprehensible how this formation could reach us in the rear without any sighting by us and in such a good attack position. Later we learned that the British were at that time already in possession of a kind of radar that could guide them exactly in height and direction.

Sergeant Fred Roberts

ARMOURER, 19 SQUADRON

We didn't really discuss death – if a pilot was killed, it was horrible to think that half an hour before we'd been strapping him in a plane. But he'd gone – and there'd be a replacement tomorrow. That was as far as our thoughts went. There was no such thing as stress in those days, there was no counselling or anything like that. It was an act of war – they died, they were killed.

Pilot Officer Nigel Rose

602 SQUADRON

On 13 August we left for Westhampnett which was a grass airfield for Tangmere. We landed at Westhampnett at about five in the evening and there was a terrific battle going on at the time and aircraft limping in. The squadron we were relieving – 145 – had really been shot to pieces over the last few days, and were in a sorry state. I think there were only five serviceable aircraft and a few more serviceable pilots out of probably, say, seventeen of each. They had an awfully hard time of it – they were ready to be posted up north for a rest. The Germans had already been sending over these vast arrays of aircraft for some two or three weeks by then. Churchill and Dowding's advice not to run the squadrons down too much going to France was probably right because they needed all they could find back in this country.

It was a lovely summer's afternoon and I remember having tea out in the garden when we arrived, wasps all round, and writing a note to my parents when I said we'd bagged five before supper – five wasps. I don't think we flew that first day after we landed – we let the aircraft get serviced and got ready. I didn't fly for the next two or three days. The squadron generally got into action the next morning – we used to do three or four sorties each day if the weather was OK and the Germans were sending planes over. You could get quite tired at the end of all that – partly the emotional strain.

That time of the year you could be called up to readiness at four in the morning and the airmen had already been out and got the engines warmed up and ticking over. You might not have a patrol until breakfast time because the Germans probably wanted to have their breakfast before they set off. The first sortie would be around breakfast time, but some of the big formations they sent over – huge fleets of bombers accompanied by equally huge fleets of fighters – fifty, seventy, ninety – sometimes over a hundred at a time. Sandy Johnstone mentions one hundred the first time in his book.

That was my first baptism of fire, around 17 August. We were split into two by Sandy – he kept the bombers to himself and 'B' Flight and we went off – 'A' Flight – to look after the fighters and keep them away as much as we could. I remember we were looking down on them – which was a good thing – so the controllers had got us up in time – and the flight commander – Micky Morant – said select your aircraft and off you go. I remember getting a feeling for one of the chaps right at the back – the stragglers were the ones to go for – so one turned one's gun button to fire, which meant the button on the top of the control column and you were all ready set to go. You had eight machine guns in the Spitfire 1 in its early days – no cannon there. We were at a disadvantage with Me 109s which had the cannons and firing through the nose – and that was a thing in their favour because it was easier for them to demolish their prey if they managed to get a lucky hit or a carefully thought-out hit.

I remember coming down on to this chap and I must have opened fire at what I thought was getting close enough, but my camera for once was working and so ultimately I had the film developed and sent back with comment that I was out of range when I opened fire. I wasn't altogether surprised. I don't know how close I got to him, but probably not terribly close for a first time, given these Me 110s which were rather bigger than 109s and possibly more menacing-looking although much slower.

He flipped on his back very suddenly and went down – there was smoke coming out of one of his engines – whether I'd got it, I imagined I did. Perhaps there was a lucky one through the radiator – but there was a cloud of white smoke coming out. He flipped over on his back and went down almost vertically. I thought, 'Gosh, this is fighting!' But as often happened I followed him a little way but by the time I levelled off, there was nobody in the sky. One minute there are masses of aircraft all flying in one direction and then there's nobody to be seen. You wander home feeling rather proud. I don't know how much ammunition I used of the 14 seconds' worth, firing all eight guns, each firing about 20 rounds a second, I think – 1,200 rounds a minute – there was quite a lot of fire-power there if you could bring your guns to bear.

I think to me this was the thing about not going to an OTU, where they would have said, 'Rose, if you think you're close enough, you're not. You're miles out of range. You've got to get in close behind – and watch your rear because there's probably somebody close behind you – so watch out – but get in close behind, get him in your sights and then squirt, at 250 yards, because then the guns are synchronised.' Well, I didn't get this wisdom imparted to me –

or if I did it wasn't strong enough and I forgot. I never really got within murderous range but I did later on get these trails of smoke from planes and I did get them to turn over and go down, so at least I must have frightened some.

But on this first occasion one went home feeling quite happy at having made the chap possibly dive in – but later on when I got a little wiser, I thought he was probably going home to lunch. These Me 110s were two-seaters, and the chap probably said to his pilot, 'We'd better get the hell out of here – we've got a Spitfire after us!' So I suppose they may not have thought much more about hanging about – Spitfires were quite revered, even by the Germans, so I think he may have been getting away into the cloud and haring off home. You don't know if you might have got in a lucky shot . . .

Johannes Steinhoff

LUFTWAFFE FIGHTER PILOT

The English had ingeniously found a way to defend their island. Every pilot, except a small group of night flyers and bomber pilots who were the nucleus of the coming night bomber fleet, was retrained as a fighter pilot. It made no difference if he was a liaison plane pilot, a bomber or fighter-bomber pilot, he was retrained. Industry was instructed to concentrate on fighters. And in this way it was possible to seal the gap – and more! In one stroke, the lost air superiority was regained, and henceforth we did not own the airspace from Calais to London.

Pilot Officer Tom Neil

249 SQUADRON

After leaving Yorkshire we went down to Boscombe Down in Hampshire. We got there on 14 August, and we were thrown into the maelstrom of fighting fairly quickly. On the next day, 249

Johannes Steinhoff, one of the Luftwaffe pilots who survived to fly operationally throughout the war.

Squadron gained its first Victoria Cross of the war for Fighter Command – which turned out to be the only Victoria Cross. That was the day I lost my first aeroplane, which I loved like a brother – P3616.

I'd been on duty the night before and the following day my flight commander, who was my good friend, Nicolson, forbade me to fly – which irritated me no end, because I hated handing my aeroplane to someone else. I had to loan it to a chap called King, who was also nineteen.

The squadron took off and intercepted a large group of aircraft roughly over Southampton. It's probably due to the inexperience of our squadron that Nicolson and his formation were bounced and Nicolson was set on fire immediately and got his Victoria Cross when he apparently was overtaken by the bloke who shot him down, and he stayed in his burning cockpit and shot whoever it was down – so this was a famous act. He baled out and, on reaching the ground, he was shot by the army and was peppered with bullets.

Fortunately he had his back turned to the chap who did the firing, so he collected most of the shot in his rump. King, who was flying my aeroplane, was also shot down, and came down by parachute. The same army shot at him and destroyed his parachute, and he fell in somebody's garden and was killed. The third person who was in the group of three was the squadron leader – also called King – who was damaged too but fortunately managed to get back to Boscombe Down. That was our first real engagement.

Many of the army on the ground were Home Guard – the LDV – and they were lunatics – they fired at everything they saw in the air. The British public in those days were unused to aeroplanes – any aeroplane in the sky was an enemy aircraft and they didn't distinguish between friend and foe. Many of the people who were shot down at the Battle of Britain who came to the ground in a parachute – and I was one of them – ran a serious risk of being mutilated and attacked by people on the ground.

Some people in Kent were East Enders who had been bombed, and they weren't very sympathetic to any Germans that came down by parachute – and they couldn't distinguish between them and the RAF.

When I came down by parachute I was in a semi-unconscious state, listening to a conversation going on by various sets of feet around me, and they were discussing whether or not I was German or British. I got the impression that things wouldn't have gone well for me had they decided that I wasn't British. A lot of people had their equipment and belongings pilfered by people on the ground. They'd been filled with all the stories of how the Germans had parachuted into Holland during the invasion – so they weren't very sympathetic to people in parachutes.

I learned fifty years after the event, when I unveiled a memorial plaque to Nicolson at Boscombe Down, that the fellow King, who was shot down in my aircraft, had also been killed as a result of friendly fire.

Ludwik Martel

(POLISH) 54 AND 603 SQUADRONS

Everything happened so quickly – it was the beginning of the battle for me, and the way you survived you were lucky. You had to be good – and lucky. You had to be good at your job – the job is that you had to get on the enemy's tail – and the 109 is quite manoeuvrable. You had to make an effort – but when you get it . . . I had two or three successes later on in the battle – but the beginning was a bit frightening until you realised that you're not on your own – the other person is trying to do exactly what you're trying to do. If you were prepared for it you knew how to do it.

We had the objective to go for the bombers and destroy them – but no matter how you try, you have to be so bloody careful who is behind you, and check if you've got someone chasing you. It was a good idea to go for the bombers to prevent the damage they were trying to do, but you didn't always succeed and sometimes you were left with the 109s – and you had to deal with the fighters. The idea was that we should fly in formation, all together, but I personally thought it wasn't a good tactic – you were so limited in movement and in observing and you had to be careful you didn't collide with your number two because of the close formation. This tactic was changed later on. One of the problems was that having a big formation taking off, it took a long time – it was a question of experience.

We were ordered in the air – the Operations' job was to direct us. To take off when the enemy was already there was very dangerous and there were a lot of people shot down taking off – you were vulnerable beneath them. The main objective in the battle was to get the squadron up as soon as possible so you have the advantage in the attack. Being below was a dead loss.

The timing was very important. The aim was to be in company – no doubt about it. You didn't need to be stuck together – but whenever you get involved, you'd look around for company – it gave you a different feeling. A number of times I found myself on my own – but then you had to defend yourself because you are a target.

The main idea was that you relied on information from the Operations Room – they knew where you should go and what target you should defend. It was important that the Germans were picking up the targets to destroy – aircraft factories and things like that. I think our radar was efficient but we didn't make the maximum effort to be able to cope with it. Quite often we were being directed the wrong way – which was very frustrating. During the battle you always looked for the most convenient situation for yourself. You don't always have to be successful and shoot something down but you always look to be in a safe position and to be able to defend yourself or be able to shoot the enemy.

We were very happy to be among the British pilots, but it was only natural for the Polish pilots to stick together – and we tended to do that.

Pilot Officer Tim Vigors
222 SQUADRON

We slipped into a routine which was to be our daily life for the next ten weeks. There were busy days and quiet days. Some days we would be scrambled as many as four times, some days only once, although the latter was rare. We had good days and bad days. More often than not we managed to cause more damage to the enemy than we received ourselves. But there were days when the reverse occurred also. On one really bad day the squadron had nine aircraft either destroyed or damaged with only four confirmed victories to our credit. Death and wounds among our companions became commonplace and were taken with an exaggerated lightness which we found was the only possible way to bear the losses and remain sane.

Tiredness started to creep over the survivors and, in some cases, a resignation to the fact that soon one's day would come. For myself, I would just not let a fatalistic attitude take hold. I was absolutely determined to survive.

About two weeks after we had arrived at Hornchurch, Hilary failed to return from a morning fight over the south coast. None of us had seen him get into trouble and I waited anxiously for news. Deaths had become everyday occurrences by now, but as I paced up and down outside the dispersal hut with Snipe, I found it difficult to treat the possibility that my good friend had been killed with that same studied lightness which, like everybody else, I learned to affect in these circumstances.

'Please God, let him be all right,' I said to Snipe who seemed to sense my worry and was walking along beside me with his head down. Living lives of such contrast, between extreme danger and normal daily comforts, it was natural to crave the close companionship of another human being. With them, one could share one's hopes and fears. Hilary and I had grown very close over the past few months and now, confronted for the first time by the stark reality that he might have been killed, I suddenly realised how much I relied on his sympathy and humour. Luckily my anxiety on this occasion was short-lived.

'He's OK, Tim!' yelled Johnny Hill from the doorway of the dispersal hut. 'Biggin Hill have just called to say that he baled out and landed nearly on their airfield. He's got a bit burned, but they say not too bad.'

Pilot Officer Nigel Rose

602 SQUADRON

We had the local vicarage or big farmhouse on the edge of the airfield, and Westhampnett was a parish with a church of its own. It was on the borders of Goodwood, and when this airfield was given runways it began to be known as Goodwood, then it became a racetrack for racing cars and after the war a private airfield.

There were hard standings where we could taxi the aircraft out and park them for the night. I don't think the Germans ever found Westhampnett – I don't ever remember getting bombed there. We had a few airfields around and Ford was fairly close and there was a night-fighter station there – which was probably why we never did night patrols there. Once one section took off – when I was on sick leave – three of the chaps who had never flown a Spitfire at night – they took off at dusk and it got pretty dark by the time they arrived, and all three overran the airfield and crashed their aircraft. I don't think any of them were injured, but they made a sad mess of the front end of their aircraft. We weren't really trained for flying Spits at night – not many people were.

When we were off duty we went to pubs – though I joined a squash club in Chichester. The officers were made honorary members, and soon after we arrived they asked us if we would like to join. Everything was very pally in those days, and we saw some of the female population there. I fell for a girl I met there called Pamela Anding – I fell for her in a big way. She lived in Bognor with her parents and her sister, and her sister used to come to the squash club too. A friend of mine also rather fell for her. So for a lot of my time off I would go to Bognor and occasionally they used to have a party at the mess in Tangmere – they would want to have a dining-in night and get rid of some of their hard-earned cash. We were paid only a pittance by today's standards, but the mess had a decent sort of peacetime cache of cash, and we could invite the girls along. My Pamela had to be home by twelve o'clock, which was reckoned to be rather strict; however, we got married four months later in Canterbury.

Relations with the locals were very good indeed – they were very nice all round, whatever one was doing in the neighbourhood. By day the NAAFI used to send a coffee urn in. It was very nice when you met people from outside – and they were the kindest of kind people – as they were everywhere in the country. If you were in the services they couldn't do enough for you. You were wearing uniform and felt rather proud . . .

We were in the flicks one day and it flashed on the screen – 'Will Pilot Officer Rose please report to his airfield at once' and we got this posting up to Scotland, which was cancelled for some reason, so I needn't have fled. One felt rather proud of getting up in the cheap seats and walking out with one's shadow reflected on to the screen.

Sergeant Pilot Iain Hutchinson
222 SQUADRON

In our free time we'd have a sing-song – drink beer in the mess. I used to play the piano in the mess, and during an air raid you had to have your tin hat with you – so I had mine on top of the piano, upside down. We didn't take cover when the air-raid sirens went, normally, but we only took cover in the shelters when we were warned that an attack on the airfield was imminent – then we scarpered, top rate. On one occasion I was a bit slow as I wanted to finish the piece I was playing – and when I looked up, my helmet had gone. After everything had settled down, we came back to the mess, somebody asked me if I put my helmet on. I said, 'No, no.' He said, 'Well, oh, pity, I put half a pint of beer in there.' I never found out who had got it.

Flight Lieutenant Johnny Kent

303 AND 92 SQUADRONS

We climbed to about 11,000 feet and then, without any warning, there was a loud bang as my engine blew up and caught fire. Flames were licking around the canopy and sparks darted around inside the cockpit. I switched off the ignition, turned off the fuel, turned up my oxygen supply and started sideslipping in an effort to keep the flames from reaching the reserve petrol tank situated just behind the firewall bulkhead. My aircraft rapidly lost speed and the other aircraft shot past me – or all except one which came in to tight formation. It was Hilly Brown, who called me on the RT, saying, 'Haw, bloody haw! You getting hot in there, Bud?' This was a reprisal for a lot of ribbing I had been giving him for having been shot down and burned a few days before – but I thought he could at least have waited until I got down.

I was, in fact, in a bit of a predicament as I was right over the centre of London and, if I baled out, the machine would crash into a densely populated area – though why I should think that this would be worse than the bombs already falling there, I don't quite know. I decided to stay with the aircraft and hoped that the fire would be blown out, and that I might reach open country or possibly even my own airfield. I called the controller and told him what had happened and what I was trying to do. Nothing much was said for some minutes and then the station commander came on to the radio and asked if I was going to bale out.

By this time it was too late and I was already starting the final approach and had pumped down both wheels and flaps. Although the smoke had died away quite a bit, I was far from happy, but it was good to see two beautifully sited fire engines converging as I touched down. They started to throw foam at me but the operators had never been given instructions in deflection shooting – while they were aiming at the engine they managed to hit me, so stopping ten yards from the spot where I had started my take-off, I got out looking rather like a snowman.

Flying Officer Harold Bird-Wilson

17 SQUADRON

I was at about 15–16,000 feet, watching a raid coming in above us – and I got anoxia. Something had gone wrong with my oxygen system and I felt terrible. It affects one's balance and physical well-being. I started diving down and I found myself over the English Channel – and there was a German aircraft, right down by the water, flying as hard as he could back to France. I did two or three attacks on him before the French coast came up. I severely damaged him and decided it was about time I got back. So I turned round and flew home but I felt so ill that I had to land at Southend. They looked at my oxygen and found something wrong with the connection.

Flying Officer Jeffrey Quill

65 SQUADRON

One thing that we hadn't discovered in the course of test-flying was that when you had been flying at high altitudes for some time and then you dived rapidly down, you'd bring this great chink of freezing cold glass with you. As you descended into the moist warmer air, the moisture condensed on the inside of the screen and promptly froze up. That was very awkward for you – you couldn't damn well see.

Flight Lieutenant Eustace Holden

501 SQUADRON

On two occasions, I was getting myself in a splendid position to shoot Messerschmitts down when my windscreen clouded over, owing to the change in temperatures from very high where I'd been, coming down into higher temperatures lower down. I was very angry and I let fly at the chaps who designed them. In no time, we had a heated windscreen.

Flight Lieutenant Robert Stanford Tuck

92 AND 257 SQUADRONS

With what speed I had left I managed to pull up to around 1,500 feet. I was only about 16 miles out, but I felt sure I'd never get back to the coast. I can't understand why that engine didn't pack up completely, there and then. Somehow it kept grinding away. I was very surprised, and deeply grateful for every second it gave me.

As I coddled her round towards home I glimpsed a Ju 88 skimming the waves away to port, streaming a lot of muck. In fact, he was leaving an oily trail on the water behind him. I had the consolation of thinking the chances were that he wouldn't make it either.

I trimmed up and the controls seemed quite all right. The windscreen was black with oil. Temperatures were up round the clocks and pressures had dropped to practically zero – but she kept on flying after a fashion. Every turn of the prop was an unexpected windfall – that engine should have seized up, solid, long before this.

I knew it couldn't last, of course, and I decided I'd have to bale out to the Channel. It wasn't a very pleasant prospect. Ever since my pre-war air collision I'd had a definite prejudice against parachutes. But the only alternative was to try to 'ditch' her, and a Spit was notoriously allergic to landing on water – the air scoop usually caught a wave and then she would plunge straight to the bottom, or else the tail would smack the water and bounce back up hard and send you over in a somersault. Baling out seemed the lesser of two evils, so I opened my hood, undid my straps and disconnected everything – except my RT lead.

It got pretty hot about now. The cockpit was full of glycol fumes and the stink of burning rubber and white-hot metal, and I vomited a lot. I began to worry about her blowing up. But there were no flames yet, and somehow she kept dragging herself on through the sky, so I stayed put and kept blessing the Rolls-Royce engineers who'd produced an engine with stamina like this. And in no time at all I was passing over Beachy Head.

I began to think after all I might make one of the airfields. The very next moment, a deep, dull roar like a blowlamp started down under my feet and up she went in flame and smoke.

As I snatched the RT lead away and heaved myself up to go over the side there was a bang and a hiss and a spout of hot black oil hit me full in the face. Luckily I had my goggles down, but I got some in my mouth and nose and it knocked me right back into the seat, spluttering and gasping. It took me a little while to spit the stuff out and wipe the worst of it off my goggles, and by that time I was down to well under a thousand. If I didn't get out but quick, my chute wouldn't open in time.

It wasn't the recommended method of abandoning aircraft – I just grabbed one side with both hands, hauled myself up and over, and pitched out, head first. As soon as I knew my feet were clear I pulled the ripcord. It seemed to open almost immediately. The oil had formed a film over my goggles again and I couldn't see a thing.

I pushed the goggles up, then it got in my eyes. I was still rubbing them when I hit the ground.

Sergeant Pilot Iain Hutchinson
222 SQUADRON

During the battle I didn't have any nightmares – until after the last time I got shot down – and then I had nightmares which have persisted the rest of my life. It was simply that I was stuck in the aircraft, and it was going down rather rapidly. I didn't think I could get out and I was just waiting for the big bang, and that did something in my head. I remember wondering whether the bit of me that was sticking out of the aircraft would be more pulverised than the bit that was inside – which was rather an odd thought – but you think about odd thoughts at these times. Then I found myself floating through the air and that was it. The nightmares started after hospital, when I went back on to the airfield.

Sergeant Frederick Gash
264 SQUADRON

We felt we had to stop the Germans if they tried to invade. I did talk to several of my 264 friends and comrades and colleagues about that. 'What're we going to do if the Germans do get here?' And most of them said, 'We've got to stop them from getting here – so why talk about what are we going to do if they get here? We've just got to stop them.' And that was the mood of most people, and I think that was the mood of the civilian people. We would stop them.

Flight Lieutenant Brian Kingcome
92 SQUADRON

One had to realise that there was an invasion pending – but equally, one knew there wouldn't be one. I was quite convinced, and I think most fighter pilots were, that there was no way they could go through us. So there was no sort of nervousness in case the Germans invaded. If they did invade, we thought, 'What a marvellous opportunity to slaughter all these barges coming in.'

Sergeant Ray Holmes
504 SQUADRON

We built up a sort of synthetic hate against them, which was a bit artificial. I wanted to shoot an aeroplane down, but I didn't want to shoot a German down. I really did not. We did hear stories of Germans shooting our fellows in parachutes, and we used to think that was pretty horrible – but we weren't sure whether it was true or not. I know I had an experience of a German aircrew getting draped over my own wing – he baled out of a bomber and got caught on my wing with his parachute, and I was jolly careful to get him off as easily and as quickly as I could, manoeuvring the aeroplane and shaking him off. And I was very glad when I heard he'd dropped down in Kennington Oval safely. So I had no feeling of wanting to kill that fellow personally.

Flying Officer Geoffrey Page
52 SQUADRON

After being shot down on 12 August, I spent a few days in Margate hospital and then I was taken up to the Royal Masonic Hospital in London, and then later on I found myself in Sir Archibald McIndoe the plastic surgeon's hospital in East Grinstead, where I spent two years undergoing plastic surgery.

I was there with Richard Hillary, who wrote a book called *The Last Enemy*, and there were six RAF fighter pilots. We got together and formed a little club, which we called the Guinea Pig Club. And from the six of us who started it, about seven hundred have been through that hospital. We thought, well, when we were allowed to get out of bed and walk a few yards, there was a little hut, and we said, 'Why don't we form a little sort of club in there, where we can have a glass of beer and get away from the ward for half an hour or so?'

Flying Officer Al Deere

(NEW ZEALANDER) 54 SQUADRON

On 15 August, when the battle was going strong, I did a stupid thing and was shot down again. We intercepted some 109s over Dover who were escorting some Ju 87s. They were dive-bombing Dover. I'd already got one down when I got on to the tail of another. When he turned for home I followed him, shooting. I realised in the end that he was getting too far out to sea and I was getting too far away. As I turned I ran into some more 109s. They set about me and shot me up rather badly. By the time I got back to the coast my aircraft was smoking badly and it was clearly going to burn. I jumped out and I landed in a field not very far from Dover, where by this time it was dusk. It was my fifth sortie of the day and I was pretty tired: I'd hit my wrist badly trying to bale out and was in terrible pain. It happened that an RAF ambulance came by the field I landed in, and they picked me up and said they'd take me to Kenley. Well, they got lost in the blackout. We went around and around and around. They finally dropped me at East Grinstead hospital at midnight, with my wrist throbbing like hell.

We started to complain about operating from Manston because it was so far forward that, in order to get to the height of the Germans – some 20,000 feet – we had to climb inland. As well as that, we had been bombed on the ground. We'd had a hell of a time. I think it was a morale thing: Churchill had apparently said we mustn't give up any piece of land. It was an expensive way of gaining the moral victory: in the end we were losing chaps taking off and landing. Eventually the powers that be gave in and we went back to Hornchurch, which was much more comfortable because we climbed straight up to height. But by this time it was well into August and the Germans were getting further and further inland. They started bombing the London perimeter airfields, of which Hornchurch was one.

The third time I was shot down was by a Spitfire. I was pumping away at a 109 when the Spitfire jumped me from behind. I was filled full of holes, but I was still flying. I headed for home, but I could see I wouldn't be able to keep airborne: the engine was rough, I couldn't move the controls properly, and I couldn't see what was wrong behind. So I decided to bale out.

At this time I was somewhere near Hawkinge airfield, on the way back to Hornchurch. I'd had a rough experience getting out the previous time, because I had hit the tail. I tell you it takes a lot of guts to turn your Spitfire upside down, knowing your harness is undone. So this time I put it on an even course and went over the side. I landed in a field, 5 or 10 miles from Detling. It so happened that the raid we had intercepted had bombed Detling airfield.

I arrived at Detling to find that they had had quite a few casualties and the place was chaos. But there was an Anson there, on the airfield, and a chap called Desmond Garvin, a fellow pre-war RAF rugger player, who was commanding the Defiant Squadron and had been shot down in the same do. We were flown back to Hornchurch together: he to discover that his Defiant Squadron was no longer, the Germans having massacred the lot of them in two sorties; and I to find that we'd had pretty severe losses again. Once again I thought I might get a break. But I was told it was impossible, we had no one else who could lead.

Flight Lieutenant Peter Brothers

32 SQUADRON

The hardest day was 15 August. That was a very big raid. There was a change of tactics and it took us by surprise. Quite a few aircraft were caught on the ground. They were bombing Biggin Hill from high level, a raid against which I was involved, but they also ran a low-level raid at Kenley, which was next door to Biggin Hill.

Wilhelm Raab was on the Kenley raid, and his squadron suffered tremendous losses. His gunner was wounded, and he landed at the first base he reached in France to off-load the wounded crew. In fact, I shot him down later, on 15 September. His unit lost most of its aircraft on that low-level raid. Meanwhile, we were unaware of the low-level raid at Kenley. The Germans threw everything they had at us. We did three sorties that day, all around midday, one of them was fifty minutes long, one was an hour, and the other was an hour and a bit. I got a 109 and a Do 17 at high level. The Germans lost seventy-five aircraft that day. Although they attacked all four fighter groups, their bombers caused some damage, but no great success. They never came again in such numbers.

Pilot Officer Bob Doe

234 AND 238 SQUADRONS

On 15 August 1940 we were ordered up to Middle Wallop. We flew up there but I was feeling very strange in the sense that everything was distant; we hadn't been involved, it wasn't real. We landed on the grass airfield, were put into a lorry, and halfway up to the mess, they bombed the airfield. One of the hangars was hit, and a WAAF was killed in a trench. Up to that moment we had been seeing war from a spectator's point of view.

A bit later that day we were scrambled over Swanage. I really had the worst inferiority complex at that time. I felt I was the worst pilot in the squadron, and I was convinced I would not survive that trip.

We took off and formed up into four Vics of three in sections astern, which is the stupidest formation you could possibly fly in. There's only one person looking round, everyone else is formating. And we patrolled up and down the sun, which, again, is a stupid way of flying. At one point, we turned back down-sun to find we were only nine strong. We had lost three; our rear section had disappeared, one killed and the other two shot down.

Then, all of a sudden, we found ourselves in the middle of a gaggle of Me 110s and 109s. God knows how we got there; we just landed in the middle of them. I was flying at number two to Pat Hughes, who turned off after a 110, gave him a quick squirt, then turned on his side, and pulled away. But it didn't look quite right to me, so I formed on the 110, got quite close to it, and kept on firing until he went down into the sea. This was the second time I'd used my guns, the first was into the sea to try them out. I thought, 'This is something! I'm not dead and I've done something!' That feeling was really fantastic. I followed him down, pulled up from the sea, and another 110 overshot me from behind. I just closed on him and shot him down.

I shot two down without really knowing anything. I realised on the way home that I'd been so lucky it was ridiculous. So I drilled it into my head that if I saw anything coming past me from behind, I would just hit the stick. I wouldn't think, just hit it. I then started thinking about why we had found ourselves in the middle of a gaggle of the enemy. I realised that I had to see them before they saw me. And I couldn't be in formation if I was going to see them: I had to get away on my own.

The following day we met a load of 109s high up over the Isle of Wight, and I found one on his own. I settled down on him. Now, although I'd shot two down the day before, I was not certain about shooting. I couldn't trust my judgement and distance, and I couldn't trust my shooting. So I aimed above him first, then below

Pilot Officer Bob Doe 234 and 238 Squadrons.

and eventually I shot him down. But I had been so involved that I hadn't seen another 109 behind me. Fortunately Pat Hughes had spotted it and shot it off my tail. I was dead lucky.

I followed the plane I'd been concentrating on down and saw him plunge into the sea. I circled the crash, and found someone shooting at me. It was a Do 18, a flying boat, out there looking for survivors. He put a bullet slap into the middle of my spinner, but didn't do any damage so I had a go at him. That was the first time I was hit. After that, almost every time I was in action I got hit, so I always knew I'd been close to it somewhere.

Aircraftwoman Jean Mills
WAAF, PLOTTER AND TRACER AT RAF DUXFORD

From the little rooms, the little wireless and radar rooms behind the controller, we could hear the crackling voices of the pilots come back, and although we had headsets on and the work was quite intensive and required a lot of concentration, we used to manage to ease one earphone off so we could hear what was going on, and then we could listen out for 'Tally-ho', which meant they'd sighted the enemy, and then you could hear them talking to each other, like, 'Look out, Blue Two, bandits to your right.' And things like that, which seemed to bring it right into the room. There was an indescribable tension about the whole thing. When there was something going on, the atmosphere was electric. We were all rooting for our boys to come back. They were very much our pigeon.

Flight Lieutenant Tom Morgan
43 SQUADRON

In 43 Squadron, right from its formation in the First World War, the spirit in the squadron between pilots and ground crew was always good. I regarded it as the first priority to maintain that squadron spirit – and indeed the squadron became well known for it. I had an extremely good relationship with them and I encouraged the view that we were a team of three – Tommy Poole my rigger, and Bill Littlemore my fitter and me the pilot. I encouraged this through my flight sergeants in the flights to have the same sort of camaraderie. I lost track of Tommy Poole after the war, but Bill Littlemore and I stayed friends until he died. Our ground crew would take an aircraft in and they'd work on it all night to get it serviceable for the next morning – we had a great team spirit.

Sergeant Pilot Iain Hutchinson

222 SQUADRON

I thought our ground crew were terrific. On one occasion I landed, to rearm and refuel the aircraft, and the airfield was being attacked. The ground crew came out, they got the bowser out, I got out of the cockpit and they got the machine-gun rounds out. I could hear this banging going on all over the place. I got under the wing, ostensibly to look and see if the guns had been reloaded, but basically I was trying to keep clear of any shrapnel that might come our way. I was very glad to get back into the aircraft and take off again – but they were out there in the middle of it, ignoring it all. They were really fantastic.

They were unsung heroes, and you could depend on them to the last man. The great thing about it was they were engineers of different skills, but they did an absolutely precise job. There was no skimping and every job was done to perfection. They looked after their pilots better than anybody else could have done.

Pilots and gunners of 264 Squadron, a Defiant-equipped squadron, pass the time with a game of draughts.

Hans-Ekkehard Bob

LUFTWAFFE FIGHTER PILOT

While I was flying my 109 slowly alongside the bombers over Canterbury, I received a hit on my cooling unit. The engine's cooling system didn't work any more and it overheated. The engine was about to start burning and I was forced to switch it off. In the event of situations such as this, we had been ordered to switch off the engine and to switch the propeller to the gliding position. At an altitude of 4,000 metres, you might be able to glide about 40 kilometres – but over Canterbury, that would have taken me either to the English coast or into the water so I thought, 'I won't do that, I'll try something different.'

It occurred to me to leave the engine idling until it had cooled down again, and then, once it had cooled down a bit, I would switch on the ignition and accelerate at full speed, ascending as high as possible. Then, when the engine overheated again, I would switch it off again, and carry on doing this. Using this method got me 80 kilometres, as far as the French coast, and I was able to perform an emergency landing on the sand at the French coast. People were astonished that I had advanced so far, having begun at such a low altitude. The incident was crowned with success and I was commended for my ability to cope in this way.

Pilot Officer Geoffrey Page

56 SQUADRON

I don't think at any point morale was low, because the facts of life were, we would be flying many times during the day, having taken off in the darkness, and then, as the dawn came up, we'd fly to a forward base such as Manston or Hawkinge or Rochford – and then we'd be at readiness all through the day. Then in the evening, just as the light was beginning to fail, we'd fly back to our base at

North Weald. Then there'd be a mad rush to get down to the local tavern before the pubs closed. Don't forget, we were all nineteen, twenty, twenty-one years of age. We were just overgrown schoolboys.

In all squadrons, fighter or bomber, during the war, there were commissioned officers and there were non-commissioned officers of sergeant rank. But while we were lying around our aircraft or in the air, there was no differentiation between ranks at all. I always felt it was a little unfair that after a hard day's fighting and you landed, one lot of us – the commissioned officers – we would go off to the officers' mess, and the sergeants would go off to the sergeants' mess. I think men who take an equal risk, you know, should live the same.

Unknown pilot
56 SQUADRON

What made war tolerable – exciting – even pleasurable – was this. It was as if you went out for a day's sport from a pleasant country house in which you had the privilege to live. We lived together – and of course there were cliques and private jokes – a language of our own, superimposed on the general slang. It created a feeling of separateness – snobbishness – if you like. North Weald had an air of its own, yet London was only 17 miles away. There was a feeling when war came that we were living in a comfortable microcosm. We never thought of wider issues – we were wrapped up in our own lives. You never heard politics discussed – and we read only newspapers – and if a book, then it was a novel. We talked about aeroplanes, but not so much shop as today. We were wilder, drank more, enjoyed ourselves more. We didn't doubt that we wouldn't lose – although I don't know that we were all as anxious to get to grips with the enemy as we made out. I wasn't. Deep down we didn't know what was going to happen – what it would be like. I never saw anyone show he was frightened, although we probably were. 'Frightened' is a bad word – we were 'keyed up' – 'tensed' in readiness.

The bell went – the moment of running to the aeroplane was worst. The nearer you got to it, the less you thought about what was going to happen. Strapping in was a nervous moment – then climbing, in those bright, clear skies – lumbering along, trying to get height.

Flight Lieutenant Robert Stanford Tuck
92 AND 257 SQUADRONS

I remember an enjoyable incident that happened on the morning of 14 August. Up at 15,000 feet over Cardiff, I picked up three Ju 88s which were heading as if for Ireland. My stern attacks didn't seem to make the slightest impression on them, so I hared past them, turned, and carried out head-on attacks. That worked all right *but* by the time I had accounted for two of them, the third had disappeared in the cloud.

A few days later, when I was on my way to an aerodrome to get a few of the holes in my Spitfire patched up, I struck the first of the big daylight blitzes on the south coast, and ran into a couple of Ju 88s off Beachy Head. I chased one of them about 35 miles out to sea before I shot him down. By that time, we were right down on the water, and as I turned to climb, the other Hun turned to fire at me with his cannon. He shot my oil and glycol tanks away, and part of my propeller, which caused excessive engine vibration.

I climbed for all I was worth and pushed the engine flat out. Very soon, it was on fire, but even so, it got me back 60 miles before it went up in smoke and I had to bale out. I was smothered in oil and I couldn't see a thing – but perhaps that was just as well because if I'd realised I was only a few hundred feet up, I'd probably never have had the nerve to jump. As it happened, my chute opened with a bump, and it was a second or so before my feet hit the ground. Some Observer Corps men I spoke to later told me that I was not more than 500 feet when I jumped. I still go hot and cold when I think of that jump.

After I had returned from a spell of sick leave, I had an experience that made me angrier than anything I can remember for a long time. I was shot down by a lone bomber – a most undignified experience for a fighter pilot. It was a Dornier, and I ran into him as he was bombing shipping about 15 miles off the south coast of Wales. I shot him down all right but as he went seaward, the rear-gunner got in a burst which put two holes in my cylinders, and I just managed to bounce on the very edge of a cliff near Tenby. I was knocked out in the crash – but fortunately not for long, and I leapt out of that cockpit pretty quickly when I heard petrol sizzling on the engine.

Flying Officer Roland Beamont

87 SQUADRON

On a scramble on 15 August, the controller said, 'Bandits now 20 miles ahead of you. You should see them directly ahead.' Almost immediately the clear sky ahead started to turn into a mass of little black dots. It could only really be described as a beehive. This mass of black dots appeared, developing ahead. Our CO continued to lead us straight towards it. I just had time to think, 'I wonder what sort of tactic he's going to employ? Is he going to turn up-sun and try and dive out of the sun at them, or go round to the right and come in behind? What's he going to do?'

While I thought that, it was quite apparent he wasn't going to do anything. He bored straight on into the middle of this lot until we seemed to be going into the biggest formation of aeroplanes you ever saw. Then his voice came on the radio and said, 'Target ahead. Come on, chaps, let's surround them.' Just nine of us!

I fired at a Ju 87 at point-blank range, and I hit it. I don't know what happened to it. But I could see my tracers going into it. Then I came under attack from directly ahead and below. It turned out to be an Me 110, doing a zoom climb straight up at me, firing as he came. He missed me. I rolled away from him straight behind another of his mates, a 110. I fired a long burst at him and his port engine stopped and started to stream smoke and fire, and pulled away from that.

Pilot Officer Douglas Hamilton Grice

32 SQUADRON

15 August was my last operational flight, and we'd taken off from Biggin Hill to patrol somewhere over east Kent. I was flying what the air force called 'arse-end Charlie' – in other words, by myself – a thousand or a couple of thousand feet higher than the rest of the squadron and slightly behind. Weaving like mad, looking right, left, centre, up, down – and mostly back – when suddenly, out of the corner of my eye, I saw a flash over my left wrist. The next moment, the cockpit was full of flames. The heat was enormous, and I'd done two things absolutely instinctively. My left hand had gone to the handle of the hood, my right hand had gone to the pin of my harness, and I was pulling with both hands. The next moment I was out in the open air. I'd made no attempt to jump out of that aircraft – well, I was straining back from the flames and the heat. What I think had happened was, I was doing a left-hand turn, and my aircraft had gone on turning over on its back, and I had just fallen out – unless I'd kicked the stick which would have jerked me upwards and out.

Anyway, there I was, falling away – and I did actually remember my parachute drill, which was to wait before pulling the ripcord for two or three seconds. I pulled it, and there was a jerk – and there I was, floating down under a marvellous canopy, about a couple of miles inland. I could look down and see the land, and I thought, 'Well, at least I won't be going into the sea.' Well, very shortly after that, I was over the coast – and a few minutes later, I was a mile out to sea – and a few minutes after that, I was 2 miles out to sea. Well, before that, I'd taken my helmet off and dropped it, and that gave rise to a moment of immense panic. I actually watched my helmet drop from, I suppose, 12–13,000 feet, until it disappeared from view. I suddenly realised how high I was, and how much space there was between my toes and the ground. So I hung on to my straps like mad.

Flight Lieutenant Brian Lane
19 SQUADRON

I saw some gleaming specks a mile or two ahead and 2,000–3,000 feet above us. I opened the throttle wider and began climbing hard after them. Glancing down, the glint of sun on water showed the position of the Thames.

The specks grew larger and resolved themselves into Me 109s, their yellow-painted noses shining golden in the sunlight. Ahead and below them was a formation of Me 110s and, in front of them again, the bombers. Twelve Spitfires slid in under the 109s and crept up towards the 110s in front. It was obviously out of the question to get to the bombers as they were too far ahead.

The only thing to do was to wade into the 110s, of which there were about two squadrons. As we got into range I singled out a target and the rest of the formation spread out and followed in. I opened fire from almost astern and the Hun went into a steep turn. As I followed him I noticed a stream of tracer apparently going straight into him. For a moment I thought it must be from another Spitfire, but suddenly realised that it was coming just over the top of my cockpit from behind me! My heart missed a beat.

Pulling sharply round out of the way, I found another 110 on my tail. How he got there I don't know for I certainly did not see any of the Huns break formation until I opened fire. Keeping in the turn, I got away from this gentleman, and feeling rather like a replica of that famous petrol advertisement, 'That's a shell, that was!' had a good look round. Nobody seemed to be after me and I turned in after a 110 ahead, coming in from the side at him. I got a good sight on him and fired a long burst until a large portion of his port engine came right out of the wing. He lurched over on his side and fell half inverted towards the glistening water far below. Keeping a good look round, I managed to watch him on his last journey and was rewarded by the sight of a huge splash of white foam as he hit the sea just off the coast.

Squadron Leader Sandy Johnstone

602 SQUADRON

Whilst in the midst of a break at lunchtime, 602 Squadron was scrambled to deal with an enemy raid approaching the Isle of Wight at 15,000 feet. In spite of the short warning, we made the interception before the bandits reached the south coast. They consisted of some fifty-plus Ju 88s and Do 17s, with a sizeable covering escort of Me 109s and 110s.

I immediately despatched Findlay Boyd to take 'B' Flight against the escorts whilst I led 'A' Flight into the bomber formations. A free-for-all soon developed and I managed to down a 110 by blowing its tail unit clean off. I saw the pilot baling out of his spinning aircraft.

As I pulled up to rejoin the fray, an Me 109 got on my tail, firing tracer but, in my anxiety to climb away from him, I accidentally stalled my aircraft and almost flipped over on top of my adversary. Indeed I was presented with such a point-blank target that even I could not fail to hit it, thus notching up my second confirmed victim in the one action.

Squadron leader 'Sandy' Lane (facing camera), the CO of 19 squadron, relaxing with some of his pilots in the crew room.

The squadron tally that day amounted to thirteen enemy aircraft destroyed and four probably destroyed, without loss.

Sergeant Rosemary Horstmann
WAAF, BASED AT HAWKINGE

It was very dramatic, because several of the girls who were working with us had boyfriends who were pilots, so they would find themselves monitoring a battle in which their brothers and fiancés were fighting, and we were writing down what the German pilots were saying – things like, 'I've got him,' or 'He's down!' Sometimes you would hear people screaming.

Flying Officer Harold Bird-Wilson
17 SQUADRON

I was both worried and frightened at times. We were praying for bad weather – probably the only time anybody in England prayed for that! Somehow during the battle we had beautiful weather – sunshine and blue skies most of the time – and we did pray very hard. Fatigue broke into a chap's mentality in most peculiar ways. My chaps had the jitters and facial twitches. I had nightmares and used to wake up in the dispersal hut about twenty-five yards from my aircraft. That was when I was night-flying my Hurricane.

Flying Officer Richard Hillary
603 SQUADRON

On the morning after our arrival I walked over with Peter Howes and Broody. Howes was at Hornchurch with another squadron and worried because he had as yet shot nothing down. Every evening when we came into the mess he would ask us how many we had got and then go over miserably to his room. His squadron had had a number of losses and was due for relief. If ever a man needed it, it was Howes.

Broody, on the other hand, was in a high state of excitement, his sharp eager face grinning from ear to ear. He left Howes at his dispersal hut and walked over to where our machines were being warmed up. The voice of the controller came unhurried over the loudspeaker, telling us to take off, and in a few seconds we were running for our machines.

I climbed into the cockpit of my plane and felt an empty sensation of suspense in the pit of my stomach. For one second, time seemed to stand still and I stared blankly in front of me. I knew that that morning I was to kill for the first time. That I might be killed or in any way injured did not occur to me. Later, when we were losing pilots regularly, I did consider it in an abstract way when on the ground; but once in the air, never. I knew it could not happen to me.

I suppose every pilot knows that, knows it cannot happen to him; even when he is taking off for the last time, when he will not return, he knows that he cannot be killed. I wondered idly what he was like, this man I would kill. Was he young, was he fat, would he die with the Fuehrer's name on his lips, or would he die alone, in that last moment conscious of himself as a man? I would never know. Then I was being strapped in, my mind automatically checking the controls, and we were off.

We ran into them at 18,000 feet, twenty yellow-nosed Me 109s, about 500 feet above us. Our squadron strength was eight, and as they came down on us we went into line astern and turned head-on to them. Brian Carberry, who was leading the section, dropped the nose of his machine, and I could almost feel the leading Nazi pilot push forward on his stick to bring his guns to bear. At the same moment Brian hauled hard back on his own control stick and led us over them in a steep climbing turn to the left. In two vital seconds they lost their advantage.

I saw Brian let go a burst of fire at the leading plane, saw the pilot put his machine into a half-roll, and knew that he was mine.

Automatically, I kicked the rudder to the left to get him at right angles, turned the gun button to 'fire', and let go in a four-second burst with full deflection. He came right through my sights and I saw the tracer from all eight guns thud home. For a second he seemed to hang motionless; then a jet of red flame shot upward and he spun to the ground.

For the next few minutes I was too busy looking after myself to think of anything, but when, after a short while, they turned and made off over the Channel, and we were ordered to our base, my mind began to work again. It had happened.

My first emotion was one of satisfaction, satisfaction at a job adequately done, at the final logical conclusion of months of specialised training. And then I had a feeling of the essential rightness of it all. He was dead and I was alive; it could so easily have been the other way round; and that would somehow have been right too.

I realised in that moment just how lucky a fighter pilot is. He has none of the personalised emotions of the soldier, handed a rifle and bayonet and told to charge. He does not even have to share the dangerous emotions of the bomber pilot who night after night must experience that childhood longing for smashing things. The fighter pilot's emotions are those of the duellist – cool, precise, impersonal. He is privileged to kill well. For if one must either kill or be killed, as now one must, it should, I feel, be done with dignity. Death should be given the setting it deserves; it should never be a pettiness; and for the fighter pilot it never can be. From this flight Broody Benson did not return.

Pilot Officer George Herman Bennions

41 SQUADRON

I was very concerned and very upset. I was annoyed at myself for having been shot down so decisively, and I felt terribly isolated. I couldn't see

188

or hear very well, and so I couldn't recognise people. I felt so very sorry for myself, which is not a good situation for anybody. I felt so deflated, that half of my life had been taken, and half wasn't worth bothering with. It was, I think, the worst period of my life.

There was one person in particular who put me on a much more even footing. He had been shot down by a Hurricane. He had sent a message to go and see him. I was on crutches at the time, and I managed to get over to where he was with a hell of a lot of struggle and self-pity. As I opened the door in Ward 3, I saw what I can only describe now as the most horrifying thing I have ever seen in my life.

This chap had been really badly burned. His hair was burned off, his eyebrows and his eyelids. You could just see his staring eyes, with only two holes in his face. His nose and lips were also badly burned. Then I looked down, and saw that his hands and feet were burned. I got through the door on my crutches with a struggle, and then this chap started propelling a wheelchair down the ward. Halfway down, he picked up the back of a chair with his teeth – and it was then that I noticed how badly his lips were burned. Then he brought this chair down the ward and threw it alongside me and said, 'Have a seat, old boy.'

It was then that I cried – and I thought, 'What have I got to complain about?' From then on, everything fell into place.

Flight Lieutenant Brian Kingcome

92 SQUADRON

It was the most enjoyable part of the war. It sounds perhaps callous – I don't know – but it was enormously exciting and tremendous fun. And we had every advantage – to begin with, we were flying over our own territory, and this was a huge moral advantage. Because first of all, it gives you a reason for being there – because when you're over your own homeland, defending your own homeland, it gets the adrenalin going.

We had two extremely good controllers at Biggin Hill – Roger Franklin and Bill Igoe – and they gave you your head. Some controllers tried to tell you exactly what to do. Roger Franklin and Bill Igoe simply told you where the enemy aircraft were and left you to decide how to attack.

5

The Battle of Britain Phase III

The Luftwaffe Targets the Airfields
24 August to 6 September

By the middle of August replacement pilots arriving at the squadrons from the Operational Training Units had flown only training aircraft such as the Master, and had as little as ten hours' flying time on the Hurricanes or Spitfires they would be expected to fly, and had no experience of high-altitude flying or attacking tactics. And there was no longer the luxury of operational training on the squadron – no experienced pilots were free to train the new boys, and although inexperienced pilots were kept out of the front line as much as possible, sometimes the controllers had no choice but to bring them into the battle. In many cases the new arrivals paid dearly for their inexperience, while those with sufficient training to get through their first combats tended to become more battle hardened and less likely to make fatal errors.

A squadron of twelve aircraft would be divided into 'A' and 'B' Flights, six fighters in each. 'A' Flight would have three 'Red' and

Winston Churchill viewing activity in the Channel from Dover Castle. Enemy attacks were in progress and two German bombers were seen to crash into the sea.

three 'Yellow' aircraft, and 'B' Flight would have three 'Blue' and three 'Green' aircraft, and in radio communication 'Red One' would identify the leader of 'A' Flight's Red Section, and so on.

Pilots had the routine of a four-day cycle – a day on stand-by when they might be called to fly within the hour, a day 'available' to fly within fifteen minutes, a day at readiness when they had to be prepared for immediate take-off, and a day stood down when, with the commanding officer's permission, they could leave the airfield. But as the pressure of the battle worsened, pilots found themselves unable to rest at all. Pilots 'at readiness' would sleep and eat at the dispersal hut on the airfield, awaiting the phone call from the Section Controller. The waiting was a period of extraordinary tension, and pilots reacted in different ways – some were able to suppress their anxiety and play cards to pass the time – others were physically sick at the sound of the phone – but there were very few who were not able to focus on the task in hand when the call came to scramble.

After Eagle Day Hitler phased his Stuka dive-bombers out of the battle, bringing Me 110s in to replace them in a dive-bomber role, with 109s as escort. Top priority was to destroy the RAF's fighters and bases, and small bomber groups with a heavier fighter escort were deployed to try to draw the fighter defence up into an uneven battle.

Goering pursued this strategy for the next few weeks, and even though the British were shooting down more enemy planes than they were losing, the Luftwaffe was slowly gaining the advantage. For a time, the Germans could afford to lose aircraft and pilots, but the RAF could not. One accidental circumstance changed the course of the conflict. In the early hours of 25 August, a lone German bomber lost its bearings and, against all orders, bombed central London. Incensed, Churchill ordered bombing raids to be launched against Berlin the next day and on subsequent nights.

Sergeant Pilot Bill Green

501 SQUADRON

I had my first flight in a Hurricane on the 12th, and on the 19th I ran into my old CO, Hogan, who said, 'How are you getting on?' I said I'd done about five hours, and he said that was too damn slow.

'You come back and we'll train you a lot faster than that.'

I asked when he wanted me back, and he said that same night. Back I went.

Three o'clock the next morning and someone was flashing a light in my face. I was put in a bed next to Ginger Lacey. I said, 'I'm Green – I've just arrived.'

The chap said, 'I know. Get out of bed – you're Green Three.'

On the way down to the aeroplane about ten minutes later I said, 'What's this Green Three business all about?' Ginger Lacey told me and we flew down to Hawkinge, and that was it.

That was 20 August, then on 24 August we were coming in behind some 88s over Manston; I was about 500 yards behind and got my gun button on to fire when, bang, I was hit, from ground flak. I crash-landed at Hawkinge. That was on Saturday and on the following Thursday we were vectored from Gravesend at about six in the evening to Deal and we were told to orbit and look out for 200 snappers coming in – and so we were all rubber-necking, watching our tail, and quite suddenly there was a crash of glass and a hole appeared in the windscreen about as big as a tennis ball. I started getting covered in glycol and I realised I had to get out. I pulled the Sutton harness which was strapping me in and got to the edge of my seat, and bang – I was out in space, rolling forwards and I heard my boots go past my ears.

I thought I'd never find the ripcord, but I did, and pulled it, and I saw a bit of white do two concentric circles in space. It didn't have any significance – but the main canopy on which you sit had nothing to drag it from its pack and the cords of the drogue chute were severed about six inches from the main canopy. It fell out of its pack and I just rolled into it, and it wrapped itself around me like a shroud, so I could see nothing. I was falling through space and really thought that I was going to die. I had only been married twelve weeks and I was seeing my end through the thoughts of my wife – and I wondered if she'd wonder if I wondered as I fell what my end was going to be like.

Suddenly I stopped rolling forward and rolled backwards and nobody ever taught me how to do that. All the wind had to get underneath one of the folds, and whoosh – the big parachute came out and kicked me back with a jolt. The secondary chute whipped away from the structure and I grabbed it as I thought that might be going as I'd seen one bit going and experienced the consequences. I looked to my left and the trees were way above me – and I thought 'I'm near the ground,' then suddenly bang – and I was down.

Two blokes came down from the farmhouse at the top of the field, carrying shotguns and asked me if I was English. I said, 'Yes I am.' I tried to get up but I was wounded in the leg so I reckon I would have been within not more than 200 feet, falling at 205 feet per second, and I would have been within a second of hitting the deck. That was it, and I didn't fly in the battle after that.

Pilot Officer Glen Niven
(CANADIAN) 602 AND 601 SQUADRONS

I'd got my commission and was acting pilot officer, then I was posted to 602 Squadron, because that was the squadron I had joined back in Glasgow. I leapt on a train and went all the way to Edinburgh and arrived at Drem, where I found that 602 Squadron had left to go south the day before, to Tangmere on the south coast. So I had to go all the way back and arrived at the squadron on 1 September 1940. I thought, 'Now I shall fly my Spitfire and show them how it's done.' Even though I'd never even sat in one . . .

Unfortunately the next day there was a call – is there anybody there who can fly a Hurricane? And unfortunately Niven had trained on a Hurricane and the CO, Sandy Johnstone, said there was me, and I was sent across to the 601 City of London Squadron, because they had lost two of their pilots. He said, 'Don't worry, we'll work on it to get you back,' so I went to 601, where most of us got clobbered – but luckily not me, because I was still effectively training. They were good in letting me follow them around. Then I got posted down to Exeter because there were only about ten pilots left out of the twenty. I phoned up the CO and said that I was down in Exeter when I should have been with 602 Squadron at Tangmere near Chichester. He said that we couldn't have that, and next day I was back with 602.

I was given three days flying Spitfires, mostly going out over the Channel looking for poor chaps who had been shot down. I would go out with a more senior pilot – in two aircraft.

They were looking for pilots at that stage, because they were losing them rather quickly – even Niven would do! You never worked out your life expectancy – if you didn't come back that was hard luck – what the hell are we going to do tomorrow? For the new ones like myself life expectancy was probably about two weeks – but if you got through two weeks, you got through three – and if you got through three, you got through five. Sheer bloody luck.

Aircraftwoman Jean Mills

WAAF, PLOTTER AND TRACER AT RAF DUXFORD

We were all pretty young – girls of only nineteen or twenty – when we got assigned to Duxford, and for a lot of us it was the first time we'd been away from home, so we were laughing and joking, because it seemed like an adventure. Suddenly we reached the brow of a hill and we could see Duxford, stretching out in front of us. It was a beautiful sunny day. As we looked, we could see that something had

Pilot Officer Glen Niven, 602 and 601 Squadron.

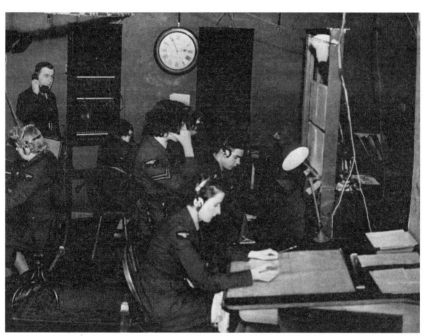

WAAFS and Airmen operators at work in the wooden huts at Ventnor, Isle of Wight.

happened. There were lots of planes – one plane seemed to hover and was nose-diving to the ground with smoke trails rising. The noise of our chatter stopped instantaneously and the mood changed. We realised it wasn't a great lark and that we were in for serious business. We were reminded of this because the pilot who was killed had an Alsatian, which kept roaming the camp looking for him. It was very sad.

Aircraftwoman Anne Duncan
WAAF, PLOTTER

There was a table with a map of England on it, and the whole of the map was marked out in a grid. The man on the other end of the telephone, when he was reporting things coming in, he'd give you two letters and four numbers, and from that you put down a little round disc like a tiddlywink. Then a few minutes later there would be another one – that would be a bit further on, and you could see the course gradually building of something coming in. You plotted everything. Everything came in over the radar tubes and the problem was to decide which was friendly and which was not. It was quite easy in the beginning, because anything that was friendly went from England outwards, and anything that was not, came from France or Holland and Belgium.

Flying Officer Alec Ingle
605 SQUADRON

The first flight you made in the morning, you would get a sinking feeling in the pit of your stomach, until you saw the enemy and the minute you'd made your first interception, for the rest of that day it didn't matter what happened. The adrenalin was flowing and certainly, as far as I remembered, it flowed in reasonable quantity. Once you pressed your gun button, you could take on the complete Luftwaffe. That's the reaction I had to it.

Flying Officer Al Deere

(New Zealander) 54 Squadron

You'd go ten days, for example, without actually seeing the mess in daylight. We'd go off to dispersal – if we were operating from the forward base, Manston, which we generally were, up till towards the end – we'd be off before first light, so we'd be landing at first light at Manston. Similarly, we'd come back in the evenings at last light. The rest of the time was spent either sitting at dispersal, which was way out the other side of the airfield with a tent or a telephone, or in the air. We used to have meals brought out to us. We never saw the public – never got off the airfield.

Pilot Officer Bob Doe

234 and 238 Squadrons

We were so confident at that time. There was no doubt in our minds. We knew we weren't going to lose. I suppose, in retrospect, we were bloody stupid, but it never entered our minds that we could possibly lose this war.

Then we had a new CO posted in, and he decided to come as my number two on a scramble. We found a lone Ju 88 over Winchester. Well, I had a go at it; he had a go at it; no effect. So I got behind it, got as close as I could, and filled it with bullets. He hit me through the mainspar, then stopped firing and went into the ground. When we landed back at base, the new CO, very keen, wanted to go and have a look for the Ju 88; it had crashed in a field very close to Middle Wallop. I'm now very sorry I went to see it, because someone informed me that every aircrew helmet had bullet holes in it, and that brought everything home to me.

I had to fly the Spitfire down to Hamble for repair. It was a lovely warm day, with interceptions going on overhead all the time. The foreman of the place invited me home to lunch, and his wife started talking to me and suddenly, for the first time, I realised that ordinary people in the street knew what we were doing, and that they admired us. She was saying things that made me blush. It really was quite something. I hadn't been aware of it; it hadn't entered my mind. People could see what was happening.

I don't know how many I'd shot down by then, but I was getting very confident. I had very good eyesight. I'd learned an awful lot about seeing aeroplanes; and was very good at spotting them. You never see an aeroplane if you are looking straight at it. You see it ten degrees off to the side. You might see movement, at one o'clock, two o'clock, and then that's it, you've got it. This became apparent to me very quickly, and probably saved my life on a few occasions. In general, I saw them before they saw me, and that is important, because you can then position yourself for your own attack. I also found that the really effective way to attack was to go straight in. Don't muck about. They never expected you to go straight in, and they scattered like wildfire when you did.

Then, too, at first I tended to be very much on my own, because our squadron never went in formation. But I found that, if you were on your own, you spent an awful lot of time looking round. After that, Sergeant 'Budge' Harker and I started flying a couple of hundred yards abreast. That way you can each see anyone on the other's tail. This was the start of 'Finger Four' flying, although the Germans had it ages before that. If we'd had any Intelligence in the air force at that time we would have known about it, and we wouldn't have lost a lot of the people we did lose.

Sergeant Pilot Don Kingaby
266 AND 92 SQUADRONS

On one occasion, after finishing a patrol, I had just landed at Manston and was walking away from my aircraft when a formation of Messerschmitts made a lightning attack on the airfield. I threw myself to the ground as I saw the flashes and felt the thud of the bullets hammer into the earth around me. I was extremely lucky to get away from this attack with only one smashed finger – it was the only wound I received throughout the whole of the war.

Pilot Officer Tony Bartley

92 SQUADRON

We did five sorties a day. We never stopped – we just went. You went to your dispersal hut half an hour before dawn, but when the Tannoy said scramble, you scrambled. You went up and you fought all day long until the sun went down. Whether it be three, four, five missions a day – you just fought and fought and fought. At the end of the day we got off the airfield, because they used to bomb us at night, so we would go down to the White Hart at Brasted and drink a lot of beer.

Pilot Officer Frank Carey

43 SQUADRON

Air fighting is a very detached sort of warfare being fought, as it were, between machines with the human factor very much submerged in a 'tin box'. Once in a while for a few fleeting seconds when someone bales out, one can suddenly be aware that humans are actually involved but, as the parachute descends, machines quickly regain the centre of the stage once more.

On one particular sortie from Wick, however, the human angle predominated for quite a while. The formation in which I was flying came upon a rather lonely He III way out in the North Sea which we naturally proceeded to deal with. After a few shots, a fire was seen to start in the fuselage and the flight commander immediately ordered us to stop attacking it. The enemy aircraft turned back towards Wick and we escorted it on its way with me in close formation on its port side where the fire was. Being only a few feet away from the Heinkel it was all too easy to become sympathetically associated with the crew's frantic efforts to control the fire and I even began to wish that I could jump across and help them. Thus was I suddenly converted from an anxious desire to destroy them to an even greater anxiety that they survive.

We had got within a few miles of the coast and had really begun to hope that they would make it, when we were all outraged to see a Hurricane from another squadron sweep in from behind and, without a single thought about us all around, poured a long burst of fire into the Heinkel which more or less blew up in our faces and crashed into the sea without any survivors.

It was all I could do to prevent myself from spinning round and having a crack at the Hurricane in response to its action. I felt a sense of personal loss as I stared at the wreckage on the water – what dramatic changes of attitude in such a short space of time!

Flight Lieutenant Tom Morgan

43 Squadron

I did have to ditch once, but that was because my engine failed. I was about 20 or 30 miles out over the North Sea, and we were attacking a Ju 88. It was very badly damaged by the time I had to break away to get ready to ditch and my number two went in and made his contribution. I saw that he hit it, so I ditched. I didn't feel any fear, I just made the best I could of it. I didn't know what was going to happen. I put the aircraft down on a wave in the North Sea and very foolishly undid my safety straps as well as my oxygen and RT. My face hit the gunsight and broke my jaw and pushed in all my front teeth.

I got the Hurricane floating, and I drifted along enough for me to get my parachute out, then get my dinghy. This was the prototype dinghy for fighters which was given to me by Farnborough – I'd been a test pilot there before the war. I then undid the CO_2 bottle to inflate the dinghy and nothing happened. So I got the hand pump – and when I inspected it, it was in pieces. I managed to hold it together enough to get some air into the dinghy – although not much – and I clambered in so my feet and head were sticking out.

My number two orbited and got a fix on me and he went off – then another two of the squadron came out as he went away to refuel. They were relieved by another two, and then my number two, Joe, came back again. I knew that the Ju 88 ditched, because every time I came to the top of a wave in my dinghy I could see three of the crew in a round dinghy about 400 yards away.

My number two flew very low over me and pointed to the west, and I could see some smoke on the horizon and then one of the pair that were orbiting went back and brought the ship to me. It was a four-funnel destroyer from a convoy and they picked me up and sent me down to sick bay. Fortunately there was a doctor on board and he took a look at me and got me wrapped up in a hammock, then the commander told me they'd put me ashore as soon as possible. When we got to Aberdeen, the commander saw the herring-fishing fleet coming in and he got hold of one of the boats. He'd explained to me that if they didn't get a boat to pick me up I'd have to go to America with them. I thought, 'God, I'll lose my squadron!'

They took me on deck – they couldn't take me down below because they couldn't get the hammock down. We proceeded as part of the fleet into Aberdeen, and then a Ju 88 appeared and started strafing and dropping his bombs. Fortunately these missed, and he didn't sink any ships. The skipper told me most of this as I was lying there and couldn't see anything except the sky. Then the Ju 88 had a go strafing us, but the crew were below. I was on deck and the skipper and I were the only two exposed. He was hit in the arm – the shooting was really appalling. I was all right and I didn't get hit. When we went ashore an ambulance was there to take me to the naval hospital where the dentist started to fix my jaw, and wired all of my teeth back into position.

Pilot Officer William Walker

616 SQUADRON

I think the only radar station that was hit was on the Isle of Wight – they were just a mast, so they weren't easy to bomb, but the Stukas had a go at it. We arrived at Kenley on 12 August, and I survived until the 26th, and then Yellow Section was scrambled – three of us – and it was the first time I'd flown with three pilots since that battle climb, and we were scrambled to patrol Dover Dungeness at angels 20, and we arrived – then suddenly we were attacked by a whole squadron of 109s.

My leader Teddy St Aubyn was shot down and terribly badly burned, but he survived although he was killed later. Sergeant Ridley was killed and I got a bullet in my leg and had to bale out. I'd never baled out before. I realised I'd been hit and had a pain in my leg, and my propeller had stopped, so I thought it was time to get out. I pulled the hood back and stood up – but when I tried to jump, I still had my helmet on, and it was plugged in and was holding me back. I took my helmet off and fell out.

I'd been sitting on my parachute so I pulled the ripcord at 20,000 feet. It took for ever to come down, and the extraordinary thing was that, minutes before, the air had been filled with planes, and the whole time I was coming down I didn't see a single aircraft. It was ten-tenths cloud and when I got through the clouds I realised I was over the sea and getting close, so I took my boots off. I could see them spiralling down for what seemed ages – and I realised I was still high up. I blew my Mae West up and landed in the sea. I could see, about 100 yards away, a ship sticking up out of the water – a wreck. I didn't know then, but it was the Goodwin Sands, and I managed to swim to that and sit on it, but I kept slipping off because it was at an angle.

Eventually a fishing boat came along and I transferred to that. They gave me a large mug of hot tea with whisky, and then when

205

we got to the shore, an RAF launch came along and I was transferred to that. By this time I can't tell you what the hot tea and whisky had done to my tummy, and I'd been in the water suffering from hypothermia, but luckily the launch had a loo on board – to which I retired. Then we arrived in Ramsgate harbour – the airmen kept knocking on the door and asking if I was all right – but I was in agony.

Eventually I was carried up the steps of the harbour. Quite a crowd had collected, and they all cheered – and a dear old woman came forward and gave me a pack of cigarettes. Then I was into the ambulance and taken to Ramsgate Hospital, which had been badly bombed.

The whole time I was there, all they could produce was a slice of bread and butter and a cup of tea because the kitchens had been bombed. On that day the drill was that I was called at 3.30 in the morning and we had breakfast at 4, and then we went straight down to dispersal. We were still there at eight o'clock, the second breakfast arrived of sausages, bacon, eggs – the lot. Wonderful smell – in the open air. That would be the last meal I would get for thirty-six hours apart from the bread and butter.

They looked at my wound and realised they couldn't cope with it so I was put under a lot of electric light bulbs and it took about twelve hours before I began to feel anything. My whole body was numb with hypothermia. Next morning we set off in an ambulance, with a driver who didn't know the way – although I knew the area fairly well. We had to pick up a shell-shock case at Manston on our way, and set off for Kenley. I'd lost my boots, so all I had was my trousers and shirt – I had to pick up my clothes at Kenley, so I did that and told the driver to take us down to dispersal so I could say goodbye to my chums. We arrived at dispersal and there was no one there – we'd lost ten pilots in ten days.

We set off across London, which was difficult because streets had been closed because of unexploded bombs. We dropped the

Pilot Officer William Walker, 616 Squadron.

shell-shock case off – he'd spent the whole journey trying to light a cigarette. We got to Kings Langley, by which time, having had nothing to eat since my second breakfast the day before, I said to the driver, 'Go into the pub and get me two pints of beer and one for yourself,' so I drank these two pints and when I finally got to Halton Hospital in Buckinghamshire at about eleven o'clock at night, the night nurse managed to rustle me up some scrambled eggs – which was rather appropriate, having been scrambled before – and then I was put to bed with painkillers and sleeping pills. When I woke up the next morning, there in the next bed was Mickey Staples. We'd been posted on the same day, and there he was.

Doctors were coming round and seeing all the patients, but no one came near me. I was getting worried because I'd heard stories about gangrene from the First World War, then about midday a group captain came to do his daily inspection and said, 'Who are you? Why are you here?'

'I've got a bullet in my leg,' I said.

'Who's looking after you?' he said.

I said I hadn't seen anyone since I arrived. He absolutely blew up! He tore everybody off a strip and within ten minutes I was in the operating theatre. When I came to after the operation the surgeon was sitting by my bed and he handed me the bullet. He said, 'You won't believe it, but I had to prise your ankle.' I still have it . . .

The doctors had a theory that they learned in the Spanish Civil War: they didn't dress wounds with bandages, they covered them in plaster and the idea was that a crust would form over the wound and it would heal, but that didn't work with me and it continued to fester. The plaster became so soft that they had to remove it and dress it normally. The problem was that I smelt so awful that I had to be put in a private room.

Flight Lieutenant James Coward

19 SQUADRON

On 31 August the squadron was scrambled from Fowlmere – a satellite of Duxford – at about 7.30 am. There were only nine aircraft serviceable and we climbed to the east to about 25,000 feet in sections of three in loose line astern. Flight Lieutenant Clouston led the squadron, I led the second section and Flight Lieutenant Brinsden the third. About 10 miles east of Duxford, I sighted a large formation – fifteen Do 215s escorted by a reported sixty fighters. Clouston instructed Brinsden to climb and engage the fighters while we attacked the bombers head-on. My foot was shot off when closing, causing no pain but just a dull thud, and I saw my bare foot on the floor of the cockpit, almost severed. The aircraft controls were damaged and the aircraft went out of control, bunting into a steep dive.

On baling out, my parachute got caught and I was forced back along the fuselage, my gloves being blown off. I tried to do a delayed drop from about 20,000 feet because I was losing blood very quickly, but was unable to stand the pain of the foot twisting in the slip-stream, so I pulled the ripcord and put on a tourniquet using my helmet wireless lead.

I drifted across Duxford airfield at about 10,000 feet towards Royston, and I saw the squadron land. Eventually the wind changed and I sailed back across Duxford and came down in a field near the roundabout at Whittlesford, on the Royston/Newmarket Road, where I was met by a youth of fifteen with a pitchfork, who thought I was a German. When my language convinced him that I wasn't, he went off at high speed to find a doctor. Fortunately the first car he met contained a doctor and in about half an hour I was picked up by an RAF ambulance from Addenbrooke's, suffering no great pain.

My aircraft crashed just beyond my home village of Little Shelford and my wife was told about it by the milkman. Fortunately the service doctor called in and told her I was all right, and she arrived at the hospital before I recovered from the anaesthetic after the amputation.

The bombers' objective was presumably Duxford airfield, but on being attacked they jettisoned their bombs which fell in fields south of the high ground to the east of Duxford, and then turned off to the south. Three of them were claimed as shot down and I learned from Flight Lieutenant Clouston that our lack of success was due to the fact that the cannons with which we had just been equipped had some teething troubles and very few rounds fired due to stoppages. In my own case, the guns went 'boom boom' and stopped.

Flying Officer Al Deere
(New Zealander) 54 Squadron

On 31 August, I was held up taking off by a new pilot who'd got himself in the take-off lane – didn't know where to go. He delayed me. By the time I'd got him sorted out, I was last off, and caught the bombs – and was blown sky high – the three of us were. But we all got away with it. I got pretty badly concussed – my Spitfire was blown up, and I finished up on the airfield in a heap. My number two finished on the airfield with his wing blown off. The number three wasn't seen for two hours, when he reappeared at the dispersal carrying his parachute, having been blown, in his aircraft, about a mile away into what we called Shit Creek, and landed the right way up and got out and walked back to the airfield. Had to go all the way round the wire to get in.

A doctor bandaged me up and said, 'Forty-eight hours and report back.' After twenty-four hours I felt all right, so I just went back because we were under tremendous stress at the time. So I was just the night off, really. I was back the next day, all bandaged up, but I felt all right. I think I was all right.

Pilot Officer Tim Vigors

222 Squadron

On the last day of August I came close to getting killed. We were diving from 25,000 feet on to a big formation of bombers. There was a lot of cloud and we suddenly found ourselves in the middle of them. I blazed away at a Dornier and then, like a fool, pulled up into a sharp left-hand turn without checking what was behind me. Suddenly there was a crash as a cannon shell fired from a 109 tore broadside into my engine. The next one struck just behind the cockpit and exploded with a bang, sending most of its particles whistling round the armour plating at my back. My instrument panel disintegrated in front of my eyes. The control column was nearly torn from my hands as a third shell hit the tail unit. Smoke and glycol poured from the engine and for a moment I was sure that I was on fire.

I was just reaching for the harness release when I found myself in thick cloud. There were no flames so, protected from the enemy for the moment by the enshrouding cloud, I decided to stay put until I could better assess the damage. My blind flying instruments had all shattered, so I had no way of telling whether I was flying upwards or downwards, or if I was the right way up or on my back. A moment later I slithered into clear air once more to find that I was diving straight at the centre of London.

I started to pull out of the dive. The controls felt funny, which was not surprising as more than half of the control surfaces on my tail unit had been shot away and most of my port aileron was missing. But the aircraft was still controllable and although there was a lot of smoke, there was no flame.

My immediate reaction was to bale out. Two things stopped me. First, the ground was still about 7,000 feet below me and while there was no reason to believe that the parachute wouldn't open, it did look an awful long way to fall. Second, and more important,

I was still smack over the middle of London. My aircraft would almost certainly crash on to a populated area, which might easily kill a lot of people, and I could end up maiming myself if my parachute landed me among buildings.

I decided to sit tight and try and land the aircraft in one piece. I started to glide in an easterly direction and, while losing height, searched desperately for a suitable landing site. I had already turned off the petrol and, although there was still a lot of white smoke coming from the broken glycol leads, I assessed the danger of fire as reasonably remote. The controls, particularly the fore and aft reactions, felt very sloppy. Also, in order to see in front of me, I had to crab the aircraft to make the smoke fly off to one side. When I was down to about 2,000 feet I spotted a large field about 300 yards square, surrounded by small suburban houses. Other than vegetables and some bushes, the area seemed clear of obstructions although some high-tension cables ran across the centre of the field.

Although the field was certainly not an easy place to land a Spitfire under the very best of conditions, by now I had no alternative and was too low to bale out. But I was going to need a lot of luck to pull it off. I only had, at the most, 300 yards of landing area and, because of the damage done to my elevators and port aileron, it was virtually impossible to get any guidance from the stick and rudder. If I allowed the speed to drop too low I would stall, dive into the ground and almost certainly be killed. On the other hand, if I came in too fast, I would not be able to get the aircraft to stall when I levelled out and would fly straight into the houses at the far end. The only way I had of making that vital assessment was visually, by watching the ground passing beneath me.

Crabbing my way along to keep the smoke away from my forward line of sight, I glided down towards the houses which lined the near side of my landing area. Passing a few feet over their roofs, I flung the Spitfire into a steep sideslip to drop off height. In order to cut down my landing run, I had left the wheels retracting the wings. Now, levelling off above the vegetables, I started to kick the rudder right and left so as to drop off speed again. About two-thirds of the way across the field I realised I was going too fast and wasn't going to make it. Emergency action was needed, otherwise I was going to end up in the drawing room of the red-brick house which was rushing towards me.

I muttered a quick prayer and took the only course open. Flinging the stick over to the left, I drove the port wing tip into the ground. There was a grinding noise as the wing dug into the soil and then I was cartwheeling. Landing on its belly, facing back the way we had come, the aircraft was now slithering backwards. The tail struck the hedge dividing the field from the small garden of a house. In a cloud of dirt and branches, we came to a juddering halt. There was a sudden and complete silence – one of the most welcome I have ever known.

As I heaved myself from the cockpit, a lady appeared through the gate from the garden. In her hand she bore a mug. 'Are you all right, dear?' she cried. 'I thought you might like a cup of tea to steady your nerves.'

Squadron Leader Peter Townsend
85 Squadron

On 31 August 1940, our Kenley controller called: 'Please come to readiness immediately.' There was a mad rush by pilots in old cars, motorbikes and bicycles to dispersal. I ordered pilots into cockpits, and to start up, and I called the controller: 'Can we go? I don't want to be bombed on the ground.' Controller: 'No hurry, old boy.' Looked round at my squadron, twelve Hurricanes, noses tilted skywards, propellers turning and glinting in the sun, all raring to go.

A moment later, controller: 'Off you go – and hurry!' As my undercarriage raised, the engine cut, spluttered, then recovered –

A formation of Hurricanes of 85 Squadron based at Church Fenton climb above the clouds, led by Squadron Leader Peter Townsend.

caused by the blast from bombs exploding just behind, where the rest of my squadron somehow got airborne, obscured by smoke. Above were Dorniers, escorted by Me 110s and Me 109s. I climbed at full boost with hood open (better to watch out for Me 109s) and reached the Me 110s first. As I attacked, a shower of Me 109s fell upon me, spraying streams of tracer from behind. A 109 turned in front, I hit him and he streamed vapour and slowed up. Then another, I hit him too and he rolled over and, streaming vapour, dived. A third just below – I could easily see the pilot, but while manoeuvring to shoot, an Me 110 came at me, firing head-on.

My Hurricane was badly hit in the windscreen and self-sealing centre tank, but mercifully there was no fire. I was hit in the foot by a 20 mm explosive shell, and momentarily lost control in a dive. I baled out low down over woods, just missing some large oaks and tumbling among fir saplings. After convincing the Home Guard and a policeman of my nationality, we all adjourned to the Royal Oak, Hawkhurst, for drinks all round and a wonderfully friendly little crowd gathered to wave me off to hospital.

Pilot Officer Denis Crowley-Milling
242 SQUADRON

On 31 August 1940, 242 Squadron, led by Douglas Bader, inter-cepted a formation of Dorniers and Heinkels escorted by Me 110s north-east of London near North Weald, estimated to be over one hundred aircraft in all. It was an eerie sight, and the first time we had seen such a mass of enemy aircraft in one piece of sky – the Me 110s on the flanks and others behind stepped up well above us as we approached their left flank. However, almost before we could take it all in, Douglas dived the squadron, sections in fairly close formation, right into the centre, causing the 110s on the flank to turn towards us, but too late to engage us before we were in against the bombers. The squadron claimed twelve aircraft destroyed in all.

Flying Officer Al Deere

(NEW ZEALANDER) 54 SQUADRON

You never knew if you were going to be bombed on the ground or not. I finished my Battle of Britain on 31 August by being blown up by a bomb when taking off from Hornchurch. Radar picture got a bit confused and they buggered around sending us off. Eventually they told us to get off as quickly as possible.

I was leading the squadron at this time. We had a new pilot in the squadron named Sergeant Davies. By this time we had practically all new pilots, for only five of us were left of the old guard. This young chap was my number two and in the excitement he taxied out to take off and, not knowing where to position himself, he stopped in the middle of the airfield right in front of me. The other nine aircraft went off. He eventually realised and moved, but before we got off the bombs came down and blew the three of us out of the sky. I went up in the air and on to my back.

That was a nasty experience. The terrifying part was that I was upside down in the cockpit, embedded in the ground. I could hardly see daylight and I could smell petrol. And I knew that I was likely to go up in flames at any moment. I heard this voice say, 'Are you there?' And it was Eric Edsall who was my number three. He had had his wing blown off, and he'd got out of his cockpit, saw me, and had crawled across to the aircraft.

The Spitfire has a little side door which drops down. Eric managed to lever this open, and got his straps and parachute undone, and managed to squeeze out of this little door – only to find that he couldn't walk as his hip was dislocated. So I got him up and carried him to the safety of the hangars, just as some 109s came down to strafe us. I was scalped and concussed – I had gone along upside down for about a hundred yards. As for the number two, he was blown outside the airfield perimeter still strapped in his cockpit, his Spitfire being dumped in a nearby creek. Miraculously, he was

Squadron Leader Douglas Bader (front centre) with some of his Canadian pilots of 242 Squadron grouped around his Hurricane at Duxford.

unhurt. The next day the squadron was moved to Catterick. For me the Battle of Britain was over.

When I went to Catterick, I think it was on 2 September, I was knackered. I was running on overdrive. I don't think I realised till I got up there what sort of state I was in. I really was pretty exhausted. And so too were James Leathart, who had been taken off earlier, and his replacement, Donald Finlay, the famous Olympic hurdler, who had lasted only two sorties. On his second sortie he was flying number two to me to get experience, and I had told him that at height it was very difficult to keep position, and if he got behind he'd had it. Well, he got behind, was shot down by a 109, and had a great chunk shot out of his bum. James Leathart, who had been released for a rest, had to come back. After a few days he took the squadron up to Catterick, and then went off for a rest. By that time there was himself, Colin Gray, George Gribble, and myself – we were the lot left out of the original 54 Squadron.

There was a tremendous amount of fatigue. It was difficult to judge who was pulling their weight and who wasn't. I had a chap on my flight, and he came up to me one morning – he'd been flying pretty intensively – and said he wasn't well and couldn't go on. I said, 'Well, I'm not well either. But I've got to go on, you've got to go on, chum.' He looked a bit pale, but I thought he'd be all right. That afternoon, he said again that he wasn't feeling well. So I said he'd better go and see the doctor. Well, he had malaria. But I'd thought he'd gone yellow. The thing was, we were all frightened and the urge was to preserve yourself and it was bloody difficult at times.

At Catterick, the squadron was broken up and we began to train pilots. I was in a mock dogfight with a trainee pilot one day when we had a mid-air collision. As a matter of fact he hit me – he chopped my tail off. I was at about 10,000 feet, and I jumped out. My parachute didn't open properly, and I was in the horizontal position when I hit. I landed in a farmer's cesspool, which cushioned the blow and probably saved my life, apart from the fact that I very nearly drowned swallowing the stuff. I hurt my back rather badly, an injury that's still with me, and after that I found my nerves were all to hell. I was made squadron leader, taken off flying, and became a controller in Station Operations.

The fear increased as the war went on. One would have thought it would get less. It's a funny thing, this. I did four tours of operations: at Dunkirk and in the Battle of Britain I was frightened but somehow not over-frightened. The next tour I did, I was less happy; the third tour I was bloody unhappy. I'd had one or two narrow escapes and I was frightened. But the fourth tour, when I was leading the Biggin Hill Wing, I somehow felt that I wasn't going to be shot down. Not because I'd had enough, I just had a feeling that I was going to be there at the end. And I was. In fact I flew right up until I collapsed in briefing.

Flight Lieutenant Desmond Sheen

72 SQUADRON

I owed Jerry one for a day when I was shot down over Canterbury by an Me 109 which jumped on me. He shot away practically all my controls and damaged my oxygen supply. I was at 25,000 feet when my oxygen supply failed, and when I came to, I found my Spitfire diving to the ground at something like 400 mph. I tried the control column but it was useless so I prepared to bale out. As soon as I undid my harness, the suction lifted me out of my harness.

Unfortunately, it did not quite do the job, and in some strange way, my feet caught under the windscreen. There I was, in a flat-out dive, lying along the top of the cockpit, with my feet fastened. I had given up hope when my feet suddenly became free. Almost by instinct, I pulled the ripcord on my parachute. I discovered afterwards that I was only about 800 feet up when I pulled the cord. I was going at a terrific speed, and I imagine that my Spitfire hit the ground before my parachute opened. By the law of averages, I should have been killed.

I fell into the middle of a wood near Canterbury and plunged through the boughs of a tree. It was lucky that I *did* hit the tree, because it slowed me down, and I got off with nothing more than a few bruises and scratches.

Wolfgang Julius Feodor Falck
LUFTWAFFE FIGHTER PILOT

Goering had many different sides to him. On the one hand, we admired him because he was a successful fighter pilot of World War I. He won the Blue Max and he was the last commander of Jagdgeschwader Richthofen. He was very nice to us and he regarded us as his young friends and comrades. But then during the war, our view changed.

Several times, I sat next to him at a dinner – and I saw the other Goering. Once, the dinner party should have been at seven but he didn't come because the Chief of Staff had been reporting to him what had happened during the day. Very late, Goering came to the dinner, smiling, and, all of sudden, he said to the Secretary of State in his staff, 'What is the situation?' The Secretary of State was concerned. 'Reichsmarschall! You've got all the information! What do you mean?'

Goering laughed and said, 'I don't want *that* situation! I would like to know the situation with the elk and the deer!' Everybody was, 'Oh my God! He made a joke!' The Secretary of State made a phone call and came back and said, 'The deer that were in the area of wood 34 have moved to wood 41.'

Goering said, 'That's the situation in which I am interested! Every night I want a report about that situation!'

That was the boss of the air force. He had such a sense of humour. Stupid, huh?

Flying Officer Dalzel Russel

(CANADIAN) 1 SQUADRON

In early September 1940, I was flying Blue Three when we sighted enemy bombers and as we attacked we were harried by Me 109s from starboard and above; as I broke away I came up under three 109s flying in line astern. I gave the last 109 a three-second burst at about 70 yards, noting strikes on his belly and he soon baled out. His leader and number two took violent evasive action and I eventually lost them. Shortly afterwards I climbed to attack a gaggle of Me 110s and fired from above and behind at the last fighter. I gave him about a ten-second burst which set his starboard engine on fire and he rolled over, one parachute came out and he crashed just south of Biggin Hill. Still above the Me 110s, I attacked another and saw strikes on his cockpit before my ammunition ran out. The Me 110 went into a lazy spiral and crashed several miles from the first, somewhere in the Maidstone area.

Flying Officer Gerry Edge

253 SQUADRON

When I took over 253 Squadron, they had just been through a very bad time. Not having been there, I do not know, but it appeared that they had a number of very good pilots, but lacked training. When Myles Duke-Woolley, 'the Duke', arrived, he and I got along very well from the start. He was obviously very intelligent and ready to give a great deal of thought to all problems, especially of aircraft in action, and we had long discussions on 'controlling' and its shortcomings. Many pilots and a number of 'leaders' accepted the instructions given on their face value. Duke and I worked out that the enemy positions given were up to four minutes out of date – that is probably up to 15 miles ahead of the positions on the controllers' table. We agreed it was vital to be in front of the enemy, as from ahead we could close on them very rapidly and get into a perfect position for attack, whereas coming from behind, we would be seen and engaged by their fighters, preventing us attacking the enemy bombers.

In addition, many controllers were not pilots, and did not appreciate our difficulties in the air, especially if leading a formation. He learned very quickly and soon became what I had requested – a top-quality pilot and leader. With only one and a half hours' experience on Hurricanes, he was not what I had hoped for – but within a couple of days, I was delighted with him.

The smaller the formation, the more manoeuvrable it is, and this is where training is so important, as the larger the formation, if defending or attacking, the more time and space is required to put them in a perfect position to be effective. One disadvantage of head-on attacks was that there was only one chance to make it fully effective and to gain a surprise, and take full advantage of sun, cloud and height, etc. These conditions do not always exist, but if visibility is a few miles and the leader can be up-sun, or in thin cloud, and be 300 to 500 feet above the bombers and put his formation into position about 3,000 yards ahead of the enemy on a reciprocal course, he has a great chance of complete surprise and causing panic and carnage to the raiders.

In September 1940, a frontal attack was aimed mainly at the cockpit, from which point the enemy crews flying multi-engined aircraft had virtually no protection, and a few bullets from ahead into the cockpit rendered the bomber out of control – and also they often crashed into each other. Their close escort of fighters had no time to intercept the attackers and their top escort were in a similar position. Had the top escort flown as a screen above and ahead of the bombers, the position would have been quite different – but this did not happen.

The attackers could open fire about 1,000 yards from the enemy bombers and, firing about 280 rounds per second as soon as they saw the cockpits breaking up, could swing away from the first targets, move their aim down the line of bombers and break away downwards before any of their escort could engage us. Inevitably our formation would have broken up and most of our ammunition been used. Had their escort followed us down, they would have put themselves in a bad position, as Hurricanes were superior in manoeuvrability and speed at low levels.

Adolf Galland

LUFTWAFFE FIGHTER PILOT

To my mind, Goering went about it the wrong way. He had nothing but reproaches for the fighter force, and expressed his dissatisfaction in the harshest terms. The theme of fighter protection was chewed over again and again. He clearly represented the point of view of the bombers and demanded close and rigid protection. The bomber, he said, was more important than record bag figures. I tried to point out that the Me 109 was superior in the attack and not so suitable for purely defensive purposes as the Spitfire, which, although a little slower, was much more manoeuvrable. He rejected my objection. We received many more harsh words. Finally, as his time ran short, he grew more amiable and asked for a series of Me 109s with more powerful engines. The request was granted. 'And you?' Goering turned to me. I did not hesitate long. 'I should like an outfit of Spitfires for my group.'

Flight Lieutenant Myles Duke-Woolley

23 AND 253 SQUADRONS

The outstanding leader was Gerry Edge. He was an auxiliary officer, and I admired the auxiliaries enormously. Too many 'regulars' before the war looked down their noses at 'those weekend flyers' whereas I thought we could learn a lot from them. Gerry had seen action

Adolf Galland, Luftwaffe fighter pilot.

during the Dunkirk period, where an intelligence officer I met told me he had shot down at least fifteen enemy aircraft, plus others 'probable' and 'damaged'. Gerry would not claim his victories and always said, 'Share them with the squadron,' but his leadership and abilities were demonstrated when he was posted to command 253 Squadron at Kenley at the beginning of September. At the time he was shot down on 26 September his score was at least over twenty-five, if not more than thirty. 253 Squadron had been stationed at Turnhouse and had been posted to Kenley on 3 September – by the 6th they had lost three COs: Squadron Leaders Starr and Gleave, and Flight Lieutenant Cambridge, as well as eleven pilots.

It was suggested that Gerry should take the squadron out of the front line at Kenley and move north to re-form, but he declined, and Group seemed very pleased to be able to keep the squadron at Kenley. It should be appreciated that Gerry was taking a considerable risk in keeping an untrained squadron in the front line, which had lost over half of their most experienced pilots in the first three days and were naturally considerably shaken, having lost the third CO on their last patrol in the morning. He was relying on his own ability to lead them to success without heavy losses. After I joined them on 12 September, other pilots told me that he had talked to them all for about an hour, pointing out that the Germans were over enemy territory and their fighters were short of fuel – and if they did as he said, they should have a very successful period . . . and they had virtually no further losses. Gerry asked for one flight commander to be rested, and for a top-quality pilot to be posted in. I was selected and I arrived at 253 Squadron on 12 September with a total of one and a half hours on Hurricanes.

Group suggested that I should be sent away for a short intensive spell on Hurricanes, but I was very keen to stay with 253 Squadron at Kenley and Gerry went along with that. I operated as number two to Gerry for about a week, and then I took over 'A' Flight.

Pilot Officer Bob Doe

234 AND 238 SQUADRONS

Once on patrol I found myself above a big bunch of 109s. If you were on your own above 109s they tended to ignore you. So, I sort of rolled over and came down to try and take one out and, as I hit him, I hit his slipstream. Well, at that time, the carburettor in a Spitfire didn't operate under negative 'G' conditions. So my engine cut dead, and there I was with a bunch of 109s getting interested. I went into a dive and headed downwards. When I was clear I pulled up, my engine started, and I caught up the bloke I'd hit and finished him off.

We continued patrolling from base, Portland or Kenley, and on 3 September over Tangmere we came across this massive circle of Me 110s. I dived across it, had two separate squirts of two seconds at 250 yards, which destroyed two of them. On my way back along the coast I was feeling pleased with myself when I saw another 110, which I got, but I had to share that one with a Hurricane.

The first London raid, they say, was on 7 September 1940, but in fact it was 5 September. That was the first one I saw, anyway. I was there when this mass of bombers dropped their bombs on the docks. This stays very clearly in my mind – it was the first real attack on London. I saw the whole docks area erupt. It was a fantastic sight, flames and smoke. I was gawping at it so much. I nearly got shot down. It was a hell of an experience, seeing it. It made me extremely angry. But they had masses of 109s there, and every time I turned there was a 109 shooting at me. I was turning like mad, and not firing my guns, so eventually I decided that, if I went down to Dover at about 10,000 feet, they'd be going home, and I should pick one, or even a brace. I headed for Dover with 'Budge' Harker, and because we were flying so that we could see each other's tail he got a yellow-nosed 109 that was right behind me. That was the first time we used that technique of flying.

The next day, 6 September, we did the same thing and met fourteen Do 17s, and a lone 109, which I destroyed. I then had a go at the Dorniers and stopped three of their rear-gunners shooting back. I then ran out of ammunition, got intercepted, and decided to go home. You could get away in a Spitfire by turning. If you went into a turn and stayed there, you were safe.

Sergeant Fred Roberts
ARMOURER, 19 SQUADRON

We used to stick patches over the fronts of the guns on the leading edge of the wings because the open guns would cause drag along the wing and slow the plane down.

If a pilot came back and we saw that the patches over his wing had gone, we used to say, 'He's fired them again, so something's happened,' you know. But unless the pilot held a couple of fingers up to us, or one finger, we didn't know if he'd been successful until the intelligence officer had finished with him. The intelligence officer was the first man on the scene – he wanted to get in while the pilots' thoughts were still fresh in their minds.

We'd start preparing the aircraft the night before. After the gun plane had been in action, and before we bedded it down for the night, the gun was thoroughly cleaned, and rearmed ready for the morning. Then the following morning, we went out again, had another look at the guns to see that everything was as it should be. Then we signed the Form 700 – which was the serviceability form. Everyone signed that – the mechanic, the engine fitter, the airframe fitter, myself. Then during the day, if the guns weren't fired, we did nothing, but if the guns were fired, immediately we'd rearm them, take the empty ammunition tanks out, put new ammunition tanks in, fully replenished. While the armourer was doing that, his assistant was cleaning the barrel out. When they were all done, we put the panels back on the plane, and that was it.

With two armourers and two assistants, this would take about three and a half minutes – and that was good. We practised and practised, before the war started – we used to be in the hangar practising, and it was one of the things on every squadron, that the armourers prided themselves on being able to rearm Spitfires quickly. And 19 Squadron was one of the fastest.

Flight Lieutenant Billy Drake

1 SQUADRON

There's no doubt about it, the fighter pilots were the pop stars of the day. But it was not necessarily just fighter pilots. There were all these great bomber boys and other RAF men being equally decorated and they saw what you did and generally speaking there was a great amount of respect and admiration for the uniforms that we represented.

There were stories of men undoing their top button to attract the ladies, but it wasn't to attract – it was just to demonstrate to everybody involved in the hierarchy of the air force that we were fighter pilots. The bomber boys didn't, but we had a great amount of respect for them as well, so there was no rivalry as such. This was just something that you did – you kept your top button undone and that demonstrated the fact that you were a fighter pilot.

6

The Battle of Britain Phase IV

The Tide Turns

7 September to 31 October

Hitler was prepared to stand by as his bombers and fighters were
gradually destroyed in the war of attrition over southern England
– but he would not countenance the bombing of the Fatherland. It
was a blow to his ego and his reaction was to order the bombing
of London – 'If the British bomb our cities, we will bury theirs.'
Night bombing raids had been launched against strategic British
industrial areas throughout the battle – but the mass attacks begun
on 7 September against the London docks and civilian targets were
unprecedented. RAF fighters were scrambled from airfields across
the country to intercept the huge waves of bombers which flew on
inexorably towards their target, accompanied by their Me 109
escorts. Pilots returned to base to rearm and refuel throughout the
day – and the Luftwaffe suffered heavy losses as bombers adhered
to their orders to keep on course to deliver their bombs and their

A Heinkel bomber flying over Wapping on the Isle of Dogs in the East End of London at the start of the Luffwaffe's evening raids of 7 September. Photo taken from another German aircraft.

escorts came to the limit of their range as they circled their charges to take on the RAF's fighters.

Throughout the battle, the people of southern England had watched the dogfights above them – they'd rooted for their RAF heroes, cheering their successes and mourning their losses. The 'Fighter Boys' were becoming national heroes – and, if ever at leisure off the airfields, Dowding's men were easily distinguishable from their bomber counterparts. As a matter of practicality, the fighter pilots did not wear uniform ties in combat – if shot down over the sea the fabric shrank, posing an unnecessary risk. Tieless young men in RAF uniform became the idols of the day in local hostelries and London clubs. No one could say they were not appreciated.

But the beginning of September Dowding and his fighter squadrons were close to exhaustion. Even if aircraft production could keep up with demand, the supply of pilots was dwindling, and with the increased attrition over airfields, radar stations and armaments factories, it had left Fighter Command and the Chain Home system critically damaged. The change of target gave the home defences the respite they needed to repair the runways, produce more aircraft, and restore the radar stations to optimum use – and although there was still pressure on pilots, they benefited from operating over their own home territory.

Morale was dropping among the Luftwaffe pilots who were suffering increasing losses among their comrades; the German pilots were becoming disillusioned with Goering's increasing demands to eliminate the RAF in time to launch an invasion across the Channel. But on 15 September, later officially designated 'Battle of Britain Day', skies over southern Britain were filled with massive flights of German bombers and fighter escorts. It was one final sledgehammer blow to annihilate the RAF and bomb London into submission. At one point every available British aircraft was airborne – and there were no reserves to protect them as they made unavoidable landings to refuel.

Dowding could not know that the Luftwaffe was also pressed to its limits. After 15 September the Luftwaffe never again launched such mass daylight attacks – the emphasis was shifted to night-time bombing. Goering had previously expressed an opinion that they might bomb Holland into submission – but it would never work with the British. He was right, and as Fighter Command regrouped, Londoners made it a matter of pride that when the battle came to them, they could take it.

It became clear as autumn weather set in that the time had passed for Hitler to launch 'Operation Sealion'. The RAF had won the Battle of Britain. Hitler's invasion was cancelled – indefinitely – and the people of Britain now had to play their part as all defences were rallied to repel and withstand the night-time horror of the Blitz.

Pilot Officer Bob Doe

234 AND 238 SQUADRONS

On 7 September – which is the day that they always say that the bombardment of London started – there were 350 bombers over London. I got one Heinkel, and then a 109 who came into my sights and left a piece of his wing behind him, but the cost to our squadron had been considerable. Of the twenty-one who landed at Middle Wallop on 14 August only three pilots remained. We were all very tired and were sent back to St Eval to rest, retrain, and get new pilots. I was out of the action for nearly three weeks.

Flying Officer Basil Stapleton

(SOUTH AFRICAN) 603 SQUADRON

Over the Thames, we climbed to about 22,000 feet – and that's when I got hit. We thought we were out of range of the 109s but obviously we weren't. I never saw the aircraft that shot me but a cannon shell hit the starboard wing in between two of the guns.

Ammunition started to come out over the wing. I opened the cockpit hood and glycol came in, so I knew that the radiator had been hit as well. I had no ailerons so I couldn't turn. I saw a straw field miles away so I aimed for it, but I came in too fast and overshot it and went into a hop field. The supports on those vines pulled up the aeroplane so that it never touched the ground.

Pilot Officer Tom Neil
249 SQUADRON

My first success against the Germans was on 7 September. I was unsuccessful so many times that I really began to feel that I wasn't suited to being a fighter pilot. Fighter pilots came in all shapes and sizes, and some were good at it, some were not so good, and some were awful. That's not to say that people were carried kicking and screaming out of the aeroplane saying, 'I can't take it,' but some were very good and some were downright poor. I honestly thought I was not very good because when you're in a battle with lots of German aircraft around you, there's a tendency to ball-watch – that is, you see 109s flashing past you and they look so pretty, you spend all your time looking at them instead of doing something about it. They were so nimble it was very difficult to draw a bead on them.

The first occasion that we'd intercepted some bombers, and I was on my own – suddenly an Me 109 came across my bows, which hadn't seen me – which was very unusual. I latched on to it and managed to shoot it in the coolant system. Normally if a Spitfire or Hurricane was hit in the coolant system and it lost its coolant, it's rather like if someone put a bullet through the radiator of your car. You wouldn't even get to the top of the road. If you managed to catch a 109 in its coolant system, it sprayed out a stream of white, and if you were hit in your coolant system it did the same, and you knew jolly well that the engine was going to seize in five minutes – so you knew a 109 was never going to get home because it took twenty minutes to get across the Channel. Most of the German aeroplanes landed in Kent because their engines had seized.

The second aeroplane I was credited with was a He III which crash-landed alongside a station somewhere in Kent. It landed in a field and some of the crew got out – and I fondly expected them to wave to me – but they didn't.

Flying Officer Alec Ingle

605 SQUADRON

We flew down to Croydon – and that was a fairly horrific sight, actually. We refuelled at Abingdon, I think it was, and then we flew right over the top of London at about 6,000 or 7,000 feet, just above the balloons – and the whole of the East End was ablaze. You could look right down the river, and the whole thing was sort of smoky and on fire. Your heart did go into your boots, when you saw that lot. It was a terrible sight.

We landed down on Croydon – 111 Squadron, I think it was, had been there. We were tucked away in the old airport hotel – but we only stayed there one night, because the CO decided this was not a very safe place to be – to have all his pilots concentrated in such an obvious target. So we organised and took over a complete street of houses on the opposite side – Foresters Drive. There were only about three of those houses occupied – practically everybody had gone and in some of them there were even the remains of breakfast on the table. We established ourselves there – we had a mess in number 39 Foresters Drive, and we lived in the various houses round about. One night the Germans dropped a stick of bombs right across our particular dispersal, and I slept through it, as did most people, I think. You just got accustomed to it.

*Gravesend, where armourers are replacing ammunition boxes for a Spitfire of
66 Squadron.*

On 8 September we met all these He IIIs, and literally we took them head-on. We were spread out – we were coming straight in, with Walter Churchill leading us. Unfortunately, his eyesight wasn't very good, and he didn't see these things as soon as most people did, so he was directing us to where they were, and we all went in that direction. We met them – and it was a fairly shattering experience. You were closing very quickly, and before you knew what was happening you had a huge aircraft just in front of you, and you were coming straight at it. We advanced on those IIIs and shot, and broke away underneath them. There was a fellow pilot, Jack Fleming – a New Zealander – he got hit directly and was just a sheet of flame. I think he was hit in the header tank, and the next thing we knew of Jack, he was in a maternity hospital some-where in Kent – he'd arrived near there, very badly burned.

It was fairly shattering to see an aircraft just go *whoof* alongside you. But it all happens so quickly, when you are closing at those speeds. You are not talking about minutes – you are talking about seconds. You are there, you fight, you break out of that particular attack and on a number of occasions, by the time you've come back again, you can't see another aircraft in the sky. The whole thing has passed you by.

This friend of mine, Passey, who was flying with me – he was rather an extrovert sort of character with a large dog called Havoc. They were a rather curious pair – but anyhow, poor old Passey – he was flying around one day, and he was shot down. He arrived on the ground in something of a hurry, and when he was found, with his aircraft, he was sitting in a seat and the aircraft – bits of the aircraft – were scattered for hundreds of yards around the place. But he was perfectly all right, sitting strapped in his seat on the ground. He had the luck of the devil.

Flight Lieutenant Johnny Kent

303 AND 92 SQUADRONS

On 11 September we suffered our first fatalities when, in a battle over Horsham, Flying Officer Cebrzynski and Sergeant Wojtowicz were killed. It was strange really, as Cebrzynski knew he would be killed and he told me quite dispassionately only two days before that he would not survive long enough to see the end of the month. He was not morbid about it, he was just stating a fact which he accepted and merely wondered vaguely when it might be. He became separated from his flight and fought a long-drawn-out battle with six 109s single-handed, and managed to shoot down two of them before he himself was shot down near Westerham in Kent.

The fight came down to quite low altitude and was clearly witnessed from the ground. He was a very gallant young man, Sergeant Wojtowicz, but, because he was a foreigner, could not be recommended for our only posthumous decoration, the Victoria Cross. Later his own government awarded him the Polish equivalent – the Virtuti Militari.

Squadron Leader Jack Satchell

302 SQUADRON

On the morning of 15 September, one of my Polish sergeant pilots had shot up a Hun and had seen him start to go down with smoke coming out, and had promptly assumed that he was going to crash and so had broken off the engagement to attack another. When he got back and learned that he was only credited with a Hun 'damaged' because he had not seen it crash, not obviously on fire, he was very angry and said that he *knew* it would crash and that there was no point in his going down to watch it do so when there were other Huns waiting to be shot down, but it was to no avail, and he only got credited with it as 'damaged'.

In the afternoon show, this particular pilot was determined to be credited with a Hun definitely destroyed. He apparently attacked a Dornier and first set the starboard engine on fire. Then he went to the other side and set the port one on fire, and not content with this, he commenced firing at the fuselage to make certain. The Huns within started to bale out and one of them, to show how close he had got to the wretched Hun, jumped straight into his prop. The prop smashed to bits and the radiator was also smashed off, but he managed to force-land the aircraft near North Weald without any further damage. When he got out, he saw that the whole aircraft was smothered with blood and bits of flesh. He was credited with that as 'confirmed destroyed'.

Sergeant Owen Burns

Wireless operator/air gunner

In a Blenheim mid-upper gunner it wasn't comfortable – the wind howled. You wore three pairs of gloves, silk, wool and then leather, and the leather was up to the elbow because you actually froze sitting in a turret for five to six hours. I did one trip of six hours forty minutes because we were searching for some VIP who had gone down in the sea. My only pleasure was that we could smoke in the turret.

When the battle started we'd had very little training, because they wanted you airborne. On 15 September – or maybe the day before we were flying out of Thorney Island. Five of us had to rendezvous to escort twelve Albacores dropping torpedoes on the German fleet in Calais. As they were very slow aircraft we had to circle them. They dropped their bombs and then out of the blue came about twenty-five-plus Me 109s and they attacked us. Our pilot Chamberlain broke away – it was every man for himself – and we lost two planes, possibly three. I was firing away as we escaped.

Pilot Officer David Crook

609 SQUADRON

Geoff was last seen on 15 September, following Michael into the attack, and after that he was never seen alive again. He had either been hit by one of the rear-gunners in the bombers, or probably, in his intense desire to destroy a bomber, he stayed too long firing at them and was destroyed by the Me 110s from behind.

For four days after Geoff's death we heard absolutely no details of the crash. However, on the Thursday, the RAF at Kenley wired to say that his body and Spitfire had been found near there. The crash had been seen by a number of people, but the machine, having fallen for about 20,000 feet, was absolutely smashed and impossible to identify by any number or letter. Geoff's body was identified only by the name in his collar band. He had made no attempt to escape from the machine, though in such a long dive he would have had ample time, had he been alive.

I don't think I have ever known anybody who appeared generally to derive as much enjoyment from life. And what grand times we have had together – the amusing evenings we used to enjoy before the war, those glorious summer days we spent rock-climbing on Scafell and Dow Crag, or sailing unskilfully but with endless amusement in the dinghy on Windermere. Then during this last summer, the good days we spent fighting together, having our practice dogfights, playing tip and run and going out every evening with the rest of the squadron. The memories which I shall always have of Geoff will be those of happiness and laughter.

Only a week or two before his death I said to him one evening that if anything were to happen to him, I should feel rather responsible because he was an only son, and I had persuaded him to join the RAF with me. He replied that he would always be grateful to me for my persuasion, because the year that he had spent in the RAF since the beginning of the war had been the best year of his life, and he wouldn't have gone into the army for anything, and missed all this glorious fun.

Looking back, I don't think that his death was altogether a surprise to me, because for some time past I had the feeling that he would not survive this war.

Flight Lieutenant Johnny Kent
303 SQUADRON

All three squadrons were sent off as a wing with myself leading. There was very little activity and we stayed on our patrol line and watched a number of small formations of 109s that were scattered about above us. Every now and then they would start down as though to attack, but always pulled up immediately we turned towards them. Then, for no apparent reason, one 109 dived right across my nose and to help him on his way I fired a short burst at him. He immediately went into an almost vertical dive and I followed, waiting for him to pull out so that I could cut the corner and finish him off. He pulled out at about 4,000 feet and I was able to catch him easily and opened fire at 50 yards.

My first burst riddled his radiators and a cloud of glycol enveloped my aircraft and splattered over my windscreen. The smell was so strong that I thought for a moment that my own engine had a glycol leak and I pulled out to one side. I saw then that it was the 109 that was spewing forth the coolant, so I commenced another attack and this time shot away part of the tailplane and pulled up on the other side of him. All this time the pilot had taken no evasive action whatever and I did not know whether he was dead or not. He just kept straight on towards the sea although he must have known that he could not hope to cross the Channel as he had been at least 6 miles inland from our coast when I first hit him. Although there were any number of fields in which he could have crash-landed, he stubbornly kept on.

240

A Hurricane of 601 Squadron being serviced on a dispersal at Exeter.

I kept attacking and shooting various pieces off the aircraft, including the canopy and, finally, when almost halfway across the Channel, a large piece of engine cowling. At this point I was getting exasperated and pulled up well above him and started a quarter-attack to administer the *coup de grâce*. I could see him sitting rigidly in the cockpit, hanging on to the control column and still flying straight and level. As I started my dive, his engine stopped and he looked at me, rolled the aircraft on to its back and appeared from behind the tail, looking for all the world like a rag-doll that had been thrown out. The 109 dived straight into the sea while he, apparently unhurt, drifted down in his parachute. I circled round him a couple of times and felt it might be kinder to shoot him as he had one hell of a long swim – but I couldn't bring myself to do it. Without waiting for him to hit the water, I turned for home.

As I approached Dungeness I saw an aircraft low over the water, about 5 miles offshore. I flew towards it to investigate and it was with some surprise I discovered it was a German machine. I immediately attacked, my first burst splattering around the rear cockpit, but I got no return fire, so I had probably killed the rear-gunner. On my second attack only a few bullets were left and my guns stopped almost immediately after I pressed the gun button. To my disgust I could do nothing but watch as the German headed towards France as fast as he could go.

Flying Officer Gerry Edge

253 SQUADRON

On 18 September, on being 'released' at midday, Myles Duke-Woolley and I decided that when our lunch had gone down, we would play squash. In the middle of our third game, over the Tannoy came the message, 'Any pilot, please phone Control immediately. Urgent.' This message was repeated several times.

There were two stages of 'released' – on and off station. On the first, all pilots had to remain on base, and for the second, all pilots could leave the station for the period of release. At the time we were released off station – but I hurried to a phone and asked the controller what was the flap, and he said that a large raid had appeared over the Channel and he had nothing to put up. I told him I thought we could put up five or six, but to keep calling over the Tannoy and tell any pilots on the station to assemble in the dispersal hut without delay, and all crews to go to their aircraft and warm them ready for take-off, urgently. Duke and I were in our squash clothes, so we rushed to our rooms and pulled on some flying clothing over the top and ran to the dispersal hut.

Arriving there we saw that one or two planes were already running. Duke and I were the first there, but other pilots were arriving and I called to them to put their helmets on and have their parachutes ready in their cockpits and to grab any spare crews available to start their aircraft and to take over from the fitter in the cockpit and keep the engine running. I picked up the phone and asked the controller what was the present position. He said a large formation of thirty-plus bombers with a similar number of fighters as close escorts, and a large top cover of fighters over the bombers, were heading towards Maidstone and London. He said there were a number of smaller raids taking place and all available squadrons were engaged. We now had six pilots, and there was another pilot running towards the dispersal.

I suggested to Duke that he get in and tell his section to close up and taxi out, ready for take-off. I clambered into my plane, which was warmed ready for take-off and running. I strapped my chute on and fastened my Sutton harness. (These two actions were greatly facilitated by my fitter and rigger, one on either side of the cockpit, holding the various straps into my hand.) I always thought of a surgeon asking for a scalpel – I didn't have to ask as the lads knew what went where, and I just had to push it forward into position. My fitter said all tanks were full and temperature and pressure OK – and jumped down off the wing. My rigger was already holding the starboard chock rope and my fitter popped up with the port-side rope. I waved them to take the chocks away.

Control cleared us for take-off as we approached the downwind position and said, 'Viceroy Leader, take off as soon as possible – you are cleared for take-off.'

Turning into the wind, I gave a last quick check round the cockpit, making sure my numbers two and three were in position just outside my wing tips. As I passed the halfway mark across the aerodrome, I eased the stick back and, as soon as the aircraft lifted off, I put my wheels up. Landing a Hurricane on grass with wheels up did little damage except to the propeller and radiator cowling – whereas with wheels down, it would be impossible to avoid running off the aerodrome and into the hedge – and probably a ditch – and turning over.

As soon as all wheels were up, I climbed up to 2,000 feet and told all pilots to open out a little and test magnetos. I set revs to 2,600, boost to plus 1 and climbed as steeply as possible.

Control asked, 'Viceroy Leader, can you see them?'

'All OK, Controller. Viceroy Sections Echelon port and Yellow Sections close to Red,' I replied. I told all pilots: 'Keep about a plane's span out from starboard and two planes' length behind. Am turning starboard now and throttling back a little. Get into line as soon as possible. We are into the sun from them, and they are not taking any evasive action, so I guess we have not yet been seen. My target is the aircraft to the left of their leader and following off down line to starboard. Try to take any bomber that has not been hit. Don't get too close. Roll over to starboard and stick back. Start aiming half a ring over target and keep firing until you break. Range now 1,200 yards. Open fire as soon as on target.'

If their speed was 180 mph, we were closing at 360 mph – around 180–200 yards per second – which gave us about five seconds to fire before breaking away – say 1,200 rounds per aircraft, so 7,200 rounds in total.

All of us were soon in position and I fired at my target at about 1,000 yards. Almost instantly his cockpit started to disintegrate and his plane swerved towards his leader crashing into the tailplane. Two gone. I left my guns firing on the port side of the formation. The bombers were breaking up and I moved my aid to my starboard and at this range I just left the guns firing, as I aimed at one cockpit after another. I was getting very close, so I rolled over and pulled the stick back and then eased out into a very steep dive. I pulled out again and felt the slight draining away from my eyes. I eased the stick forward and, as my sight returned, I looked around and the first thing I saw was a large bomber passing my starboard wing tip about eight to ten feet away. Then a second one, ten to fifteen yards ahead of me. There were no others close that I could see, and, hoping I was out of the danger area, I climbed away to port.

I could see a large number of mixed bombers and fighters heading south in the distance, but at that range I could not easily catch them, and in any case, my ammunition was nearly finished.

I reported to the controller that it appeared to me that the enemy had tried to saturate the area with small raids, so that a large raid could be pushed through the middle with us having no more fighters to engage it. It nearly worked for them, but I don't think that they saw us until too late. They took no evasive action. I did not see any of their guns firing. None of our aircraft was hit. Neither their close escort nor their top cover made any move towards us that I could see. Firing through their Perspex windscreens, we probably killed or badly wounded the pilots of the bombers, of which a number crashed into each other.

I think it must have been a great blow to their morale that an unengaged, strongly escorted raid nearing their target was suddenly attacked and, in under fifteen seconds, completely broken up with seventeen of them definitely destroyed, plus others probably destroyed and some damaged. What's more, they'd had to jettison their bombs over open ground to no effect and return to base reporting to their leaders the complete fiasco. In the same way, after such heavy losses in its first few days of action, that 253 Squadron could inflict such damage on the enemy without receiving a single bullet hole in return was a great boost to our morale.

Flying Officer Terry Kane

234 SQUADRON

On 18 September 1940, flying Spitfire Mk IIs with 66 Squadron, on patrol at 30,000 feet over Dover, we sighted a flight of Me 109s crossing our track. I attacked the rearmost which was heading for cover in thick cirrus cloud and managed to get in two short bursts of fire. The enemy aircraft immediately burst into flames. The pilot baled out, parachuting into the Channel 2 miles off Folkestone. He survived and I later learned that he was Leutnant Erich Bodendeik of JG53 Ace of Spades group.

On 22 September we shot down a Ju 88 which was seen crossing the coast towards France, and another chap and I pursued it. He had the faster aircraft – if you're the newest member of the squadron you didn't get the fastest aircraft – and he was drawing away from me. He fired on it when he got within range and bits flew off it and some smoke came out of it. He then turned to go home, and as I still had a fair amount of petrol left, I went on after it and fired at it as well. Some more smoke came out and it went into a steeper dive and went into the water. That was my half victory.

On the 23rd I was shot down – I'd gone off with another chap and a similar thing happened. He had the faster aircraft and we were flying into the sun, and my RT broke down and I couldn't communicate with the ground or with him, and I lost him. It was very difficult to pick up a single aircraft unless you're very close. I knew which way I was flying, but where I was I really had no idea. I was above cloud so I couldn't see what was underneath me.

I decided the only sensible thing to do was to bale out. This was my great adventure. I jettisoned the hood and unfastened my Sutton harness. I turned the aircraft on its back and climbed out underneath it. Then I realised I had failed to detach myself from the RT and the oxygen so I had to climb back in again to do that, and by this time the aircraft had turned on its side. I turned it on its back again, and this time I managed to get out and fall clear, then I started feeling for the ripcord, and I couldn't find it – which was alarming.

I managed to beat down the incipient panic and I decided to go to the middle and work outwards, and I found it. I pulled it and the parachute opened very nicely, then just about that moment I broke cloud and, looking down, I judged myself to be about 400 feet from the ground. Looking back on it, the terminal velocity of the human body is 120 mph – 176 feet per second – and it doesn't take a great brain to work out how long it takes to fall 500 feet. If I'd been three seconds later getting to the ripcord I wouldn't be here.

I landed in the sea – I had no idea where. To my great relief a German ship appeared over the horizon and picked me up – I didn't know it was German to start with, because I didn't know where I was. 'For you the war is over,' those were their actual words. I had just over four and a half years in POW camp. I'm a fairly phlegmatic sort of chap, and I found myself able to put up with it. I was nearly twenty-five when I got out. I finished up in Stalag Luft III. They marched us out in January '45, when the Russians were getting close: we struggled about 30–40 miles through thick snow – in about three days. I'm lucky to be here – I've led a charmed life.

Flying Officer Harold Bird-Wilson
17 Squadron

On 24 September we were flying at about 16,000 feet and suddenly, when we were south of the Thames area, a Spitfire came down through our formations – which worried us a bit, because we hadn't realised that they were being chased by 109s. The next thing I experienced was a terrific bang in the cockpit and there were flames coming from the fuel tank. There was no Perspex left in my hood, and it was getting fairly hot, so I baled out immediately.

One notices the quietness, having baled out. The battle was still going on. I could hear the rat-a-tat of the guns going off in the distance, and my fellow pilots circling above me, making sure I got down safely. I was slightly wounded with shrapnel, but I was floating down peacefully. It was then that I saw a navy torpedo boat coming out to intercept me.

Forty-two years after the event, I read in a book that I was the fortieth victory for Adolf Galland – the famous German fighter ace who was made lieutenant general of the Luftwaffe.

Flight Lieutenant Brian Lane

19 SQUADRON

On 25 September the wing was on patrol south of London and intercepted a formation of Me 109s. The Hun by now had almost completely given up large-scale bombing raids, contenting himself instead with sending over 109s on offensive sweeps, some of these fighters carrying bombs in order to increase their nuisance value more than anything else, judging by the results they obtained.

We were flying south-east at the time and some bursts of ack-ack fire ahead showed us a formation of about twenty or thirty 109s flying north in loose formation. As they saw us they turned to meet us and Squadron Leader Bader waded into them, the rest of us following. As the squadron broke up, I noticed two yellow-nosed Huns creeping round underneath us to try and attack from below and behind.

Half rolling, I dived down on them, getting in a short burst at each of them as they passed through my sights. I was coming down rather fast in the dive and felt the aircraft skidding slightly. My left

By permission of the IWM (CH1371)

September 1940: The intelligence officer of 19 Squadron (with his back to the camera) takes down pilots' accounts of a sortie over Fowlmere, Cambridgeshire. Squadron Leader Brian Lane, the CO on the left, was killed in 1943, Pilot Officer 'Farmer' Lawson in the centre was killed in 1941 and Sergeant Llyod on the right in 1942.

hand felt for the rudder bias control and wound the wheel back. Still the aircraft continued to skid and, trying to pull out of the dive, I found that I couldn't. I was doing a fair rate of knots and the controls had stiffened up a great deal accordingly, but a backward movement of the stick did not have the customary effect! Pressing as hard as I could on the left rudder pedal had little or no effect either, as it was almost impossible to move it at this speed.

A glance at the airspeed indicator showed me I was doing well over 400 mph and the altimeter was giving a good imitation of one of those indicators you see in lifts. I had started this blasted dive at 25,000 feet and the altimeter now showed 10,000. I was just beginning to think about stepping out, and then began wondering whether I could at this speed. I decided to have one last attempt at getting control.

Bracing myself against the back of the seat I put both feet on the left pedal and pressed as hard as I could, pulling back on the stick at the same time. I felt the aircraft straighten up and saw the nose rising to meet the horizon. Determined to make no mistake about pulling out of the dive completely, I kept the stick back, and not unnaturally blacked out completely as the controls regained their full effect.

Easing the stick forward again, I came to and was confronted with the sight of someone's parachute upside down and apparently ascending instead of descending. Further examination of this phenomenon drew my attention to the fact that the sun was below me. I had completed a half loop while I was blacked out without knowing it.

I rolled out the right way up and circled round the white mushroom of silk, trying to recognise the pilot at the end of the shroud lines. High above me one or two aircraft were still circling round, but the dogfight seemed to be over. Circling round, I waited until the pilot came to rest in the top of a tree, and then diving down (slowly this time), caught a glimpse of him climbing down to the ground. He was obviously OK and I couldn't help laughing at his predicament. As he reached the ground he waved, and I turned for home.

Pilot Officer Bob Doe
234 AND 238 SQUADRONS

On 28 September I was posted to Chilbolton and given a flight with a Hurricane squadron, 238 Squadron. I had two half-hour trips in the Hurricane, learning to fly it, and went into action on the 29th. It was a bit of a comedown, a Hurricane. There was much more room in it, it was far more manoeuvrable than a Spitfire, and it was a very good gun platform, but it was crude in comparison. I was in a Hurricane the day I did a head-on attack on a formation of Heinkels and got one. But I got a bullet through the wooden-bladed prop, which split it from tip to base. There was about a quarter-inch gap, and the weirdest noise, flying home. I was surprised it didn't come to bits.

The last major daylight raid of the Blitz was on 7 October, which was when they headed towards Bristol. We had five aeroplanes, I think, that day and I somehow managed to get into the middle of the bombers, and damaged a Ju 88. He started to drop out, so I dropped out as well, and did a quarter-attack on him from the beam. His tail suddenly blew up, which seemed incredible. Apparently, they stored all their oxygen in containers just in front of the tail.

Three came out, but the last one pulled his ripcord too soon and his parachute started burning. That was the last trip of the Blitz, and when I got back I found I had eleven holes in the plane. So, I was very lucky.

On 10 October we were scrambled, Hurricanes against high-flying 109s, on a day when there was solid cloud from about 4,000 up to 20,000 feet. Once in the cloud, I lost everyone. As I broke the cloud, I was hit from behind and in front. The first thing I knew, a spark came over my right shoulder into the dashboard. Then I heard a thump underneath my bottom, and a cannon shell hit my right foot and cut the Achilles tendon. I was hit in my left shoulder, which was like a blow from a sledgehammer, and I was also hit in the hand. I thought I was going to die. All sorts of thoughts flashed through my mind – I was to be married in two months and I regretted not having the chance to get married. However, I had worked out before what to do if I was attacked from behind, and I hit the stick and was back into the cloud.

Then I realised I was still alive and that I ought to get out quickly. I'd pulled the pin which holds the Sutton harness together, but due to negative 'G' the straps would not release. In sheer panic I tore at the harness, which must have pulled the straps free and I popped out like a cork from a bottle. I've no idea how I got the hood back, all I remember was the joy of floating down in the air. It was a most wonderful feeling. I looked around quite calmly for a parachute handle, found it and pulled it. I felt an almighty jerk and, still in cloud floating downwards, started looking round me to see what the damage was. I could see a load of blood everywhere; I couldn't use my left arm or my right leg. Apart from that everything seemed quite reasonable. I was just floating down. Eventually, I came out of the cloud over a blue lagoon. It was beautiful. A lagoon in England! Blue, with an island in the middle of it that I was drifting towards. Poole Harbour!

I then realised I was coming down rather fast because the cannon shell which had hit my armour-plated seat had destroyed quite a bit of my parachute canopy. I began to shout which was a stupid thing to do as there was no one around. Because I was minus a working leg and an arm I didn't land properly – I landed on my bottom and was knocked out. When I came to, I was in the middle of a quagmire on Brownsea Island with an Irishman standing over me with an iron bar saying, 'What are you?' So I used my basic

English to tell him exactly what I was. He then kindly carried me about half a mile to the jetty, where a naval boat had been sent across, and they took me into a hospital.

For me the Battle of Britain was over. I was twenty years old and had fourteen confirmed kills to my credit. On 7 December I got married.

Flight Lieutenant Denys Gillam
616 and 312 Squadrons

I left 616 Squadron and joined 312 Czech Squadron at Speke on 8 October 1940. As I was taking off in my Hurricane I saw a Ju 88 crossing the boundary of the airfield and I closed to 100 yards, opened fire and saw many strikes on the enemy bomber, which landed close to the airfield, so I completed the circuit and landed. I believe this was the fastest confirmed victory, the time from take-off to landing being about eight minutes.

Flight Lieutenant Brian Kingcome
92 Squadron

It was a beautiful clear autumn day – 15 October – and I thought, now is the time to practise a forced landing – so I throttled back and glided gently down towards Biggin Hill. I was thinking about the eggs and bacon I might get for breakfast if I was lucky after landing.

Suddenly, between 15,000 and 20,000 feet, there was a rattle of bullets in the aircraft, and one went through my leg. Three Spitfires drew alongside me and took one look and rolled away. Whether they had shot me in error – which did happen – or whether they had shot something off my tail, I don't know. So I baled out. Blood was coming out of the top of my flying boot and I was travelling fast enough for the air to suck me out and strong enough for me to get two black eyes from the force of the slipstream. I pulled my ripcord and sailed gently down and landed on one leg in a ploughed field – which gave me a slipped disc, which I still suffer from.

A number of farmers gathered with pitchforks. I was a bit nervous, because some Polish pilots who had been shot down had been set upon because of their accents, and I was wearing a German Mae West which I had taken off some pilots who had got shot down some time earlier. As it happened they were extremely friendly, because my Spitfire had landed before me. They then asked me where would I like to go? I said, 'What hospitals do you have around here?'

Squadron Leader Myles Duke-Woolley
253 SQUADRON

I was flight commander of 'A' Flight, 253 Squadron, Kenley, and early one morning in October the controller called to tell me he had an enemy singleton on the radar screen just over Dieppe. I went up with my number two, Guy Marsland. We flew our Hurricanes at 500 feet, over the railway line running south from Redhill, and started climbing at 1,500 feet per minute. As the boost pressure started to fall with altitude I maintained 'plus four' as long as I could, opening the throttle all the way. Ten minutes after starting we levelled off at 16,000 feet with Beachy Head below at one o'clock ahead. The sun was coming over the south-east horizon above low cloud.

I saw the bandit almost immediately, a black speck 2,000 feet above us, nearly 10 miles away, flying north-north-west. I steered to the left of him, letting the spot move slowly across my windscreen to my right. I waggled my wings to Guy to close formation and, when he had done so, pointed forwards and waved him out again. He opened out to fifty yards or so and thirty seconds later I saw his thumbs-up signal. As the spot became a blob I knew that we were closing, but I was aiming to cut off his retreat by getting south of him. He was turning gently westward. I continued west-south-west.

Two minutes later we were within 5 miles of him, and his silhouette was beginning to look like a He III, the workhorse bomber with considerably less speed than the Ju 88 or Do 17 which I had expected. A lone He III made no sense. I quartered the sky and the sea, but I couldn't see that he had anyone with him. We closed to within a mile, with him north-west of and still apparently unaware of our presence. Brighton was square to port and the Heinkel was doomed. Which meant I could afford to break RT silence. I called Control that we'd made the sighting.

I edged towards the Heinkel, keeping his image steady at the side of my windscreen at about two o'clock. Thirty seconds later the Heinkel turned sharply left and started a gentle dive. I turned inside him, closing quite fast. It seemed possible he still hadn't seen me, because the dorsal gunner had not yet opened fire. When they saw a fighter bearing down, air gunners would immediately open fire, as this encouraged an attacking pilot to fire back, often at an excessive range. I checked our speed to prolong the time it would take to reach our best killing range – 250 yards. If the gunner had seen me, I thought he must surely have opened fire. I closed to 600 yards.

To my astonishment, the Heinkel suddenly jettisoned his bomb load. No reconnaissance aircraft was ever burdened with bombs! That was unheard of. There was also the size of the bomb and the way it fell. The He III's usual load was four 250 kg bombs stored vertically behind the cockpit and – unusually – nose up. I had seen them drop, they came tail first and wobbled around before assuming a normal falling curve. This bomb was vastly bigger and fell away horizontally at first. Our intelligence had reported provision for the external carriage of one or two 500 kg bombs, but to me this looked like 1,000 kg. Tangmere was away to Kenley's west and almost on the coast, and I wondered if that had been his intended target.

My target was the Heinkel's port engine. In my very first encounter with a He III I had learned that a steel monocoque fuselage could take a great deal of punishment. The liquid-cooled engines were much more vulnerable. Flying trails of a captured Heinkel had revealed that it flew better on its port engine alone than on its starboard. So I was lining up my aim on the port engine in relation to the nose of the fuselage. When the two were in line, the angle was almost precisely fifteen degrees. The radius of the circle surrounding the central dot of my position gave an angle of twenty degrees. When the same tip was in line with the dorsal gun I aimed for a 20-degree shot at 250 yards.

The gunsight allowed precisely for a target crossing speed of 100 mph at correct firing range. I had to guess at his airspeed, but in a gentle dive, and doubtless in a hurry, I thought it near 300 mph, so I needed a deflection of one radius of my sight-ring. With it bisecting the port engine, and with the engine pointing straight at the central dot, I needed only to be flying with no skid or slip – otherwise there would be some sideways wind across my gun muzzles. I took a check on my turn-and-slip instrument, low down on the left of my blind-flying panel, and it showed the top needle vertical. I squeezed off a full one and a half seconds' burst at killing range.

Halfway through the burst, white smoke spurted from the target engine and became a thin stream trailing for 200 yards astern. He'd got a serious coolant leak, and if he didn't shut down that engine it would quickly overheat and seize up. Sure enough, the port airscrew stopped and I could see that the blades had been feathered.

I throttled sharply back as the Heinkel's speed dropped, and came up abreast of his port wing. From perhaps fifty yards I looked across at the pilot, a thick-set man in pale-brown overalls and a dark-brown flying helmet. He looked back at me, and for ten seconds or so we gazed into each other's eyes. Then I stabbed my finger downwards three or four times and made landing motions with my arm. When there was no response, I pulled back the hood and repeated my gestures. For a few seconds he looked at me and then, to my relief, he raised a hand in acknowledgement. I closed my hood and followed the Heinkel in his slow starboard turn.

I waggled my wings to Guy to rejoin formation. We circled and watched as the enemy bomber landed. It seemed intact. The crew of four climbed out and huddled together on the ground.

We flew back a short distance to a main road and spotted a police car, which stopped. A figure gazed up at us, hooding his eyes with his hands. We flew a half-mile west, turned and then came over him on a direct line for the Heinkel as I waggled my wings. We circled again and watched the car continue a short way and stop. Two figures got out and went into the field next to our prize.

As I flew back low over the Heinkel, I was surprised – and rather touched – to see the captain line up his crew and then salute me. On impulse, I fished out my half-smoked packet of Players cigarettes, wrapped one of my rubber earpieces from my flying helmet around it, and tied them up in a not-terribly-clean handkerchief, opened the roof, came in on a slow low run and threw them out. They fell close to the group. As I circled round I could see him handing them out to his men.

I called Guy into close formation for a final fly-past. We came in low and, as we neared them, they came smartly together to salute, and held it as we thundered past. I climbed away towards Kenley looking back at them. I have often wondered who the captain was, but I never found out.

A few days later, 253 Squadron was scrambled to intercept a 'twenty-plus', believed hostile, near Selsey, height as usual, vague. Cloud was 10/10 at around 4,000 to 7,000 feet and that raised a doubt in my mind, 'but theirs not to reason why'! We climbed to 20,000 feet and fairly soon were intercepted by around forty Me

Werner Voight, whose Me 109 had been shot down over the Channel, is seen here as a new POW accompanied by British soldiers and a member of the public.

109s, a dozen of which were carrying bombs which I saw being jettisoned. So there we were, high and dry, with the opposition having the height on us. I deployed the squadron into a long line astern and a defensive circle. Graves was number twelve in the line and was nibbled at by an Me 109, before I blew it away, which caused them to pause for thought.

I asked the controller if they thought any 'big babies' were around as the sky seemed to be full only of 'snappers'. We orbited and I scanned around, waiting for news. Now and then a snapper made a frustrated dart. I got tired of this stalemate and led the squadron for cloud cover, dipped into it, and asked them to re-form below as I steered south-west, intending to climb up into the sun and try again. I saw a green and brown camouflage wing near to my tail, but thought nothing of it. My error – it was a 109 camouflaged with our colours. Suddenly it was snowing in the cockpit, there was an almighty bang on my left foot and rudder pedal, and a powerful smell of cordite and petrol in the air.

An odd phenomenon which I experienced in moments of danger was that time seemed to slow down. Perhaps because my adrenalin-boosted brain went into overdrive – and time is relative anyway. Snow in the cockpit was the sign of tracer. I couldn't pull away to either side because of my flanking number two and three. So I slammed on the starboard aileron and slid under my number two, and discovered that my rudder controls had been shot away. The 109 broke away to port, and my Polish number two clobbered him. I had petrol sloshing about, so it was time to 'take silk'. I had always hated the thought of getting burned. I had seen men I knew well become unrecognisable through burns. I snapped my goggles down over my eyes, unclipped the oxygen tube – the RT plug pulled out easily, but the oxygen had a bayonet fitting like a light bulb into its terminal – unpinned the Sutton harness, trimmed the aircraft nose-heavy and got ready to leave as soon as the hood was open.

I slammed the hood back, and immediately the vortex of air behind the windscreen sucked the petrol out of the leaking tank all over me. As I crouched on the seat, holding the stick, I could feel it splattering on the front of my overalls and trickling down my face and neck. I took a glance all round. All I had to do was give the stick a good kick and the Hurricane would go down while I went forward.

At that precise moment the engine stopped. The gravity tank, which I'd been flying on for thirty minutes, was empty. I suddenly felt a right Charlie, half standing in the seat with my head and shoulders outside the cockpit. The danger of bursting into flames had passed, and we were not so flush with Hurricanes that one could afford to throw any away unnecessarily. So I sat down again, throttled back and switched on the main tanks. The engine picked up immediately, so I decided to fly it back to Kenley. I felt sure I could fiddle the landing somehow without the benefit of rudder, but checked for brake and differential braking which all registered.

No sweat. Kenley here I come. At least I can taxi under control. So I turned off to go home, and found I had no radio. No worry, I knew where I was, and my faithful number two was back in formation. By dumb crambo I indicated no RT and my intention to return and land. He nodded and gave thumbs up. In a routine sort of way I then flicked the contents switch to starboard to confirm that the main tank was full. It wasn't. It was barely two-thirds full, and the port tank was the same. Squinting backwards on either side, I could see a faint haze tail behind each main plane, and decided the main tanks were both leaking fast. The question was, how fast?

I timed a five-minute run after reducing revs to minimum and leaving throttle well open – a good formula for max-range flying. After five minutes I calculated ground covered, ground to go – and rechecked my fuel. About one-third full on each side. It would be a dead heat between arrival at Kenley and fuel exhaustion. Say five minutes left, check again after three. Airfield just about in sight, with Homer's wireless masts dead ahead. Exchange 500 feet for more speed – leaves 20,000 feet still for baling out.

The sensible thing to do was leap out after all. But that would really give the Luftwaffe one more victory. I thought, dear old Hurribubble, can't desert you now! I signalled to my number two a straight-in approach. The die was cast, the speed cut down, the undercarriage lowered and, as late as possible, the flaps. I throttled right back to reduce to a minimum the swing caused by change of torque from different power setting and resultant yaw, and lined the aircraft up with the runway using aileron and elevator. Got it straight and set it down. Rolled off on to the grass as the speed dropped to around 40 mph and steered towards dispersal. Eighty yards short the engine coughed apologetically and stopped and we drifted to a halt with just fifty yards or so to push.

It was a triumph for mental arithmetic and stupidity. I asked my flight sergeant, always on the spot, to check the aircraft over; longed for a cigarette but decided that smoking was much too dangerous; and cantered off to the mess reeking of 100-octane. Long hot shower and total change of clothing, and back to dispersal. My flight sergeant met me with a slow, wry smile, and passed the strange request from my ground crew that I get back into the cockpit 'to see their handiwork'. I was mystified but I climbed on to the wing and saw what they had been up to.

My rigger explained that they had been threading strings through the holes in the tail to the holes in front. There were about twenty of them. When I sat down there was no position I could find that didn't cause me to bend at least three of their strings. The flight sergeant asked me if I had discovered any holes in myself during my shower – which the grinning faces all round seemed to find absolutely hilarious!

I went on trying, with the seat up and down, but it was no good. Three bent strings was my lowest possible score. How could that have happened – don't know. Not, that is, if you discount some powerful outside agency. I never did, though. Fools and drunkards traditionally are His wards, and some traditions I totally accept.

Sergeant Pilot Donald Kingaby

92 SQUADRON

The reason I got so many Messerschmitts may be that it's just my luck to have run into more of these enemy machines than any other type. The day I shot four of them down was when they were coming over the Channel in droves. Messerschmitts in formations of fifty or more were being tackled and broken up and shot down by a dozen Hurricanes and Spitfires.

On this particular occasion, our squadron of Spitfires was sent out in the morning and intercepted one of these formations of 109s coming in over the Channel. There were fifty of them. When our leader, a Canadian, gave the order to attack, I got on the tail of four 109s at about 17,000 feet, and attacked the outside one. After I'd given him two bursts of fire, he crashed near Gravesend. When I looked round again, the sky was full of Messerschmitts scattering in all directions. We chased them back to France and returned to our station for lunch. It seemed to me a pretty good morning's work.

In the afternoon, we were sent up again and told there were some 109s off Selsey Bill. We saw them when we were about 20,000 feet. There were 40 of them about 500 feet above us. As they out-numbered us by more than three to one, I suppose they thought they were on to a good thing. At all events, they started to dive on us. We evaded their first attack, and then turned on them. I picked on three. They made off towards France – one straggling a bit behind. I concentrated my fire on him and he went down in flames. The other two Messerschmitts had not seen me come up so I closed up behind the leader and gave him a burst. As I did so the other one came right up on my tail, but I held on to the fellow I'd got. He must have been carrying a bomb for after another burst from my guns he blew up before the one behind could protect him. There was nothing left of him in the sky that you could recognise as part of a plane. Just a flash, and a puff of smoke, and bits of debris hurtling down all over the place.

I must give the third Jerry pilot his due. He could have got away – but he stayed to fight. But the Spitfire's eight machine guns were too much for him, and after a couple of turns, he went down in flames. Then I turned, found the squadron, and came home. And that's about all there was to it.

Flying Officer David Scott-Malden
603 SQUADRONS

The aerial combat which remains most vividly in my mind was over Kent on 12 October 1940, soon after I'd joined 603 Squadron. The squadron was depleted by losses and eight aircraft were directed into a large gaggle of Me 109s. The squadron split up individually and passed head-on through the enemy formation. There was a sense of shock, as a distant series of silhouettes suddenly became rough metal with grey-green paint and yellow noses, passing head-on each side. At the far end I had a few minutes' dogfight with the last 109s, scoring hits which produced a trail of black smoke. Then we were alone at 20,000 feet, the German gliding down with an engine which coughed and barely turned over, I with no ammunition and very little petrol. He glided hopefully towards the Channel and I looked for an airfield before the last of my petrol ran out. Strangely I felt inclined to wave to him as he left. But then, I was only twenty years old.

Pilot Officer Jocelyne Millard
1 AND 242 SQUADRONS

Every day we would wonder what was going to happen. My biggest fear, all through my flying career, was a mid-air collision. Nobody liked being shot down, but if you're being shot at you don't see it

263

coming. But with a mid-air collision something may come from a long way but at the last minute you see it – and I think that's frightening – terrifying. No matter where they come from, not necessarily head-on, you're bound to see it at some time. Other friends of mine, their biggest fear was being burned to death – we all had different fears.

I was not shot down – but a number of my friends were – so I was very fortunate indeed. A friend of mine who became an air chief marshal, said, 'If you're in the wrong place at the wrong time, no matter how good you are, you'll get shot down. It's just unfortunate.' A lot of good people – competent people – Bob Doe is one of them – were shot down.

Pilot Officer Glen Niven

(CANADIAN) 602 AND 601 SQUADRONS

Nobody who flew ever thought they would be shot down. It was automatic – you knew that *you* would be all right. But after some time you'd feel that you'd managed to last rather a long while without being shot down. It got a bit more sticky.

Even on 29 October, when this bugger shot my wing tip off and I had to totter back at about 500 feet, I managed to get back and the engine stopped just as I was coming in to land. On the ground they saw that I'd been hit, and I was later than everybody else – because I couldn't go flat out. I could see bits of wing flapping about, and I was praying it wouldn't fall off. An ambulance came out about ten minutes later – having gone into the hedge. The doctor leapt out – 'Are you all right, Niven?' Then the CO came out – 'Are you hurt?' When he found I wasn't he said, 'Put your parachute in that aircraft there – it's not used.' That was the aircraft I look off in half an hour later.

Sergeant Pilot Paul Farnes

501 SQUADRON

On one occasion we'd been sent up to intercept and something happened with my aircraft – perhaps the RT wasn't working, but I had to come back. I was flying past Gatwick at about 1,500 feet and I saw a Ju 88 coming towards me at about the same height. I went round and shot him down, and he crash-landed on Gatwick Aerodrome. He didn't put his wheels down – did a belly landing and went through the fence and on to the racecourse beyond. Then I landed and the CO took me over in his car, and I met the pilot. It was quite an occasion for me because I'd done all my flying training at Gatwick.

He didn't speak English and I didn't speak German, and I didn't shake his hand – they simply took him away.

Flying Officer Michael Wainwright

64 SQUADRON

On one occasion towards the end of the battle, an aircraft came along my port side and I sensed something – and there was this 109 and he was waving at me. Then he went off. I thought he was letting me know that if he had any bullets he could have shot me down, but he'd obviously run out. Nobody believed me when I told them that.

Pilot Officer Harbourne Stephen

74 SQUADRON

On 30 November 1940, the station scoreboard at Biggin Hill was nearing the 600 mark, and naturally every pilot on the station was hoping that he would shoot down the six hundredth victim – especially as most people on the airfield had subscribed to a handsome prize for the lucky pilot. Before 0800 hours, the Operations Staff rang through to advise that a small convoy in the Channel was being attacked by German fighter-bombers. Flight Lieutenant Mungo-Park, a great fighter pilot and leader, and I took off and, aided by some clever controlling from the ground, we saw a large German fighter wing returning to France at very high altitude. With skilful stalking we selected a 109 on the edge of one of the outside formations flying at the then great height of 35,000 feet. I opened fire with a short burst from the starboard quarter. Then Mungo-Park went in, and when I made my second attack I saw pieces flying off the 109, which eventually crash-landed inland from Dungeness. So a shared 109. Seven months later Mungo-Park was killed on a sweep over France.

Hans-Ekkehard Bob

LUFTWAFFE FIGHTER PILOT

To begin with we were just bombing the airfields and the ammunition factories, aircraft manufacturers and so on, all that was OK – in terms of warfare it was both understandable and important. But once London was being attacked, we told ourselves that this was something that we wanted to have less to do with.

Being fighter pilots, we were not affected by it as much as the bomber pilots were, because we didn't drop any bombs, at least most of us didn't.

If during these missions you approached Greater London, to begin with you came across the blocking barrage balloons, and then there was the concentration of anti-aircraft weapons – the sky was black with them – but even this was simpler for us fighter pilots, because we could fly either around or over them. Whereas our bombers had to get right into it, and so you would say to yourself, 'My goodness, that takes some doing!' They were flying into anti-aircraft fire when the entire sky was black from the detonations.

Julius Meimberg
LUFTWAFFE FIGHTER PILOT

Late in the afternoon of 28 November 1940, we took off for southern England from Beaumont le Roger for our second mission of the day. Climbing towards the Isle of Wight in bright sunshine, I was leading the 4th Staffel and directly ahead of us was the Staff Schwarm of JG2 Richthofen led by our Kommodore, Major Helmut Wick, at that time the leading fighter pilot in the Luftwaffe. With him were his wingman Oberleutnant Rudi Pflanz, Oberleutnant Leie and Oberfeldwebel Rudorffer. At about 23,000 feet, we were almost above the Isle of Wight when we spotted vapour trails caused by Spitfires above us at a much greater height.

Major Wick led his Staff Schwarm towards them at full throttle, with the result that the Schwarm aircraft pulled apart from each other. Climbing with my Staffel to one side, we were soon drawn into the main battle and the Staffel separated. A single Spitfire turned in front of me and disappeared behind my engine cowling as I fired off my weapons. Apparently undamaged, the aircraft went into a spin and I followed it down, expecting the aircraft to pull out at any time, but it never did. The red glow in the cockpit indicated a possible oxygen tank hit.

When we landed, Rudi Pflanz reported that Major Wick had shot down a Spitfire, was then in turn shot down by a second, which in turn had been shot down by Pflanz. We were all told that no one had seen what had happened to Wick's aircraft, which left us hoping for the safety of our Kommodore. We returned later next day, and again the following day, but there was no sign of him. What we hadn't been told was that Rudorffer had witnessed him go down, a large bullet hole passing through the starboard wing trailing edge straight through the cockpit and engine block. He felt that Wick was already dead as his aircraft corkscrewed downwards, finally plunging into the sea. After the war, I learned that his conqueror had been Flight Lieutenant John Dundas DFC, who himself only seconds later was shot down by Pflanz and killed.

Heinz Lange
LUFTWAFFE FIGHTER PILOT

I flew as an escort to the bombers. I had some opportunities to shoot the opposition down – but not the luck. For us, it was more important to stop the British planes from shooting at our bombers than to have a dogfight. I came through without being hit. We mostly attacked the River Thames as far as London – targets further away were out of our range. The British flak was very good – they almost didn't have to aim, because our route was so consistent as we were always so worried about running out of fuel. But this changed later on when we could attach extra fuel.

Aircraftwoman Anne Duncan
WAAF, PLOTTER

We didn't awfully like going into the shelters, because they were not really bomb-proof, and if a bomb landed right on one it'd leave a very nasty mess. So what we usually did was to go outside and look and see what was going on. You could see the aeroplanes overhead – you could hear them all the time. There was this special droning noise. And then one night they started dropping bombs all around us. We all lay flat. There were lots dropped on the airfield. It was very exciting. This happened night after night, so you didn't get a lot of sleep during certain periods when they were having a particular drive at London. We were right in the pathway.

Aircraftwoman Jean Mills

WAAF, PLOTTER AND TRACER AT RAF DUXFORD

I remember coming on for a night shift and seeing a great glow in the south-east, like the biggest sunset you ever saw, and we said to the guard, 'What's that?' and he said, 'Oh, that's London burning.' That was the first time, really, that I felt it in the pit of my stomach.

Flight Lieutenant Billy Drake

I SQUADRON

One has to be honest and say there were moments – the bad moments you can't even remember. They're past, forgotten – but the great moments and the camaraderie – the times that you had on leave, the friends that you made. You met such a cross-section of the British population that you would never have met at other times, other than in wartime.

As I remember the situation, there was quite definitely a class distinction in 1939, at the beginning of the war, where the majority of your pilots were officer class and not NCOs. Then around 1940, at about the beginning of the Battle of Britain, you then got the introduction of the RAFVR type aircrew who were in the majority of working-class families, so there was a gradual absorption of the working class within the framework. Your NCO and your RAFVR NCOs were being commissioned and promoted to leaders and by 1943 it was a very middle-class organisation.

Flight Lieutenant Tom Morgan

43 SQUADRON

The German aircrew and ourselves were comparable types – they weren't any worse or any better than us. Generally we were very similar and we suffered the same severe casualties they did. They too had to send up a lot of new boys.

As far as the fighters were concerned, we'd go in against each other and it was a joust to see who came out the best. But as far as I was concerned – and I think this was true for a lot of people – we didn't like the bombers. We disliked them bombing our people and there was a fair determination amongst us to get them before they could drop their bombs on the target. That was always our aim. Sometimes we didn't find them and you'd not be vectored on them until they were coming out – at least then you'd have another go at them so that they couldn't get back and bring another load.

Sergeant Pilot Iain Hutchinson

222 SQUADRON

We were very much aware that this battle was the precursor to an invasion, and we knew at that time that the British Army had no heavy weapons – no tanks, not very many machine guns, demoralised troops – so all the Germans had to do was to land on the coast and march inland. But they couldn't land on the coast if we were able to attack them from the air. Their only way of stopping us attacking them from the air was to wipe out the Fighter Command – and that's what they were trying to do – but they didn't succeed. I think Hitler probably recognised that he was losing aircraft and pilots, and they had much bigger fish to fry. He wanted to preserve his troops for the attack on Russia, which was going to be launched shortly. So I think that's why the Battle of Britain eventually petered out.

Flight Lieutenant Billy Drake

I SQUADRON

We accepted the fact that we were at war, and that there would be casualties. If a mate was killed, then it wasn't us – it was dear old Joe – let's find out if there's any stuff in his room that we could use. It was slightly stupid, but it was dealt with. A man's goods in his room were distributed amongst his friends.

I don't think we feared death – we accepted that it could happen. What we did fear was being wounded or taken prisoner of war. Those were the two immediate worries on a day-to-day basis. I think it did worry us that we could be burned or wounded in combat. We were very much aware of McIndoe's work with the Guinea Pigs – in fact we used to go up to London and see these people that had been burned. They were permitted and encouraged by the medical staff to be seen in public, in bars and in restaurants with the terrible burns, so that everybody, including the Guinea Pigs themselves, could get used to the fact – and that people didn't shy away from these very nasty sights.

I don't think we feared coming down in the Channel that much. We were a reasonably behaved bunch of youngsters and we had to look after ourselves because we had a job to do – which was to fly bloody aeroplanes. Not just to fly them, but to fight in them, because there were two jobs involved in air combat. One was to fly the aeroplane and then, having learned how to fly, we had to learn how to operate them to be an effective weapon in combat.

Heinz Lange

LUFTWAFFE FIGHTER PILOT

On the whole, the battle was conducted fairly, neither side shooting aircrew hanging from parachutes, but the strain on our nerves was immense. After the first few weeks, the wings had rest days and could be sent home until being returned to stand-by. Then we would meet at the Rio Bar in Lille, a well-known bar which the English had used before us. As the weather worsened, the crews were near the end of their strength and the battle drew to a close, but we had lost a lot of friends, many of whom had been sent to captivity in Canada. In a way we felt sorry for them, but later on there were times when we envied them.

Sergeant Pilot Iain Hutchinson

222 SQUADRON

I think we were a bit worried about burns, but I think you were probably more worried about cannon shell and bullets than fire, because you could probably get out of a burning aircraft but you can't get out of the way of a flying bullet.

You were always aware of the possibility of death, but you didn't think of it as such, in fact. You suffer from a bit of apprehension but in my case this was matched by a kind of hatred for the people who were daring to invade our airspace, so I think the two things kind of cancelled each other out.

You had to shut your mind to the friends who didn't come back – you accepted it. The second day that we were in operation, the whole of 'B' Flight was shot down – there were only two of them killed – but you were constantly aware of what might happen. But then when people came back it seemed to some extent to balance the number that were killed.

I did not expect to survive to see the end of the war. Starting off with that as the bottom line, I really felt I wanted to get this business over and done with as quickly as possible, and that was the motivation for not bothering too much about what went on round about me.

Flight Lieutenant Peter Brothers

2 AND 257 SQUADRONS

The raid on 15 September was a tough one as well, and when we went up we thought it was going to be one of those days, a hard day: one of an hour and ten minutes and one of forty minutes. I got a Do 17 and a Ju 88.

After that September raid things abated slightly. On 19 and 20 September we ran defensive and convoy patrols, but we saw no action. The general feeling was that we'd seen them off. On 28 September we did two patrols – a 'Big Wing' with 73 and 17 Squadrons. We were flying in and out of cloud, when suddenly we were jumped by some 109s. I saw one going past, attacking 17 Squadron, who were below and in front of us, leading. This 109 knocked off a Hurricane before anybody could do anything. Suddenly we realised that there were several of them about, and of course, the wing broke up and everybody got involved, but without any great success.

The sporadic raids went on into December, then they reverted to 109s carrying bombs. 257 Squadron had moved from Martlesham Heath to North Weald, and one day, when I'd gone over to the mess for tea, suddenly the scramble sounded. We were raided by 109s dropping bombs, and I dived under the table. They dropped a bomb right outside, where I'd parked my old open Red Label Bentley. It was filled with soil, but fortunately not damaged.

The winter was coming and clearly there was not going to be an invasion. The Battle of Britain had been won.

Hans-Ekkehard Bob

LUFTWAFFE FIGHTER PILOT

Some people say that Hitler had a soft spot for England, that he was an admirer of England and that he didn't want to humiliate the English and so on. There are several different variants as to why it didn't happen, but taking everything into account, it is my opinion that in that battle there were neither victors nor vanquished – only losers. We all lost.

Pilot Officer Bob Doe

234 AND 238 SQUADRONS

I wasn't fighting for the King, I was fighting for me mum – I didn't want them over here.

Bob Doe passed away on 21 February 2010, aged 89.

On 20 August, Prime Minister Winston Churchill spoke to the nation – his words were prophetic – those airmen would go on fighting through the summer and into autumn, and eventually avert the danger of invasion.

The gratitude of every home in our island, in our Empire and, indeed, throughout the world, except in the abodes of the guilty, goes out to the British airmen who, undaunted by odds, unweary in their constant challenge and mortal danger, are turning the tide of the world war by their prowess and their devotion. Never in the field of human conflict was so much owed by so many to so few.

ACKNOWLEDGEMENTS

At my publishers I would like to thank my editor Ed Faulkner for his endless patience and great support. I would also like to thank Martin Noble for his editorial comments, Sophia Brown for her fine work on the photographs and Davina Russell for overseeing the completion of the book.

My profound thanks go to Vicky Thomas whose diligent and conscientious research and editorial skills have enriched this book. I am much in her debt. My dear friends Sir Martin Gilbert and Lady Gilbert, Debbie Moggach, Susan Jeffries, Don and Liz McClen have all been steadfast in their support and I am most grateful to them, as I am to Joshua Levine whose book on Ireland, *Beauty and Atrocity* is published in June 2010.

Ruth Cowan has, as always, been wonderfully supportive. Lucia Corti has throughout brought me much delight and laughter.

I am most grateful to the following publishers for permission to use extracts from their books:

Grub Street: *Life Is Too Short to Cry* by Tim Vigors and *Spitfire Pilot* by David Crook.

David & Charles: *Battle for the Skies* by Michael Paterson.

Pen and Sword: *The Story of the Spitfire and Hurricane* by Douglas Bader.

History Press: *One of the Few* by Johnny Kent.

Vintage Books: *The War in the Air 1939–1945* edited by Gavin Lyall.

Amberley Publishing: *Spitfire! The Experiences of a Battle of Britain Fighter Pilot* by Brian Lane, edited by Dilip Sarkar.

Macmillan: *The Last Enemy* by Richard Hillary.

Buccaneer: *The First and the Last* by Adolf Galland.

Two absolutely invaluable books have been vital to the background of this book. They are: *Men of the Battle of Britain* by Kenneth G. Wynn (Gliddon Books) and *Aces High: A Tribute to the Most Notable Fighter Pilots of the British and Commonwealth Forces in WWII* by Christopher Shores and Clive Wiliams (Grubb Street).

I would like to thank Peter Devitt, the Assistant Curator of the RAF Museum, for help in supplying personal testimonies from the museum's archive. I would also like to thank the BBC for use of these recordings.

I am most grateful to the ever helpful sound archive of the IWM for their permission to use the following accounts which have an accession number after their name.

Neil 26977; Drake 26967; Hans-Ekkehard Bob 26965; Stapleton 26958; Roberts 26973; Dalton Morgan 26969, all of whom recorded their interviews for Channel 4's Battle of Britain documentary.

Martel 27233; Millard 21299; Rose 29076; Hutchinson 26970; Bamberger 27074; Bird-Wilson 10093; Kingcome 10152; Dundas 10159; Hamilton Grice 10897; Holden 11198; Quill 10687; Evans 13348.

Finally I owe a debt of gratitude to Group Captain Patrick Tootal and his wife Janet of the Battle of Britain Fighter Association who kindly arranged for me to interview surviving pilots of the battle.

INDEX